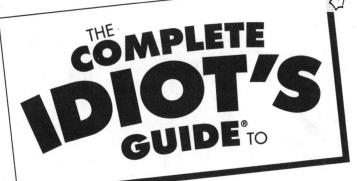

THE COMPLETE IDIOT'S GUIDE® TO

Project Management

Third Edition

by Sunny and Kim Baker and
G. Michael Campbell

ALPHA

A member of Penguin Group (USA) Inc.

International Standard Book Number: 1-59257-119-0
Library of Congress Catalog Card Number: 2003111790

05   04   03   8   7   6   5   4   3   2   1

Interpretation of the printing code: The rightmost number of the first series of numbers is the year of the book's printing; the rightmost number of the second series of numbers is the number of the book's printing. For example, a printing code of 03-1 shows that the first printing occurred in 2003.

Printed in the United States of America

Note: This publication contains the opinions and ideas of its authors. It is intended to provide helpful and informative material on the subject matter covered. It is sold with the understanding that the authors and publisher are not engaged in rendering professional services in the book. If the reader requires personal assistance or advice, a competent professional should be consulted.

The authors and publisher specifically disclaim any responsibility for any liability, loss, or risk, personal or otherwise, which is incurred as a consequence, directly or indirectly, of the use and application of any of the contents of this book.

Most Alpha books are available at special quantity discounts for bulk purchases for sales promotions, premiums, fund-raising, or educational use. Special books, or book excerpts, can also be created to fit specific needs.

For details, write: Special Markets, Alpha Books, 375 Hudson Street, New York, NY 10014.

Publisher: *Marie Butler-Knight*
Product Manager: *Phil Kitchel*
Senior Managing Editor: *Jennifer Chisholm*
Senior Acquisitions Editor: *Renee Wilmeth*
Development Editor: *Jennifer Moore*
Production Editors: *Megan Douglass, Billy Fields*
Copy Editor: *Cari Luna*
Illustrator: *Chris Eliopoulos*
Cover/Book Designer: *Trina Wurst*
Indexer: *Brad Herriman*

Contents at a Glance

Contents

Foreword

Projects are everywhere—they are an integral part of modern life.

In preparing for my wedding a few years ago, I introduced my wife-to-be as the "project manager." Weddings come with all the excitement and challenges of a complex project, including the pressure to meet a schedule.

My wife coped with this all admirably, with much advance planning, attention to detail, and management of risk (have you ever tried to do a seating plan?). This was all going really well until two days before the wedding, when the Groom and the Best Man stepped naively and somewhat unprepared into the action. We were quickly allocated our tasks. "Could you turn the field behind the house into a parking lot, pick up your clothes for the wedding, and get your hair cut?"

Unfortunately 24 hours later, due to a slightly slow start, and a minor miscommunication with the barber, we had achieved none of these tasks well, and were asleep on the floor of my mother-in-law's living room. It was at this point that we received the key motivational talk from the project manager emphasizing how important the project was and our role in making it successful. You can imagine!

From this point forward the wedding went without a hitch, or at least with only the one important one.

We can all benefit from managing some of the key things we do at work and at home with proper project discipline. I am sure you can think of a number of projects that are already under your belt.

For new project managers it often feels like you need to be paying attention to everything at once. This book helps you focus on the right things that will make your project successful. Now most projects will run into difficulties at some point. The methods in the book will help you recognize when a project is going off the rails and systematically get it back on track. (I just wish I'd read the section on "Making Your Communications Count" before asking the barber to "Just take a little off the top.")

A lot of what makes projects seem complicated is the language that is used. ("Could you update the Gantt, based on the revised dependencies, take out the padding and get it cross-checked?) Kim, Sunny, and Michael do a great job of demystifying the language and showing how you can use it to your advantage. Once you speak the language, you'll find that the know-it-alls in to your office know less than you might think.

As a leader, one of the best things is to have project managers you can depend on. They understand all the dimensions of what makes projects successful, they are diligent, and they drive the project through to execution. If things are not going well, they are ahead of the game, coming to you with solutions, not problems.

So be brave as you tackle your projects. Your confidence will grow with each one you complete. It's amazing the opportunities that come your way having a successfully managed project under your belt!

And to all the would-be grooms out there, make sure you pay attention to your project manager.

—Andy Smith, CIO, North America Gas and Power, BP.

Andy Smith is the Chief Information Officer of BP's North American Gas and Power business. He has worked for BP for 14 years in finance, planning, and information technology. These roles have taken him around the world to Glasgow, Anchorage, London, and Houston.

Introduction

Many project managers use the term SWAG as a way to estimate the level of effort for a project. For those of you who haven't heard the term, it's an acronym (with mild profanity) that ends with "guess." You can imagine what the other letters stand for, but if you are curious, just ask an experienced project manager.

However, there is a better way than "SWAGing" to manage projects, and you don't need to be a genius, or even have an MBA, to understand how. It doesn't take a special certification to manage a project, but it does take special skills to bring projects in on time and within budget. Yes, there's some planning and charting involved in moving projects from start to finish, but this book takes the practical approach to the process and puts you in control. The road to successful project management is mapped in the following pages.

This book explains in easy-to-understand language how the power of time-proven project management methods can help your mission-critical projects come in on time, on budget, and on target. You'll learn how project teams, in spite of politics and personalities, can be pointed in the same direction; and how changes, no matter how frequent, can be managed to keep projects on track. You'll learn that it's skill, not luck or fancy degrees, that makes the difference in making your project a success.

How to Use This Book

The book has seven parts, which we recommend you read from beginning to end. The parts work together to provide you with the steps and tools behind successful project management and offer practical advice that can be adapted to the needs of today's fast-moving, ever-changing organizations.

Part 1, "Project Management Power," explains how to balance all the different needs that all project managers must satisfy. You'll be introduced to steps that can be used to bring any project to a successful conclusion, on time and within budget, and to the three secrets to success behind any project: the project manager, the team, and the plan.

Part 2, "The Project Initiation Processes," presents techniques to start a project off on the right foot with a clear scope and a motivated project team. This part is especially important because the way a project starts off usually defines the way it will end up.

Part 3, "The Project Planning Phase," explains the basic planning processes central to successful project management. You'll observe how tasks are defined, scheduled, and budgeted using powerful charting and analysis tools that can help you scope out projects of all sorts and sizes. This is the most technical part of the book, so you might want to read it twice. Mastering the tools in this part is important because no project is ever better than the plan used to manage the effort.

Part 4, "The Execution Phase," presents proven techniques to transform the plan into action focused toward meeting the project requirements. This is key to successful project management. The end result of a project is always related to the way the plan is translated into actual work in the real world.

Part 5, "The Controlling Processes," talks about ways to monitor, track, and adjust each project so that you can keep everything on schedule, within budget, and with the right quality. You'll also find easy-to-follow guidelines for dealing with the most common project problems and for minimizing the impact of the changes and conflicts that are part of almost every project.

In **Part 6, "The Close-Out Phase,"** you discover how to finish your project and reap the rewards of a job well done. This is the most often ignored part of project management, but you'll see why it is so important.

In **Part 7, "The Organization and Tools to Make Project Management Prosper,"** you'll be introduced to some software packages that can help you and find out how to put the discipline of project management to work throughout your organization.

Extras

To add to the material in the main text, a series of boxes throughout the book highlight specific items that can help you understand and implement the material in each chapter:

> **Words from the Wise**
>
> These quotes and tips include observations from our experience and other experts that may help inspire you to greater achievements, or simply help keep you motivated to do your best, even when the project seems impossible.

> **CAUTION** **Risk Management**
>
> Sometimes things just go wrong, no matter how well you plan your project. Luckily, there are usually warnings before things get too bad, if you know how to recognize them. In these boxes, you'll learn how to read the danger signs before you get swamped with problems.

Project Lingo

These boxes define the most important definitions and concepts in project management. These are the words you should use in meetings to impress your boss and your co-workers, because it will demonstrate that you know what you are talking about.

Time Is Money

Use the suggestions in these boxes to keep your schedule up-to-date and your budget under control. Hopefully the advice will spare you the embarrassment of running out of money before the project is completed. You'll also pick up on a variety of tips used by veteran project managers to run projects of all sizes and kinds.

Along the Critical Path

Stories or information related to project management appear in these boxes. (You'll learn about critical path—an actual project management term—in Chapter 12.)

Acknowledgments

All of the people at Alpha Books—especially Renee Wilmeth and Jennifer Moore for their professionalism, skill, and good ideas—deserve our thanks. We've appreciated the opportunity to work with them.

Just as important, we want to thank you, the reader, for purchasing this book. We understand how important your projects are to your personal and professional success, and we feel a deep sense of gratitude that you believe that we can teach you something about becoming a better project manager.

In addition, G. Michael Campbell would like to thank Bill Nash and Henry "Skeeter" Lieberum, who have been the best mentors a person could hope for, by encouragement and example, as well as introducing him to the discipline of project management and the Project Management Institute. And any acknowledgement would be incomplete without recognizing Michael's wife, Molly, and her undying patience he worked to complete this book. Her support, and the love of his children, is the rock upon which everything else is built.

Trademarks

All terms mentioned in this book that are known to be or are suspected of being trademarks or service marks have been appropriately capitalized. Alpha Books and Penguin Group (USA) Inc. cannot attest to the accuracy of this information. Use of a term in this book should not be regarded as affecting the validity of any trademark or service mark.

Part 1

Project Management Power

Each year, organizations launch mission-critical projects involving millions of dollars in capital investment plus significant requirements for project-savvy human capital. The processes and methods of project management provide the structure, focus, flexibility, and control to help guide investments to outstanding results, on time and within budget.

In this section, you'll be introduced to the processes and life-cycle phases of the project management discipline and the successful techniques of experienced project managers. You'll also learn how to get started on the project, the first step in consistently bringing your projects in on time and within budget. If you can do that, you'll be a rising star within your organization. That's the power of project management.

Projects, Projects Everywhere

In This Chapter

- Why project management is vital in today's competitive world

- Projects versus ordinary work

- Project harmony: a balancing act

- Six features shared by all projects

- Identifying projects that need better management

- Common project questions to ask yourself

The twenty-first century is here along with tighter budgets, less time to get things done, and fewer resources. Sure, building warp drives that allow faster-than-light travel are still *Star Trek* fantasies, but rapid change, expanding technologies, and global marketing are real today.

To compete, you'll need to do more with less. Competition will continue to pressure you to come up with better ideas. You won't have time to waste on stale methods or wimpy techniques. To captain your business in the future, you'll need to build things faster, cheaper, and better. And you'll need to get things done right the first time.

Projects are becoming the way of the working world. Computers and automation have eliminated many types of repetitive work. This has freed people to focus on building new things—new products, new services, and improved organizations. And where there are things that need to be created, there are projects.

> **Project Lingo** _____
>
> A **project** is a sequence of tasks with a beginning and an end that is bounded by time and resources and that produces a unique product or service. This means that a project produces something that has never existed before; a deadline or target date when the project must be done; and a budget that limits the amount of people, supplies, and money that can be used to complete the project.

But before you can use any of the advice in this book, you need to distinguish the projects in your business from the ordinary, repetitive work. In this chapter, you'll not only learn how to recognize the projects in your business, you'll also see why projects need a special kind of management to get them done right.

All Projects Are Work, but Not All Work Is a Project

Like most people in business, you are responsible for ordinary work and projects. In business, we could probably break down the work that is done and call the repetitious, day-to-day work "operations," and the work that is unique and only lasts for a short time as a "project." You probably don't even think about the difference. You just think you have too much to do.

Okay, you're right. There's always too much to do. But people often fail at managing projects not because projects involve too much work, but because the difference between routine work and projects isn't clear.

Projects vs. Operations or Ordinary Work

Pretend for a moment that you're a salesperson at Pyramid Products Company. You're already working full-time, day in and day out, trying to sell Pyramid's products to your customers. Then your boss asks you and one of your colleagues from each of the other four regional offices to plan the upcoming sales meeting in San Diego. Every day you respond to customer requests, make sales calls, and write trip reports after your client visits. It's pretty easy to figure out that setting up the national sales meeting is different than your day-to-day sales activities. But what exactly is it that makes the job of arranging the national sales meeting a project and the work with your customers operations?

Both the project to set up the sales meeting and the everyday operations of contacting customers may involve similar activities such as making phone calls, writing reports, and going to meetings, but projects have different goals than ongoing, day-to-day job activities.

Time Is Money

Using project management (PM) techniques to control a project may seem like an additional burden, but it saves time and money in the long term. Properly applied, PM techniques allow you to meet the expectations of the stakeholders (we'll talk about them later) in your project. Too often projects disappoint people because the project manager was too busy working on project activities without making sure the project met the requirements the "customer" wanted.

A project has a definite start date, and a distinct end date. You certainly will have a deadline to finish the planning for the national sales meeting because everyone will want to know when to show up in San Diego!

The second characteristic that distinguishes projects from operations is that projects create something unique. The San Diego sales conference will be unique because the agenda and topics will be different from any other sales conferences, as will the list of attendees.

In addition, projects have specific budgets. For the sales conference, your budget probably won't be big enough to allow you to plan a cruise down the coast of Mexico as part of the conference, for instance, but it may allow you to include some on-site entertainment.

So there you have it! Projects have deadlines, unique deliverables, and budgets.

To better understand the differences between operations and projects, consider the following comparisons. Note that the projects all have definable goals. They also have a beginning and an end. Most ordinary work must be done over and over again, whereas most projects are done only once (if they're done right the first time).

Operations (Ordinary Work)	Projects
Responding to a customer's request	Producing a sales brochure that will introduce a new product or service
Making coffee for the office	Catering the inaugural ceremonies for the president

Operations (Ordinary Work)	Projects
Writing a letter to a prospect	Writing and publishing a book
Hooking up a printer to your computer	Implementing a company-wide computer network
Meeting with an employee to discuss a new procedure	Hiring a sales team for the new office in Madison
Attending a conference	Promoting your product in a two-week program across the country

Projects vs. Assignments

Now that you know the difference between operations and projects, let's throw another term into the mix: assignments. Let's suppose that you are a member of the corporate communications department and you are responsible for producing the monthly newsletter that will go out to everyone in the company. At first glance, it may seem like this task is a project because it has many of the same characteristics that projects do: It has a deadline, a budget to produce it, and the content will undoubtedly be unique for that month. However, it is really an assignment, not a project. Why? Because you will develop a process for producing the newsletter that you will follow each month. And while the content is unique, the format, size, and distribution will probably be the same month-after-month.

So we need to change our perspective when we talk about an assignment versus a project. The goals and deadlines of the business routine are general. Routine work is defined within the scope of a department or functional job description. A good example is the newsletter. You probably schedule the month to ask people to contribute articles, create deadlines for the print shop to produce the newsletter, and review the content with key people to make sure you have the right content for that month. All of this is part of your ordinary work.

Another way to look at it is this: Every day companies must run the business to ensure that the customers are happy and products and services are being produced. At the same time, companies are working to change their business to stay ahead of the competition, or catch up to the competition, and they almost always use projects for "changing the business." As one of our clients once said, "the hardest job I have is to run the business today so that we can eat this month, while simultaneously changing the business so that we can eat this time next year. Refer to the following model to see what we mean.

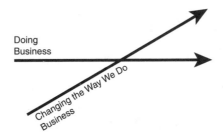

Doing
Business

Changing the Way We Do
Business

The dual perspective needed for simultaneously running the business today and changing the business to meet future needs.

The basic problem with the project approach used by most companies is that less than 30 percent of the projects that companies employ to change their business are successful! *Less than 30 percent!* That is clearly unacceptable. Those projects include mergers and acquisitions, major technology initiatives, or reengineering, to name a few. According to the research, over 30 percent of IT projects are cancelled. Over 50 percent of projects will experience cost overruns. And only about 16 percent will be completed within the desired timeframe and budget and achieve the desired results. Amazing!

The good news for you is that if you work to master the techniques that are in this book, you will be seen as a rising star in your company. Why? Because you will be successful in completing a project, and the contrast with so many other failed projects will be striking.

That's why many people see the advantage to becoming a *project manager.* The Project Management Institute (PMI), an international organization dedicated to the advancement of project management, has nearly 100,000 members at the time this book is being written and will probably exceed that number by the time you read it. It has established standards and certificates to raise the knowledge and professionalism of project managers worldwide.

Project Lingo

The **project manager** is the person who takes overall responsibility for coordinating a project, regardless of its size, to make sure the desired end result comes in on time and within budget.

Project Lingo

A **program** is a group of projects managed in a coordinated way so that the benefits are greater than if these projects were managed individually. For example, in many electronic companies, a program manager will be responsible for the development of a new product (a project) and all the revised versions that will be released over the next five years (a program).

Project Success: A Balance Among Time, Resources, Results, and Perceptions

One of the hardest tasks any project manager will face is balancing a project's time, cost, and quality. If you look at the three elements in the accompanying pyramid, it becomes clear that if the time begins to slip (so that you may miss your deadline), you impact the other two elements. For example, you can get the project back on track by getting more people involved (and increasing your costs), or reducing the quality that was originally designed into the project. Or you have to ask for more time!

A good project manager will make sure that he or she understands which of these three elements is paramount. In other words, what is most important—the deadline, the budget, or the quality? Once you know that, you can understand how you will need to keep the other elements in balance as the project progresses.

This pyramid demonstrates the balance among time, resources, results, and customer satisfaction that is required to bring a project to a successful conclusion. If you change one of the elements in the pyramid, you automatically change the scope of the project.

The Universal Project Pyramid

This brings us to the factors that are essential to the success of all projects. These factors include the following:

◆ Agreement among the project team and the stakeholders (which include internal and/or external customers and management) on the goals of the project. Without clear goals and agreement among everyone involved, the results can be devastating. You'll learn ways to develop clear, agreed-upon goals in this book. No project can be a success unless everybody agrees that they want the same thing produced.

◆ Support from management to supply the *resources* and to remove organizational obstacles. Without management support, project managers rarely have enough authority of their own to execute the decisions and policies necessary to complete a project. To get that support, you'll need to manage "upward" as well as manage the project team. You'll also learn ways to do this as you read through the book.

◆ Communication that is effective, appropriately delivered, and ongoing throughout the project. Almost every project management technique involves some form of communication. Without clear, concise communication, the people on a project team will never be able to agree on goals and then meet them. The project plan is one major component of this communication, but there are many other components required for project success. This book not only explains how to plan a project, it also examines the ongoing communication necessary to keep a project focused and on schedule.

> **Words from the Wise**
>
> Project management methods are useful if they can be placed in the context of today's trends, impacts, and technology. If we merely forge ahead and use them as they were used 30 years ago, we will meet with, at most, limited success.
>
> —Bennet P. Lientz and Kathryn P. Rea in *Project Management for the 21st Century*

It's Not Magic

Great project managers weren't born that way. They have learned to use the methods that have been successful for other project managers and adapt them to their particular situations. Sometimes they were lucky and had an opportunity to watch a great project manager at work or even have one as a mentor. However, most of us are not that lucky. So we can either muddle through it by trial-and-error, or we can use tried and true techniques.

Remember that the information in this book takes the most successful techniques of hundreds of project managers, not just one! And because all projects share similar features and require a balance among time, resources, and results, similar formal project management techniques—the science of the great project managers—are also necessary to bring your projects to successful conclusions. These techniques are what you're going to learn about in the rest of the book.

The tools and techniques for project management were originally developed to handle construction projects. However, these same methods will work whether you're training a team of new employees, creating an ad campaign, developing a new software product, or reorganizing a corporation. Project management tools also can be used to correct midcourse problems that would otherwise go undetected and undermine the success of any project.

Projects Change, and We Must Manage That Change

Of course, in spite of their similarities, all true projects really are unique. Projects involve different goals, employ different people with distinctive personalities, take place over varying time frames, and produce different results.

No two projects, even projects with the same general objectives, are ever identical in planning or implementation. People who manage projects successfully quickly learn to become managers of change because there are always plenty of surprises, even in small projects. Thankfully, the project management toolbox offers techniques for identifying and managing the unique attributes of every project. You will learn about these techniques throughout the book.

When you master the techniques of project management, you'll see that the project of setting up a national sales meeting and the project of building the NASA Space Station depend on many of the same project management tools, even though the projects are on vastly different scales.

How Many Projects Are You Responsible For?

Projects are the means by which companies change and adapt to meet the needs of changing markets, new technologies, and expanding opportunities. Given that business is becoming more project-oriented, almost everyone will benefit from learning the project management skills in this book.

As you start reviewing the activities in your business, you'll see that the business endeavors that meet the project criteria are endless, varying from small to large and from simple to complex. If you try listing all the projects in your area of responsibility, you may discover a lot more on the list than you anticipated.

All Projects Great and Small

It's usually easy to identify the most complex projects in business, such as developing a new model automobile, installing a new financial reporting computer application like Enterprise Resource Planning (ERP) tools, or building an overseas manufacturing facility. But smaller and more mundane business endeavors can also be projects, even though they may not be called by that name.

Consider the job of hiring a new marketing manager for your company. Most experienced managers wouldn't consider this a project because they know how to plan and schedule all the steps in their head. You simply put an ad in the paper, interview some people, and make a choice. But hiring a new marketing manager involves deadlines, people, money, and time—and hopefully, you only have to do it once. You'll probably use a team of people to interview the candidates as well. And when you're done with the project, you'll also have something you didn't have before—a new marketing manager.

When viewed this way, hiring a marketing manager is a project and deserves to be treated like any other project. Good project management will help you hire the right marketing manager in the shortest period of time—and that could make a big difference to your company.

Sure, it won't take as long to plan the project of hiring a marketing manager as it will to plan how to build a new bridge across the Potomac. You probably won't have to use a computer program to create the schedule or to manage the budget (although you might). But using good project management techniques is still important because the choice of the marketing manager is important to your business.

You can't afford to treat even a small project, such as hiring a new employee, like ordinary work. Now would be a good time to identify two small, but important, projects that you have been postponing. For practice, you can apply to them the techniques you learn in this book.

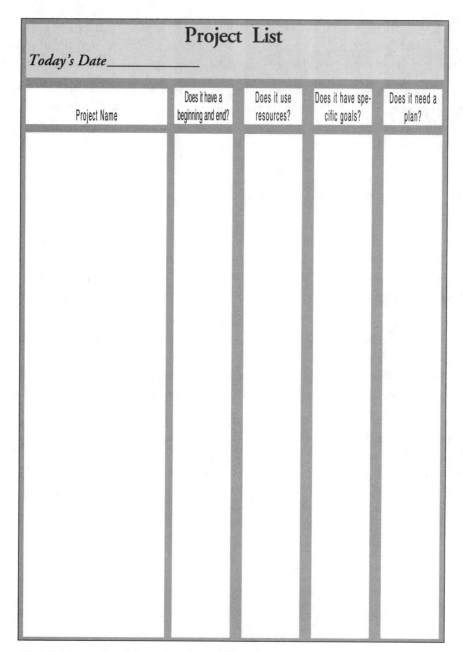

Project List

Today's Date_____

Project Name	Does it have a beginning and end?	Does it use resources?	Does it have specific goals?	Does it need a plan?

Use this form to list all the projects in your business.

The Next Step

In the following pages, you'll be taken step-by-step through the fundamentals of planning, scheduling, tracking, and controlling the costs and resources of any project—whether the project is mundane or technical or multifaceted and complex.

These practical techniques are applicable to the projects that people in sales, marketing, human resources, finance, and general management positions are responsible for, yet they are based on the same general, accepted methods employed by engineering project managers in building skyscrapers, satellites, or software systems.

> **Words from the Wise**
>
> Project management skills transcend industry boundaries, and add a lot of opportunities for those people who are willing to learn the ropes. Those additional skills are added job security for those who are worried about their current job or company.

After learning about project management techniques, you'll be able to answer questions like these:

◆ How can I best define the work that needs to be done to make the project a success?

◆ How can I gain ongoing consensus about the goals and scope of the project?

◆ How long should the project really take to complete, and how much should it cost?

◆ How will I attain enough authority to get things done?

◆ Who should I put on my project team?

◆ How much work can be expected of each person on the project?

◆ How can I control cost overruns?

◆ Where are the risks that might cause the project to fail?

If you can answer all these questions, who knows? Maybe with good project management you really could build that warp drive.

Beam me up, Scotty! We're ready to go.

The Least You Need to Know

♦ Projects differ from ordinary work—called operations—and thus need special management techniques to make them successful.

♦ The factors of time, resources, results, and customer satisfaction are interrelated. If you change one of these, you must change the others to keep things in balance.

♦ Even though projects share attributes, they are still unique because of their different contexts and their particular use of resources, time, and results.

Chapter 2

What? I'm a Project Manager?

In This Chapter

- ◆ The role of the project manager
- ◆ The knowledge areas possessed by effective project managers
- ◆ The skills of successful project managers
- ◆ Seven traits of effective project managers

Regardless of what your business card says, if you manage projects, your company is depending on you to deliver a successful project. In this chapter, you'll learn what it takes to be a good project manager, because your company's success depends on successful project managers.

The Business Connection

Most companies decide to begin a project for one reason and one reason only: They hope to make more money. So that means that every project is linked to the business strategy in some way. A project is usually begun to meet the future business requirements of customers. And the final end result is better performance from the business. What does that mean for you as the project manager? It means that you must understand the business context or strategy that prompted your management to hand you the project in the first place. Without that understanding, you are like an architect who is designing a building without knowing what the business to be housed there will do!

So What Are My Responsibilities?

As a project manager, you are the one person assigned to lead the project management process, and in most cases, you alone are ultimately responsible for the project's success. (The project sponsor is often the person paying the bill for the project and so wants to make the project a success too, but we'll talk more about that later.) Even if you have other work to do or if you manage the project as part of a project team, you need to make sure the project gets done as specified.

So how does a project manager go about doing this? First of all, he or she must work with the customer to determine the requirements. When I use the term "customer," I am not necessarily referring to someone outside the company who will buy the product or service. If I am the project manager for a project that is designed to reconfigure the warehouse to get the products boxed and shipped faster, my "customer" might well be my company's manufacturing general manager. And I want to make sure that I have a steering committee of *all* the potential customers (or stakeholders) so that I make sure they all approve of my plan. (We'll talk more about steering committees and stakeholders and how to define them in Chapter 5).

CAUTION

Risk Management _____

If your boss or someone else asks you to add projects to an already over-loaded work schedule, you'll need to politely employ a tactic that has been successful for other project managers in similar situations: Before you say "yes," review with your boss the project or projects you are currently working on. Discuss the priority of the new request in the light of what you are currently doing. It may be that your boss will decide to have you stop working on something that he or she perceives as less important. Other times, they may decide to give that project to someone else or, if the manager is really clueless, stick you with it without making any changes to your workload. Only as a last resort would I suggest you turn down the opportunity to work on the project. However, you may need to do so if the request is unreasonable and you have done all the steps suggested above.

Once you as project manager have the requirements from the customer, you must make sure that the steering committee is on-board with the requirements. In my warehouse reconfiguration project, I would want the sales manager on that committee. Why? Because it is the sales manager whose sales team is promising outside customers delivery within certain timeframes. If the sales manager doesn't like the reconfiguration, I will have trouble no matter how satisfied the manufacturing general manager is.

What Do You Need to Do?

Being a successful project manager means that you must master two very different skills. First, you must be very creative in solving problems, because all projects, by definition, are unique. However, it also requires that you are very self-disciplined in your approach and employ technology, charting techniques, and budgeting tools to define the project. The bottom line is that to be truly successful as a "project" manager, you must first establish yourself as a competent manager.

Time Is Money

According to the Project Management Institute (PMI), project managers must integrate four areas of knowledge: cost, time, scope, and quality; and four support areas: communications, human resources, procurement, and risk management. Whew! That's a lot of stuff to handle. No wonder project management was invented.

Learn to Plan and Act

Project management as a discipline evolved because of a need to coordinate resources and technology to secure predictable results. The common project management tasks include establishing objectives, breaking work into well-defined tasks, charting the work sequences, scheduling, budgeting, coordinating a team, reporting, and communicating throughout the project. These tasks involve two general types of activities: planning and definition activities and implementation and control activities.

As we go through this book, we will look at each of these areas in more detail so you will know exactly how to plan and act at each stage in the project.

Focus on the Project's End

In the 1990s, Stephen Covey's *Seven Habits of Effective People* became a best-selling book. Covey wrote that one key to success was keeping the end in mind as you decide what to do and how to do it. This is an essential habit for successful project managers to develop. Instead of looking at a project as 50 tasks, always keep the end in mind. That way, the project is less likely to stall midstream. It also makes you a stronger project leader. If you have a clear vision in your mind about how the product will look at the completion of the project, you will be able to steer your project through difficult times and still succeed.

Be a Manager and a Leader

Good project managers can handle both the authority and the responsibility necessary to guide the project. Management of the project and leadership go hand in hand. As a leader, your team will expect you to be honest, competent, and inspirational as well as skilled in the use of project management techniques. On the individual level, you will need to motivate, delegate, mentor, and coach at various times. So having those skills plus the ability to help your team members resolve conflicts will be critical elements to your success (and the success of the project). But most of all, to be an effective project manager, you need to lead the project with energy and a positive attitude that make you the catalyst for moving your project forward. Never put the techniques of project management above your attitude—it's your attitude that gives you power.

It is possible to complete the management part of the project—the meetings, assignments, audits, reports, and other communications—and not attain the status and influence of a leader. To be a successful project manager, however, you must be both a manager and a leader. You must develop administrative procedures for ensuring that work is getting done on time and within budget, but more important, you must gain the trust and respect of the project team so that people feel comfortable taking your direction.

Let's take a closer look at project managers as leaders.

Words from the Wise

The most important quality in a leader is that of being acknowledged as such.

—André Maurois, *The Art of Living*

Time Is Money

A project manager who views the responsibility of managing a project as one of guiding, facilitating, negotiating, and coordinating will do better than will one who views the project management responsibility as one of ordering, dictating, and coercing.

The Leadership Roles of the Project Manager

As part of your responsibility for leading the various phases of the project, you'll need to assume a variety of roles with other people. Accomplished leaders move effortlessly among various roles, which we discuss in the following sections.

Interpersonal Roles

To be perceived as a leader, you must be regarded as honest, capable, and dependable—as well as personable. In your interpersonal roles, you'll need to do these kinds of things:

♦ Deal effectively with people from various professional backgrounds and create team unity.

♦ Solve team disputes.

♦ Focus and motivate team members to achieve milestones on the way to achieving the project goal.

♦ Build positive relationships with project stakeholders.

Informational Roles

You need to assume informational roles to keep people up-to-date and on track. When you do so, you'll need to accomplish these sorts of tasks:

♦ Arrange and lead team meetings.

♦ Create and maintain work schedules for other people.

♦ Communicate project vision to upper management.

♦ Provide feedback regarding results, quality, and project deliverables.

Along the Critical Path

After a seminar on project management, one of the attendees (a wag, obviously) ran up to us and told us that, after listening to our presentation, she had finally figured out how to be a perfect project manager. "All you have to do is have the intelligence of Einstein, the patience of Job, the integrity of a Supreme Court judge, the negotiating skills of a Mongolian horse trader, the savvy of James Bond, the appeal of Marilyn Monroe, the charisma of Sir Ralph Richardson, the communication skills of Tom Peters, the ideas of Stephen King, the planning skills of Colin Powell, the personal drive of Bill Gates, the financial acumen of Alan Greenspan, the skin of an armadillo, and the ego of Mother Teresa." Maybe she's right. Maybe we should shorten our seminars to give attendees less time to think up stuff like this ...

Decisional Roles

To move forward, projects demand that countless decisions be made, ranging from trivial to critical, at every phase of the project. When a decisional role is required, you'll need the expertise to do the following without alienating the people who may be affected by your choices:

- Distinguish between features and benefits.

- Appropriately allocate resources if a project falls behind schedule.

- Strike a balance between cost, time, and results.

- Prevent scope "creep" (when the project keeps getting bigger and more complex) and budget "slippage" (when the money starts running out).

The Other Business Management Roles

In addition to the roles detailed already, project managers will need all the general skills required of any competent business manager.

One of the most critical is human resource management. In building your project team, you will need to do some team building, and not just at the beginning of the project. Throughout the project, you should analyze how the team is functioning and make decisions about the best times to reinforce the "team" aspect to complete the project. No one will be able to do the project without it.

Time Is Money

The following are some ground rules for conducting meetings.

- Turn off all cell phones, pagers, Blackberries, and other electronic devices.
- Start and stop the meeting on time.
- Never hold a meeting without distributing an agenda in advance.
- Limit each person's speaking time.
- Criticize ideas, not people.
- Once a topic is covered, discourage people from engaging in "me too" speeches.
- Don't discuss items not included on the agenda and don't include on the agenda items where resolution will not be possible during the meeting.
- Have an end result (e.g. decision, actions, assignments) in mind for every meeting.
- Work on major differences one-on-one outside the meetings.
- Review meeting results before the meeting adjourns.
- Rotate the note-taking assignment for meetings.
- Distribute notes of each meeting highlighting what decisions were made and any action steps that were decided upon, the responsible party for those steps, and their due dates.

Some of the symptoms you might see that indicate a need for teambuilding include frustration, conflict, unnecessary competition, unproductive meetings, and/or lack of trust in you, the project manager. Team building will be a key integration element in project execution.

The Seven Traits of Good Project Managers

In addition to having knowledge of project management processes and an understanding of your various roles as a project manager and leader, research and experience point to seven additional traits that can help you become a successful project manager. These seven success traits are shown in the following figure, and we will discuss each of them in turn.

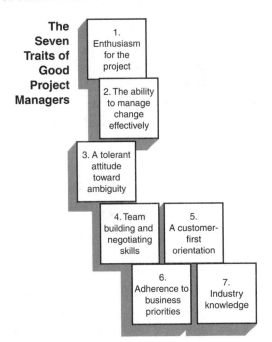

The Seven Traits of Good Project Managers

1. Enthusiasm for the project
2. The ability to manage change effectively
3. A tolerant attitude toward ambiguity
4. Team building and negotiating skills
5. A customer-first orientation
6. Adherence to business priorities
7. Industry knowledge

As project managers gain experience, the successful ones develop these traits to make their work easier and more satisfying.

Trait 1: Enthusiasm for the Project

Good project managers want to do a good job. Your enthusiasm for the project permeates to other people on the team, making it easier to keep people motivated and involved.

Trait 2: The Ability to Manage Change Effectively

Change is inevitable in projects. Customers change their minds about the end results. Managers decide to make changes to the scope of the project. Team members need to change their schedules. People who manage projects successfully learn to become managers of exceptions because there are always plenty of surprises, even in small projects.

Trait 3: A Tolerant Attitude Toward Ambiguity

Project managers often have ambiguous authority. This means that people may have other bosses to report to during the project and may not consider you a manager (unless you earn their respect as a leader). In fact, many of the roles in large projects are not clear-cut.

Some of the team members may make more money or have more senior jobs than the project manager; customers may get involved as team members; other departments may have a stake in the project. A good project manager must feel comfortable with these ambiguous roles and expectations and must learn how to manage them to see the project to a successful conclusion. If you need clear authority and an absolute plan, your project management days are numbered.

> **Time Is Money**
>
> Talk to experienced project managers. They'll tell you (if they admit it) that at least one of their first projects was a dismal failure. If this happens to you, don't kick yourself. Instead, pick up the pieces, learn from your mistakes, and move on.

Trait 4: Teambuilding and Negotiating Skills

A project manager needs to build coalitions among the various stakeholders in a project: management, customers, the project team, and suppliers. Power is only granted to a project manager who builds these relationships. Project managers must negotiate authority to move the project forward, so the success of any project depends on the project manager's ability to build a strong team among internal and external players.

Trait 5: A Customer-First Orientation

In projects that involve customers or clients (and most do), a good project manager puts the customer first and understands the customer's perspective regarding the project. After all, the ultimate measure of the project's success is the customer's satisfaction with the results. In a partnership with a customer or client, a skilled project manager crafts a vision for the project that can be communicated to the rest of the project team. Through alliances, team building, and empathy with the customer or client, the project manager is ultimately able to turn changing expectations into satisfaction with the completed project.

Trait 6: Adherence to the Priorities of Business

Earlier we talked about the project's connection to the overall business strategy. You'll also hear this called a "bottom-line" orientation, but paying attention to the budget and costs is only part of the business equation. The other business priorities involve maintaining competitive advantage, integrating the project into the culture of the organization, managing stakeholder issues, and ensuring both productivity and excellence as the project proceeds. However the business connection is served up, you should never lose sight of it during the project. It should be your compass point that tells you that you are heading in the right direction.

Trait 7: Knowledge of the Industry or Technology

Even though most project management skills are industry-independent, as a project manager, you'll need to have both project management skills and some experience or specific knowledge relevant to the industry you're working in. For example, if you're managing software projects, you'll need experience with programming concepts. If you're managing the development of a new shopping mall, you'll need a background in construction. However, you don't need to be an expert in the field, because you shouldn't be doing the work; you should be managing the work. We once worked with a project manager who insisted on supervising every move his project team made because he knew so much about the topic. However, he was actually a hindrance to the projects he managed because, for all practical purposes, he was doing everything himself!

> **Words from the Wise**
>
> Every man is the son of his own works.
>
> —Miguel de Cervantes

Be the Best Leader You Can Be

Of course, there are other traits that project managers would be wise to develop such as written and verbal communication skills, computer literacy, and above all, dependability. When you make a commitment to a stakeholder or team member, your reputation is at stake. Don't take that type of commitment lightly or you will damage your credibility and put the entire project at risk.

If you work at being all the things talked about in this chapter, you'll reap the rewards of your labor with the help of project teams that respect your efforts as a leader. As a result, your projects will meet their goals more often than not.

The Least You Need to Know

- You need to coordinate and prioritize your ordinary work along with your projects so that both get done effectively.

- To be successful as a project manager, your team must perceive you as a leader.

- You need people skills, communication skills, business skills, and technical skills to be an effective project manager.

- As a project manager, you'll need to assume interpersonal, informational, decisional, and business management roles, depending on the phase and the needs of the project.

- Being a good project manager takes ongoing, enthusiastic effort.

The Rules of the Project Game

In This Chapter

- ◆ Universal project success criteria revisited
- ◆ Standard reasons for project failure (and how to avoid them most of the time)
- ◆ The 12 golden rules of project management success
- ◆ Simple ways to help you follow the rules for success

We know you're just chomping at the bit to get started managing your projects. But before you become convinced that project management is more about process than substance, you need to know that all the ingredients that make up the project management recipe for success boil down to only 12 rules that you need to follow.

These 12 golden rules have been honed from years of experience by all kinds of project managers responsible for all types of projects in diverse managerial and political environments. So whether your projects involve building spaceships or building ships in bottles, you'll get better results by paying attention to these rules from the initiation phase to the closing phase of every project.

Universal Project Success Criteria

You may recall from Chapter 1, that for almost all projects, success is defined as meeting three criteria:

1. Finishing the project on schedule.

2. Keeping costs within budget.

3. Meeting quality outcomes (or goals) that have been agreed upon by the project team and the project stakeholders.

Quality may be difficult to define in some cases, but in project management, quality is always defined as meeting the requirements of the customer. If my project is to design a container that can hold an internal pressure of 500 pounds per square inch (psi), then a quality bottle will meet that expectation. A bottle will not meet the quality standard if it holds 400 psi or 600 psi.

Project Failure: The Reasons Are Simple

According to research done by the Project Management Institute, there are seven key reasons why projects fail; in addition, there are some basic strategies that people can employ to avoid those problems. They are as follows:

♦ **Poor project and program management discipline.** To avoid this problem, you will want a well-defined project plan using a proven methodology and use project management tools to track and control your project.

♦ **Lack of executive level support.** This is an all-too-frequent project killer. To avoid this problem, you must enlist the executive leadership. At least find a project sponsor among that group. Provide the executive team with regular communications and constantly reinforce the need for their involvement.

♦ **No linkage to the business strategy.** Provide a clear business direction that is understood by everyone who is impacted by the project. You will need to make sure everyone knows *why* this project is important, *what* it will mean when it is complete, and *how* you plan to implement that finished product.

♦ **The wrong team members.** Sometimes people are selected for a project because they "have the time." That should be the last criteria for choosing someone for the team. Pick the best players and give their day-to-day load to those who have the time. If the right people aren't available, hire contractors or consultants who do have the knowledge and experience. You'll be glad you did!

◆ **No measures for evaluating the success of the project.** Too often, no one has determined exactly how they will know if the project is a success. These are the measures that should be contained in the business case for the project (we'll discuss the business case in Chapter 7). If you haven't been given those measures, then you must develop them yourself and get the project sponsor and the steering committee to agree to them before you get too far into the project plan.

◆ **Lack of a robust risk strategy.** All good projects have a well-defined risk plan. You will need to identify as many potential risks as possible and develop a plan for mitigating them.

◆ **Inability to change.** All too frequently the organization is simply not prepared to accept the changes that a project might entail. For example, if the project is to install a new software system to capture orders and schedule delivery, you will likely meet with major resistance to this change. You will need to develop a robust communications and change management plan to get the organization ready to use the new system.

Words from the Wise

He enunciated no rules for success but offered a sure formula for failure: Just try to please everyone.

—E. J. Kahn Jr.

People don't start a project hoping it will fail, yet projects fail all too often because project managers disregard the 12 basic project management rules that can help avoid the seven reasons for failure.

12 Golden Rules of Project Management Success

The 12 basic rules of project management define the focus you'll need to get things done on time, within budget, and to the expectations of the stakeholders. As you read this book, you'll see how project management techniques are designed to help project managers put the 12 golden rules into action over and over again.

In the sections that follow, you'll be guided to the chapters of this book that offer specific advice related to the rule being discussed. Of course, if you consistently break or ignore the rules of project management, regardless of your diligent use of charts, plans, and reports recommended in the rest of this book, you'll probably doom your project to failure anyway—or at least cause a lot of problems that otherwise could have been avoided.

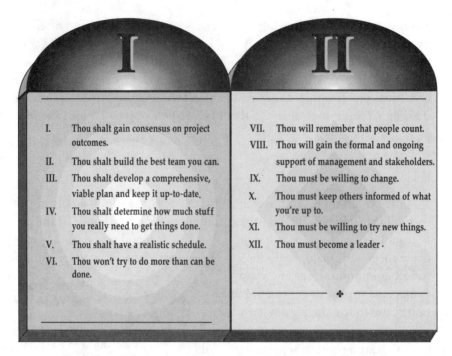

The 12 Rules of Project Management

You'd be wise to keep this list of rules in front of you throughout your projects.

Rule 1: Thou Shalt Gain Consensus on Project Outcomes

If you don't know what you intend to accomplish, it's not likely that you'll accomplish anything of value. A project without clear expectations is really just a bunch of work without a purpose. To be considered a success, a project must have clearly defined goals that specify what the project looks like when it's done.

It's not enough, however, for you to know exactly what you want to do. You also have to reach consensus with the stakeholders and team members on the project that the goals and expectations are the right ones. In Chapter 7, you'll learn how to set clear project goals and expectations, and you'll get tips for gaining the consensus required to ensure that the project you finally finish is the project people wanted to get done.

Rule 2: Thou Shalt Build the Best Team You Can

A willing, skilled, appropriately organized project team is the key to success. This is a group of people you'll have to develop because the perfect team almost never starts out that way. A good team starts with good choices on your part; however, sometimes the people you pick may turn out to be total dummies or uncooperative blockheads.

It's your challenge to make sure the project team gets smart really quickly and stays ambitious in spite of inadequate experience and training, family problems, or conflicting priorities. If people must be trained to get things done right, that's one of your responsibilities as project manager. Of course, the people must also be willing to work on the project and learn the new skills. That means you'll have to use your best management skills and motivational tactics to guide them in the right direction. (That's the direction you want them to go.)

Time Is Money

Review the 12 golden rules at least once a week, and you'll have a much better chance of getting things done the right way, on time, within budget, and to the specifications agreed upon by customers, management, or other stakeholders. Of course, the schedule and budget may change over time, but as long as people agree on the changes, you're still getting things done the right way. A review of the rules will remind you of that.

Rule 3: Thou Shalt Develop a Comprehensive, Viable Plan and Keep It Up-to-Date

A complete, appropriately detailed project plan is central to successful completion of any project. The plan helps you guide the project. It is the document that communicates the overall intentions, tasks, resource requirements, and schedule for the project. Without a plan, it's almost impossible to lead a group to achieve a common goal. You'll learn about creating the various parts of the project plan in Chapters 9 through 16.

Of course, creating a plan isn't enough. Because you can't see into the future any better than a fortune teller with a broken crystal ball, the plan you develop and get approved will probably change many times from project initiation to project closing. As you gain more information about the realities of the project and as the stakeholders change their minds about what they need, your plan will have to be reevaluated. Be forewarned (you'll hear about this again in Chapter 24), if you don't update the project plan—and negotiate these changes with the stakeholders—you're going to be responsible for the budget and schedule of the original plan.

Along the Critical Path

Think about all the really smart people who use project management techniques, develop detailed plans, and still seem to fail in getting projects done on time and within budget—consider the project in Boston, Massachusetts, that has been nicknamed the Big Dig. Construction on the project began in late 1991, and it is still not completed as of this writing. Furthermore, there is considerable debate as to when, exactly, it will be finished. The project was designed to replace the six-lane highway called the Central Artery that runs through the center of downtown Boston with an underground expressway of eight-to-ten lanes. At the time of the project initiation, the budget was $11 billion and was scheduled to be completed before the end of the decade. That budget has grown to $14.6 billion and the new schedule for completion is now December 2004. This project is similar in scale to the building of the Panama Canal or the English Channel Tunnel (dubbed the Chunnel). However, for the poor citizens of the Boston area, this has been an expensive, inconvenient project that must seem like it will take forever to finish.

Rule 4: Thou Shalt Determine How Much Stuff You Really Need to Get Things Done

No matter what your boss says, you can't squeeze blood from a turnip. Without adequate people, capital, and equipment to complete a project, there is no way you can make it happen. You must get sufficient resources allocated to the project, or you must renegotiate what is going to be done so that fewer resources are required (refer to Rule 1). Getting sufficient resources (including equipment, people, and supplies) for a project is an ongoing problem in most companies—and one of the most important responsibilities for all project managers. In Chapter 15 you'll learn how to scope out what you really need to get a project done. In Chapter 24, you'll discover some techniques for negotiating when you don't get everything you need the first time around.

Words from the Wise

Time waits for no one, and nowhere is that more true than when managing a project.

—Project manager and PM teacher Jim MacIntyre

Rule 5: Thou Shalt Have a Realistic Schedule

Without a realistic schedule, you'll never succeed—and you'll run out of time before you get to try again. You may be able to bring more people on board and buy more supplies, but you can't produce more time no matter what you do. (Of course, if your last name is Wells and your initials are H. G., you might be the exception.)

There's no faster way to lose credibility as a project manager than to change the schedule without a really good reason. Then again, if you follow Rules 1 and 8, you can get more time for yourself by getting a new schedule approved. In Chapters 12 and 14, you'll learn how to develop a schedule you can meet (and how to change it when necessary).

Rule 6: Thou Won't Try to Do More Than Can Be Done

You must have an appropriate scope for the project. The scope of the project involves more than goals. For example, the goal could be to build a two-story building on the location of the back parking lot by next December. But the scope of the project could range from putting up a prefabricated metal building with a cement floor to building a miniature Taj Mahal for the chairman of the board. While the first scope is feasible, the second is not. Make sure the objectives and the scope of the project are clear to everyone if you want to be considered a success when the project is done. While *gold plating* the project might score you bonus points, it should not be one of your primary goals.

Time Is Money

Learning to work with people takes a lifetime—and at the end, you'll still be wondering how people really work. Even with all the good advice in this book, people will surprise you in mysterious and wonderful ways. That's what keeps project management interesting.

Project Lingo

In project management jargon, doing more than the project requirements call for is called **gold plating** the project.

Rule 7: Thou Will Remember That People Count

Sometimes, in focusing on the process of project management, you may forget that projects are mostly about people. Project success depends on people, not on reports or charts or even computers. To be a successful project manager, you must accommodate people's needs and priorities. People manage the project. People do most of the work. People enjoy (or curse) the end results. Projects also put stresses on these people because projects almost always involve new group structures, deadlines, and extra work. If a project's end results don't serve people, then the project has failed.

Another way of stating Rule 7 is this: Do no damage to the people on the project! Don't overwork the staff; don't demand the impossible; never lie to anyone (even if it seems like a way out of a tight situation).

Projects almost always incorporate built-in priority conflicts between ordinary work and project work. The bad news is that you must eventually satisfy people's needs, priorities, and conflicts for the project to come to a happy ending. The good news is that, in Chapter 23, you'll learn some techniques to help you deal with the inevitable conflicts among the people and the priorities in your projects.

Rule 8: Thou Will Gain the Formal and Ongoing Support of Management and Stakeholders

It's obvious (or at least it should be) that you must have approval from management and the key stakeholders before you initiate a project. This involves not only communication skills but also negotiation skills. This rule is a lot like Rule 1, except that it means you must add a formal approval stage to the general consensus you gained in keeping Rule 1. You need to get all the people who have to contribute resources (time or money) or who may be impacted by a project (if it will change their job or life) to formally endorse your project and to agree that the project is worth doing. You also need to get formal agreement on some basic rules from the stakeholders for dealing with issues of authority, changes in project scope, and handling basic communications.

For many of the stakeholders, support requires signed approval, but it doesn't stop with a signature. Keeping this rule also demands that you ensure the stakeholders' ongoing interest in your project. If you start a project for your boss and your boss has no real interest in the project even after he or she has signed on the dotted line, it's unlikely you'll get any praise for finishing the feat. Remember to review Chapters 5, 23, and 24 whenever support wanes for your projects.

Rule 9: Thou Must Be Willing to Change

This rule goes along with Rule 3. You must be willing to adapt the project plan and implementation to guide the project where it needs to go. Sometimes things change for justifiable reasons, such as a rainstorm that stops the work on a construction project. Sometimes things change because you get new information, like the time researchers in Utah discovered cold fusion in a test tube, which changed the whole perspective on building fusion reactors and stopped projects worldwide (for a while at least—the whole experiment was found to be erroneous and unscientific). As one researcher put it, "It was like we were trying to invent the biplane and someone shows us up with a 747." Sometimes changes are simply the result of peoples' whims, like the advertising agency's customer who now wants a videotape instead of a brochure to promote a new product—even though the brochure is almost ready to go to the printer.

You'll also learn in Chapter 24 that change is an important part of controlling a project. The main thing to remember here is that it is not the project manager's job to say "no" to a change; rather, it is his or her job to tell the stakeholders the impact that the change will have on the time, cost, and quality of the project and to let them make the decision about the change.

Rule 10: Thou Must Keep Others Informed of What You're Up To

You must keep all the relevant stakeholders informed of your progress, problems, and changes. The way to obey this rule is simple: communicate, communicate, communicate. As things change on the project (and they always do), you'll find through your communications that the stakeholders may want or need to introduce their own changes into the project. You'll have to refer frequently to Rule 9 while adhering to Rule 10.

> **Words from the Wise**
>
> Graham's Law: If they know nothing of what you are doing, they suspect you are doing nothing.
>
> —Robert J. Graham in *Understanding Project Management*

Rule 11: Thou Must Be Willing to Try New Things

Because every project is different, with different people, goals, and challenges involved, it would simply be inappropriate to use the exact same methods, software, charts, graphs, or other aids on every project. The standard methods and tools can be used with all projects, but not all projects involve the same risk or complexity. Thus, not all the techniques in this book should be used on all of your projects.

Large, complex projects will likely use more methods or tools than smaller projects. Too many methods *or* too few tools can doom a project. You must adapt the processes, technologies, tools, and techniques to the needs of the project at hand. For example, you obviously need to put more detail into the network diagram (see Chapter 10 for more on these) for building a new corporate headquarters from scratch than you would for setting up a new sales office in a rented building.

Rule 12: Thou Must Become a Leader

Leadership is an art that comes naturally to some, but the rest of us have to work at it. Chances are, you have to work on your leadership role, too. Reading management books won't be enough to bring your projects in on time and within budget. As a project manager, you must put what you read into action. You need to become a leader as well as a team member. You must not only plan, track, and control the project, you must also be a source of wisdom and motivation for the team members and stakeholders. Without leadership, even a well-coordinated project can fail to meet its goals—the people in the project won't feel they have the support or guidance they need to make things happen. That's your job as the project manager. Chapter 2 details the skills and traits of a good project manager.

Keep Your Eyes on the Prize

Projects help further personal goals as well as those of companies and organizations. If you keep the 12 golden rules of project management in front of you throughout the project phases, project failures can be minimized if not eliminated.

Yes, there will be times when fate plays a role, and you can't do everything to everyone's satisfaction. But if you remember the 12 golden rules throughout the five phases of the project management process, you'll succeed more times than you fail. Keep working at it. The prize for your effort will be projects done on time, within budget, and with less stress on mind and body.

The Least You Need to Know

- When projects fail, it is usually due to one or more identifiable reasons.

- Follow the 12 golden rules of project management to help guide projects of all sizes and complexity to more successful conclusions.

- Your first loyalty is to your project even though you may be pressured from all sides for change.

- Keep a list of the 12 golden rules of project management on your desk or, better yet, put the list on your office wall to keep you focused on the success factors during the tough times of a project.

- Remember that the success of a project always depends more on people than on process, but some processes and structures (like the ones you'll learn about in this book) are important in helping people stay on track.

Chapter 4

Starting Off on the Right Foot

In This Chapter

◆ Learning the project life cycle

◆ Introducing the All-Star Cable case study

◆ Project life cycle phase one: defining your project

No matter how big or how small a project is the simple fact is that as a project manager you are operating within a larger context. That context is the environment and styles that exist within the organization where you work. Any project manager who doesn't recognize how significant that can be is in for a rude awakening. In this chapter, we'll take a look at how to organize the project and factor in the environment, too!

> ## Words from the Wise
>
> Imagine a (theatre) director who has no master schedule for the work to be done to transition her theatre company from the old play to the new one. When asked about the calendar dates for key transition events, she answers, "Well the situation is much too fluid to put things done on a calendar. We'll just have to wait to see how things play out, won't we?"
>
> —Dutch Holland, *Change Is the Rule*

The Project Life Cycle

All projects can be broken into distinct phases. Taken together, these phases comprise the project life cycle.

> ## Words from the Wise
>
> Be not afraid of greatness: Some are born great, some achieve greatness, and some have greatness thrust upon them.
>
> —William Shakespeare, *Twelfth Night*

> ## Project Lingo
>
> The conclusion of a project phase is generally marked by a review of both key deliverables and project performance to date, to determine if the project should continue. These phase-end reviews are usually called **stage gates.**

Since all projects are unique by definition, they all have a large degree of uncertainty associated with them—remember that you are creating something that has never existed before. One of the techniques that can help us to develop our project plans effectively is to use the project life cycle as a guide.

Project Phases and the Project Life Cycle

There are four phases in the project life cycle, as you can see from the following diagram. The four phases are labeled according to what occurs in them:

Phase 1.   Project Definition Phase

Phase 2.   Project Planning Phase

Phase 3.   Project Execution Phase

Phase 4.   Project Close-Out Phase

① Project Definition Phase	② Project Planning Phase	③ Project Execution Phase	④ Project Close-Out Phase

① Project Definition Phase

- Initiate the project
- Identify Project Manager
- Identify initial project concept
- Develop Project Charter
  - Describe Project Strategy
    - Establish Initial Direction
    - High-level Project Outcomes
    - Project Guiding Principles
  - Define Project:
    - Refine Project Concept
    - Concept Scope Planning
    - Strategic Plan Fit
    - Business Rationale
    - Opportunities/Benefits
    - High level risks
- Conduct Feasibility Study
- Define Planning Phase Schedule & Budget
  - Identify Planning Team Members
  - Determine contracts, as needed
- Deliver Project Charter Memorandum to Decision Authority

② Project Planning Phase

- Organize and Staff Project
- Develop Project Plan
  - Finalize Scope Definition
    - Project objectives
    - Project requirements and specifications
  - Develop Work Breakdown Structure (WBS)
    - Identify work activities required
  - Develop Organizational Breakdown Structure
    - Match project work activities and performing organization
  - Project Scheduling and Cost Estimating
    - Identify activity dependencies
    - Sequence activities
    - Develop Project Schedule
    - Estimate costs
    - Develop budget/funding profile
    - Determine scheduled start dates
    - Set project milestones
    - Establish measurement baselines for schedule and cost performance (project metrics)
  - Originate Subsidiary Management Plans
    - Risk Plan
    - Project Change Control Plan
    - Issues Resolution Plan
    - Quality Assurance Plan
    - Organization and Human Resources Plan
    - Procurement Plan
    - Monitoring and Reporting Plan
  - Develop Organization Transition Plan
    - Project Communications Plan
    - Change Leadership Plan
- Deliver Project Plan Memorandum to Decision Authority

③ Project Execution Phase

- Execute Project Plan
  - Manage the project scope
  - Monitor and report project status
- Manage Project Plan
  - Execute and refine management plans:
    - Risk Plan
    - Quality Assurance Plan
    - Project Change Control Plan
    - Issue Resolution Plan
    - Organization & HR Plan
    - Procurement Plan
  - Activate Project Controls
    - Scope - Cost - Schedule - Quality
  - Maintain Project Plan:
    - Incorporate Lessons Learned.
    - Add approved Scope Changes
- Implement Project Results
  - Verify Scope Completion
  - Execute Organizational Transition Plan
  - Transition to operations
- Deliver Project Completion Memorandum to Decision Authority

④ Project Close-Out Phase

- Document Project Lessons Learned
- Schedule After-implementation Review
- Provide performance feedback
- Close-out contracts (as needed)
- Complete administrative close-out
- Deliver Project Completion Report to Decision Authority

The four phases of the project life cycle. Note the deliverable at the end of each phase.

Each phase has a *deliverable* that marks the end of the current phase and gives the project manager authority to continue. To better understand the project life cycle, let's take a look at our primary case study for this book. Once it's been introduced, we can follow through the four phases of the project life cycle.

Project Lingo

The **deliverable** for each project phase is defined as a tangible, measurable, or concrete result that must be produced as part of a project.

The Case Study: All-Star Cable

All-Star Cable is a 30-year-old company that started in South Texas. It began as a basic cable company offering standard television channels but with better, more consistent transmissions than traditional reception methods. It was able to take advantage of larger companies' equipment and lines as a result of deregulation of the industry. It was an excellent business that grew rapidly because it offered great, simple service at a better price than the larger companies. All-Star prided itself on being a small company that could respond very quickly to customers, both in problem resolution and installations.

In the mid-1980s, All-Star realized that its growth had virtually stopped, and it was starting to lose established customers. The company was slow to respond to this trend. By the time managers studied the market and their customer base, All-Star was almost bankrupt. Its problems centered on a few key issues:

◆ Its customer base was doing better economically and wanted more options than All-Star could offer.

◆ It had become to be perceived as the "cheap" company—the one you went to when you couldn't afford anything else.

◆ Its competitors had geared their sales efforts to tiered offerings that attracted the same customer base All-Star previously had relied on.

All-Star hired a marketing manager and an information technology manager, who remapped company strategy and operations and developed new product offerings that turned the company around. They contracted with premium channel companies to offer their subscribers HBO, Showtime, ESPN Sports, and a host of packages that the customers were seeking. They were able to offer those at a cost below the larger companies by reducing standard margins, thinking that volume business would offset their declining customer base. It started working immediately.

In addition, the IT manager was able to automate the company's billing system and office functions, allowing All-Star to run its business operations more efficiently and cheaply. Its fortunes rose, and All-Star was soon regarded as the "best deal" company. The marketing manager and IT manager were promoted to vice-presidents.

Within a few years, managers at All-Star saw Pay-for-View as the coming attraction. The company invested in new equipment, upgraded current equipment, and expanded its IT department. It took awhile to become efficient and have customers start using the service. The marketing VP took aggressive action, and revenues and profitability increased. This was the first service that All-Star offered that it didn't have to discount to be competitive. Its customer base grew to the point that the company is no longer the small competitor. It had become one of the largest cable companies in South Texas and was expanding its market further.

Time Is Money

According to the Project Management Institute (PMI), project managers must conduct a feasibility study in the Project Definition Phase that will provide some evidence that the project can be successful. In a feasibility study, project managers should evaluate the alternative solutions along with the associated costs and benefits. The objective is to provide predictable results for a specific project. (See Chapter 7 for more details.)

The Project

All-Star has identified Movies-on-Demand as the new direction for the company to take. Movies-on-Demand (MOD) is a revolutionary concept. Whereas Pay-for-View allows a viewer to key a code into their controller box to "turn on" a movie that is being broadcast globally, MOD allows customers to view menus of movies, pick the movie they want to watch, and watch at a time they designate.

These movies would be stored digitally in a data warehouse owned by All-Star. Customers will be able to sift through menus that list movies by title, actor/actress, or genre, then drill down to the specific movie they want to order.

The marketing director and the company president believe that their MOD service will make All-Star an industry leader. They have suffered through the pains of catching up in a market, and they've seen the benefits of delivering new products. This time, they have an idea that is a conglomeration of ideas from nationwide cable companies. Not everyone in the company agrees with this vision. They are concerned about their internal IT capability to develop it, and they're very concerned about development costs.

The current system allows customers to access their billing information, make traditional pay-for-view movie selections, and access the Internet using their All-Star controller box. The controller box will be the access device to the new menu driven selections.

The billing system will require modification to include the cost to the customer of viewing these digitally stored movies. Menus will have to be built. The anticipated cost of viewing any single movie will be $6.00. There is no discount planned for customers who order large numbers of movies.

The Project Manager (That's You)

As the project manager, you have been introduced to the concept by the president and marketing director. They are looking to you to find out how feasible the concept is. They also are looking to you to determine what this project might cost to rollout. After acceptance by the board of directors, the project will start. Unfortunately, the president and marketing director have established a go-live date of six months from now.

You will be presenting the concept to the board of directors next week. While you have come to believe that this move is essential to the company's growth and long-term survival, you have many concerns. These concerns are based on the fact that you don't have a lot of information that you feel you need. You are feeling the pressure of "carrying the ball" on this project, without all the information you'd like, with a specific time deadline. It's time to start planning this project and getting ready for the board of directors' presentation.

Project Definition Phase

As the project manager for the All-Star Cable project to make Movies-on-Demand a reality, you will now be responsible for defining the project. The first thing you'll need to do is make sure that you understand what the project is about and whether or not it can even be done!

You will need to interview key people, some of whom will be stakeholders, but others who may be experts in information systems, to see if it will be possible to deliver movies through All-Star's cable system using the existing cable boxes that customers have already. You will need to interview the president and vice president of marketing to find out if All-Star is going to offer "adult" videos as part of the selection that its customers can order. As you continue and your project team continue to work on the project, you will undoubtedly come up with more questions that you will need to research or ask others.

At the same time, you need to think about the various risks that are involved in this project. While you can't anticipate all of them, you can certainly think of some. For example, what if you miss your schedule and another competitor introduces the idea first. *Remember, this has never been done before* and therefore it is, by definition, a project. Essentially, at this point, you are trying to build a case that allows the board of directors to decide if they should go ahead with the project, or drop the idea right now before any more money is spent.

Time Is Money _____

As part of the Project Definition Phase, you will need to ...

- Identify the basic idea behind the project.
- Develop a project charter that defines what the project will include, and what it will not include.
- Conduct a feasibility study to see if its even possible.
- Plan a preliminary budget and schedule for delivery.

Project Life Cycle Flow

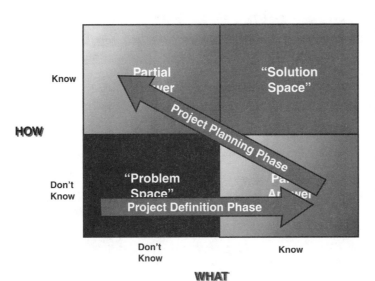

In the figure, the definition phase of the project moves from the space where you don't know what you will do or how you will do it, to the space where you have defined what you will do. In the planning phase of the project, you will move to the space where you know what you will do to how you will do it. During the execution phase, you move the project into the space where the solution resides.

Focus on the Project Team

Now that you have some idea of *what* you are going to do, you need to begin to think about *how* you will do it, and with *whom*. In other words, you need to start thinking about the people that you'll need who can do the work that will make Movies-on-Demand a reality. You will need to think about people's technical skills, perhaps the experience they have in the industry or within the company, and determine if you will need other resources that are not available inside the company, such as consultants or contractors. We'll take a closer look at the people involved on projects in Chapters 5 and 6.

The Least You Need to Know

- ◆ Since you are working on something that is new and unique, use the project life cycle as a way to get organized.

- ◆ Deliverables are part of every project phase and determine whether you can move on to the next phase.

- ◆ Getting clear on the project and beginning to define it is a critical step to success.

- ◆ You will be expected to develop a feasibility study as to whether the project makes sense at all.

- ◆ Once you know *what* your going to have to do, you need to begin to think about *who* you're going to do it with.

Part 2

The Project Initiation Processes

You may think it's easy to get a project started, but starting a project off right takes some hard thinking and involves some tough decisions.

First, you need to identify who the players are—these people are the stakeholders who'll help you define the project. As you begin to define the project, you'll need to pick some smart, talented people to help you—some for the entire duration of the project. Next, you begin the tough process of defining what is included, and what is not included, in the project you have been assigned. After that, you need to define the specific goals for your project and identify all the risks and constraints that may cause problems for the project once it is started. You'll then need to create and get approval for a project charter or statement of work, which defines the project you're going to plan and the rules by which you're going to play.

Identifying Stakeholders and Defining Their Roles

In This Chapter

- ◆ Identifying the key project stakeholders

- ◆ The roles of the project stakeholders

- ◆ Learning to work together with the stakeholders

Always remember that projects are successes when the *stakeholders* on the project are satisfied. Thus, identifying the right and complete list of stakeholders must be the first step in getting your project moving and should be an ongoing responsibility throughout its life cycle. These key stakeholders will make all of the important decisions during the project. In this chapter, you'll learn how to identify the key stakeholders—those people who will have the greatest influence and authority as you proceed in defining and planning your project.

Start by Identifying the Stakeholders

The first stakeholders you need to identify are those who will make a meaningful contribution to a project. Thus, the stakeholder list includes:

- You (as the project manager)
- The managers in your company who are involved with approvals
- The customer
- The project team

Project Lingo

A **stakeholder** is someone who has a vested interest in the success of a project. The Project Management Institute identifies stakeholders as individuals and organizations who are actively involved in the project, or whose interests may be positively or negatively affected as a result of project execution or successful project completion.

There may be other stakeholders, as well. For example, when the project involves building a chemical plant, government regulators at the local, state, and national levels are stakeholders. Environmental action groups, community and neighborhood groups, labor unions, and a variety of other groups might also be stakeholders.

Key Stakeholders and Their Contributions

Project Manager	Leads and manages the project; plans, monitors, tracks, controls, documents, and reports project activities.
Sponsor (may be a customer representative or functional manager)	Provides authority for project to proceed; guides and monitors the project in partnership with the project manager; key organizational advocate for the project. Typically, the sponsor will approve the project charter.
Core Project Team	Provides skills, expertise, and effort to perform the tasks defined for the project; assists with planning and estimating project tasks.
Customer (may be internal or external)	The individual or organization that will use the product created by the project. Establishes the requirements for the project; provides funding; reviews the project as milestones and deliverables are met. Ultimately accepts the finished product.
Functional Managers	Establish company policy; provide people; some will provide review and approval authority.

Organizational Stockholders

Potential stakeholders for any project.

Sometimes the various stakeholders' roles will overlap, such as when an engineering firm provides the financing for a plant it is designing.

It's your job to manage the stakeholders by keeping them informed of any key decisions that are made. You must also communicate with them regularly on the status of the project. As a rule of thumb, stakeholders should never be surprised by any key decisions or project status. However, not every customer representative or manager in the company is or should be considered a stakeholder.

Each stakeholder might have his or her own objectives for the project, and that can often lead to conflicts of interest. For example, the line manager of a department may request a new management information system and want it at the lowest possible cost. However, the vendor of that system is interested in maximizing their profit, and the IS manager is mainly interested in emphasizing technical excellence.

The Customer

The customer is the person or organization who pays for the project. In some cases the customer may be a department or division of your own company. In other cases, the customer is external. In either case, the customer contributes both funding and project requirements. When defining the customer stakeholders, be careful to distinguish between the people with final authority for project approvals and changes, and those who must simply be kept informed.

Stakeholder	Roles	Approvals
Project Manager: Joel Baker	Defines, plans, controls, monitors, and leads the project.	Makes recommendations for approval; signature authority for any purchase under $1500.
Sponsor: Joe Macdonald, Director of Engineering	Authority for most operational project decisions; helps guide the project; assists project manager with planning and approvals by other stakeholders.	Approves personnel requests and hiring decisions; signs off on SOW and project plans before submitting to the customer; signature authority for any purchase under $15,000.
Customer: Managers Sarah Goodwin, Vice President Fred Catwalk, Director of Finance	Helps define the project; authority for all major project plans and changes; budget approvals.	Final approval for SOW and all project plans; initial budget approval; signatures required for any non-planned purchase of $5000 or more.
Customer: Experts Allen Strange Jell Elsewhere	Experts who help define the project and develop product specifications.	Works with project manager and team; makes recommendations; not formal signature authorities.

A simple chart like this can help you identify the roles and authorities of the key stakeholders on your project.

The Project Sponsor

The project sponsor is your most important ally in the project; this is the person who shares responsibility for project success and helps everyone on the project team be successful. The sponsor doesn't usually have the title of sponsor—but it's important that you identify the person who has the role. If the project is internal to your organization, it is usually a senior manager within the organization. If the project is for an external customer, the sponsor is usually someone from the customer organization who has authority to make decisions and provide money for the project.

This authority, and the person's support, are the person's primary contributions to the project. The sponsor supports the project through approving the project charter, advising you as the project manager, assisting you in the development of the statement of work (see Chapter 7), helping to secure the people needed to complete the project, and consulting on the development of other project documentation.

A good sponsor will also assist you in overcoming organizational and political obstacles. Many times the sponsor will be your direct manager, but other times it will be a person from another department or a customer representative with a primary interest and assigned authority for the project. Developing and maintaining your relationship with the project sponsor is key to making the overall project and its implementation successful—in many ways it's a partnership. The sponsor will always be the first person you should confide in when you need help or think you're in trouble.

The project sponsor's role for All-Star Cable includes the following:

- Has the ultimate authority, responsibility, and accountability for the success of the project.
- Resolves cross-functional organizational issues.
- Promotes innovation to achieve the project goals.
- Provides guidance, support, and direction to the project.
- Signs project charter and business case.
- Signs project plan and statement of work.
- Is responsible for quality of the implementation.
- Contributes to and approves the responsibility matrix.
- Assists in developing project policies and procedures.
- Approves project deliverables.
- Approves changes to project scope and provides additional funds for those changes as required.
- Monitors the progress of the project, the project budget, and schedule.
- Works with the steering committee.
- Makes business decisions for the project.
- Provides user resources to the project as needed.
- Shields the project from corporate politics.
- Works to resolve conflicts.

Steering Committee

The steering committee (sometimes called review and approval team or a project governance board) is the group of stakeholders who must approve and agree on project scope, schedule, budgets, plans, and changes.

Obviously, one or more key customer representatives, either internal or external, will be included in this group, but it will likely include selected functional managers and executives from your own organization who must approve aspects of the project. The key is to keep this team limited in size and scope to those people who really do need to approve project documents. On a large project you'll need to develop an approval matrix that describes the people who will have a say in, review, and approve each type of document and project change.

The steering committee for the All-Star Cable project is expected to perform the following roles:

♦ Advises on the business architecture

♦ Monitors the project and maintains priority relative to other projects

♦ Settles priorities between related/competing projects

♦ Provides organizational support

♦ Provides timely decisions

♦ Resolves major issues of significant risk to the enterprise

♦ Disposes of issues and change requests that impact the organization beyond the commercial area

♦ Executes formal reviews and management reviews

♦ Approves changes in budget and/or schedule

♦ Provides feedback to the project sponsor and the project managers

♦ Manages environmental factors beyond the control of the project

Project Lingo

It's common for people to devote only a percentage of their time to projects. This is usually identified as a **matrixed** organization. That means that they may work on projects part-time and have dedicated duties in a functional group, while they work on your project. In these cases, it's very important that you work with these people's functional managers to ensure their support of the project.

Functional Management

Functional management, also known as line management, is made up of the company officials with an interest in your project. These may include department supervisors, managers, or vice presidents. With the exception of companies that are organized based on projects, these managers are responsible for organizational units within the company, such as engineering, marketing, or finance. Usually, they are the people who will supply the people who will be working on your project team. You must work closely with these people to ensure that you get the best people for your project. You also need their commitment to *continue* to support the project with resources. Too often functional managers cut back the time that they allow their people to spend on a project.

Therefore, as the project proceeds, you must keep the relevant functional managers informed of project progress and personnel performance issues. These managers can help you out of personnel jams if you let them; but if you don't keep them informed, they can derail a project from underneath you.

After identifying the obvious functional authorities for your project, you'll need to identify those people who will have informal veto authority on decisions that will affect the project. Many of these managers will be involved in approval processes even if they don't have a formal stake (such as required signatures) in the project. For instance, if you have a contract administration function within the organization, they are not really involved in a direct way with the project. However, they control the process you will use to manage procurement activities. It's your job to identify these people to make sure they are included at strategic points in the project initiation, development, and execution.

CAUTION

Risk Management

On large projects that may affect many departments within a company, line managers might indicate that their organizations don't need to be involved. At first, you can accept this view and proceed with the project—but we recommend that you still return to these people periodically and provide them with an update on the project and invite them to participate again.

All-Star Cable Case Study

For our case study, review the following list of people. They are the key players in the Movies-on-Demand project.

The Key Players

Name	Position	Personal Characteristics	Background
Martin Swift	Board of Directors	Male, age 55	First Board Member. Helped define the strategy that brought the company back on its feet. Doesn't understand or trust technology. Believes the company should stay as basic as possible.
Michael Solis	Board of Directors	Male, age 45	Been on the board 10 years. Has a successful retail business. Is very attuned to sales, customer service, and product delivery. Understands IT to a degree, but is very cost sensitive.
Sarah Mayo	Board of Directors	Female, age 48	Vice-President of a large San Antonio bank. Been a friend of the company for many years, providing key financial support during hard times. Been on the board three years. Open to new ideas and understands the cost of IT.
David Gonzalez	All-Star President	Male, age 55	Founded the company. Lot of personal time and money invested. Fearful of business decline. Started the board to give direction and has given the board approval/veto power. Doesn't totally trust IT, but understands the need for innovation. Concerned about passing the company on to his family in solid condition.

Name	Position	Personal Characteristics	Background
Micky Nash	VP Marketing	Female, Age 37	High energy, high influence marketing VP. Not concerned with anything but company growth and profitability. Visionary who sometimes alienates others who take their time with decision making. Has the ear of the president. Has become a friend of Sarah Mayo.
Michael Puerto	IT Director	Male, Age 40	Brought on several years ago to provide in-house IT capability to operations and back-office functions. Has developed a very capable staff with a lot of experience specifically in the cable business. Is aggressive and confident. Feels rising IT costs are the cost of doing business. Knows IT is the key to the delivery of products in the future. Has run sideways with the president and the board at times with direction that he felt necessary, but they felt costly.
Southside Citizens Groups		Wide variety of people	Vocal force to local businesses. They don't feel like the company has kept their interests in mind. Want to return to a cheap, basic cable service affordable to many. Feels like they have to bear the cost of business expansion and the company doesn't consider their needs anymore. Powerful lobbyists who can change public opinion. Helped the company a lot during their troubled times.

Working Together: The Magic Success Formula

The project manager (that's you) will have responsibility for ensuring that the stakeholders on the project work together and gain consensus on project decisions.

Not only at the beginning of the project, but as it continues through its phases, the project manager must continue to clarify who the key stakeholders are and the roles they will play.

Many of the stakeholders, including the sponsor, the functional managers in your company, and the customers will have more formal authority than you—but even so, you need to lead them. Your leadership will be embodied in the tough questions you ask, the facts you provide, the ideas you inspire, and the enthusiasm you convey for the project. You'll need to coordinate the stakeholders and guide them through the various project stages. Some experts call this "managing upward." Your ability to do this is at the heart of successful project management.

The Least You Need to Know

- ◆ The identification of key stakeholders on your project is an ongoing process and is key to the implementation, planning, and execution of the project.

- ◆ At the very least, the project stakeholders include you (the project manager), the customer, the project sponsor, company functional managers, and the implementation team members.

- ◆ Coordinating and communicating with the stakeholders is a primary role of the project manager.

- ◆ As a project manager, you'll need to "manage upward," to guide the key stakeholders through the project phases.

Chapter 6

Selecting a Project Team

In This Chapter

- ◆ Selecting the team members for each phase of the project
- ◆ Identifying and planning for project roles and responsibilities
- ◆ Getting the right people working on the project
- ◆ Developing the team to get the performance you want

As you build the project team, you will need to carefully consider the knowledge and skills of each individual and what they can contribute. You'll also need to think about which phase(s) of the project life cycle they will be involved in.

The largest number of people will be required during the execution phase, and smaller numbers in the definition and planning phases.

Because people will be coming on and off the project at different times, your human resource planning will be very important. Otherwise, building a cohesive team will be difficult and the project will suffer.

The First Step

The first step in building your organization and human resource plan is to determine what kinds of people you will need. To help you consider the kind of background your team will need, we have developed a series of questions to help you think through your requirements. The questions are as follows:

◆ What kinds of experience do they have/need?

◆ What is their availability?

◆ What knowledge and skills will they need?

◆ Do they have a personal interest in the outcome of the project?

◆ Will they work well in a team environment?

You will probably think of other questions, but this list should help you begin to sort through the possible candidates and select the appropriate ones.

Sometimes organizations will have policies or guidelines that govern how you can recruit team members for your project. When you have these guidelines or policies, they can often act as a *constraint* on your ability to get the people you want or need.

Time Is Money

Look for people who can work within an ordered system of checks and balances. Avoid people who might impose their own agenda on the project. If you have a choice in the matter, choose individuals who will accept your role as project manager without resentment or hostility.

Project Lingo

A **constraint** is any restriction that will affect the performance of the project or any factor that can affect when an activity can be scheduled. Chapter 8 includes information on managing constraints.

Responsibility Assignment Matrix

For complex projects, it's useful to have a tool to help you determine your personnel needs and match those needs with qualified individuals. One such tool is the responsibility assignment matrix (RAM). In addition to helping you match individuals to tasks, you can also use it to help figure out who needs to be consulted on particular decisions or issues and who will actually be responsible for carrying out certain duties. Signature authority is usually reserved for managers who control critical aspects of the organization that the project will depend on. They are key stakeholders, and you will not be able to use their facilities or people without their approval. Bob is a case in point in the following matrix.

Responsibility Assignment Matrix (RAM)

Phase	Ali	Bob	Callie	Diane	Ed	Frieda
Requirements	A		P		I	R
Design		S		P		A
Development	A	I	P	A	I	
Testing	A	S	A	A	P	A
Training	P	I				A

P = Primary   A = Assigned   R = Review Required

I = Input Required   S = Signature Required

In the matrix, the primary responsibility for certain tasks are given to those who have the knowledge or experience you need. Often, project managers will give them a title such as team leader. For example, Callie is an experienced developer who has worked on projects that were similar to the development needs that you anticipate will be important for All-Star Cable's MOD. Therefore, Callie becomes the team lead for development. Ali, on the other hand, is less experienced and would need someone like Callie to help direct her work, or assign work for her, at times. And Bob is the manager for infrastructure at All-Star Cable, so he will need to be consulted, or be asked to sign-off on, certain aspects of the project.

You may also decide to use the RAM as a tool to help you bring new people onto the team, or as a way to determine who to recruit if you happen to lose people along the way (which almost always happens!).

The Core Project Team

Choosing the *core team* could be the single most important decision you make as a project manager. Strong team leaders effectively combined with knowledgeable experts (where necessary) build the momentum required for successful project planning—and good planning is paramount to a successful implementation of the project.

The core project team usually consists of the most important players, who will be associated with the project from start to finish. On small projects, the core project team might be only

Project Lingo

The **core team** members work on the project from start to finish while other workers come and go as their tasks are completed.

you and another key person with whom you will be working on the project. The core project team will be involved in the project design phase and the planning phase, and then they will bring others on board for the implementation phase.

Rank is not always a consideration in forming the core project team; for a larger project, skill or experience might be more important factors.

The core project team doesn't usually have signature authority for the project, but this group of people is directly responsible for the overall success of the project planning and implementation phases.

The membership of the core team may change slightly as you move from one phase of the project and you begin the next phase. For example, Ed may be the team leader for the testing plan during the planning phase, but Diane may take the lead for testing during the execution phase of the project. Throughout the project, however, your core project team should consist of your most trusted employees and central advisors.

Other Project Team Members—Who Are They?

As noted in Chapter 5, the project team members are stakeholders in the project—they'll all make a contribution of one sort or another toward project completion. In addition to your core project team, on a large project you will likely have many other staff working on the project. You might also need outside consultants and specialists. Generally, these people perform a role during one part of a project and then are phased out once their work is completed. In addition to these players, administrators and other staff play a role in most projects, but because their roles are generic and they are replaceable, they are not considered to be core team members. Nonetheless, even team members with minor and replaceable roles should be kept informed as progress on the project proceeds, just like all the other stakeholders will be.

Risk Management

When taking over an ongoing project and its staff, check out the team before you accept the job. Make sure you have the authority to make changes to the team as necessary. There might be good reasons why there's an opening for a project manager. A poor-quality team could make you the project scapegoat instead of its savior.

Use Teambuilding Activities to Develop Your Team

People trust one another only after they know them. Because trust is an important element in any team, you'll need to encourage your team members to develop trusting relationships. Make team-building activities a regular part of your project review meetings or even set aside an entire day for it. If they respect and trust one another, they will be more likely to be able to work together to solve difficult project issues. And they will be more likely to cooperate with each other and not waste their time and yours on needless competitiveness. We'll talk more about team building later and give you even more specifics to work on in Chapter 19.

Building the Project Team for All-Star Cable

So let's go back to our All-Star Cable example. In deciding to build the project team, the project manager decided that specific kinds of people were required to make the project a success. He developed the following list of people that he needs to begin the planning phase of the project:

- ◆ A person with experience in building and modifying information technology network architecture capable of handling the Movies-on-Demand

- ◆ Programmers with application development experience who have also done systems testing as part of that experience

- ◆ Someone with billing and accounting knowledge and experience to help decide the best way to interact with customers and possible vendors

- ◆ A marketing person who would know how to reach the markets that the project team decides to target

- ◆ Someone with experience in developing the drop-down menus that the customers will see on their TV sets

- ◆ A database administrator with experience in extracting data for generating reports

- ◆ A security expert who will address confidential customer and company information

Armed with this information, the project manager is now able to begin identifying and recruiting the people who best match the requirements.

The Least You Need to Know

- ◆ Pick your project team members carefully by creating a staffing management plan.

- ◆ Use a responsibility assignment matrix to match your needs with people's skills.

- ◆ Pay particular attention to your core project team—the people who will work on the team from start to finish—as they will be the key to your success.

- ◆ Use teambuilding exercises to develop relationships among team members so that they will work together effectively.

7

Scoping Out Project Goals

In This Chapter

◆ Why specific goals (also known as objectives) are important to project success

◆ Six criteria of all good project goals

◆ Steps for establishing project goals

◆ Choosing a scope for a project that meets the project goals

◆ Creating the statement of work (SOW) to establish clear expectations among all project stakeholders

Even a good idea can be a bad idea if its goals and scope are not clearly defined before major resources are committed to it. Smart project goals identify specific, measurable, agreed upon, realistic, and timely results. Fuzzy goals can be interpreted differently by different people; thus, stakeholders may never agree on whether you're done or whether you've succeeded or failed. It's not enough to say you're going to build the next version of a software product; you need to establish what the new version will do, how much it will cost to build, and how long it will take to design it, among other goals for the project.

In this chapter, you'll learn why you need to get very specific about what you expect to accomplish on your projects. You'll also learn how to set goals for your project that no one can argue with.

Why Bother with the Goals?
I Know What I Want to Do!

Okay, okay. Patience isn't always a project manager's best virtue, and lots of projects get started without clear goals. Please don't let this happen to you. Slow down. Don't rush into further planning until you have consensus on the goals. The time you spend on setting goals will help ensure that the project you deliver is really something worth crowing about.

Start developing your goals and objectives for a project during project definition phase. At that time, you will want to establish the business rationale for the project and how it fits into the overall strategy of the company or the division, depending on the size of the organization.

You may even go through a feasibility study to see if the project makes sense, from an economic or business point of view. Normally, you will develop a business case study that outlines the pros and cons of going forward with the project. This is especially useful if you are not the person who will decide whether to go forward if, for example, you have a steering committee or governance board that will oversee the project.

Suppose that you are in the new development division of a utility company and you have been asked to construct a new power plant that will bring power to a new auto assembly plant that was just announced. You will need to do a feasibility study to answer four distinct questions:

♦ How do we know that the owner of the new auto assembly plant will need more power?

♦ Why do you believe that we can deliver the power that they need?

♦ How will you manage the risks for this plant? (For example, perhaps a competitor may also build a power plant, or the automaker might back out and drop the idea because car sales drop off.)

Time Is Money

Many project managers are eager to get to the "meat" of the project. It frustrates them, and their project team sometimes, to work on planning and scoping the project. However, our experience is that a project that hasn't been planned well is almost certainly a disaster waiting to happen.

◆ What will be the return on the investment (ROI) that you can expect from the plant? (Based on certain assumptions.)

In this example, the organization will spend an extraordinary amount of money if they go through with the power plant project. Before spending millions of dollars, you will need to be able to answer these four questions in some detail.

For All-Star Cable, the project manager should be able to answer some very specific questions:

◆ How do we know that our customers will buy Movies-on-Demand versus going to Blockbuster to get them? How do we know that they will prefer Movies-on-Demand over pay-per-view?

◆ Why do you believe that we have the capability to deliver movies on demand? Is the technology in place?

◆ Will you, as project manager, be able to manage the risks associated with this type of project? What are the risks you have identified so far?

◆ How much do you estimate it will cost to develop movies on demand and what is the payback period? What kind of return will All-Star Cable see on this investment?

Words from the Wise

Winners make goals; losers make excuses.

—Anonymous

Examples abound of companies that initiated major projects and then flushed millions of dollars down the drain because of poor project planning.

The city of Denver spent millions of dollars on a state-of-the-art baggage handling system at its new airport. When the system was finally tested, it not only failed to deliver baggage to the right places, but it shredded and mangled the luggage en route! The project was over a year late and millions of dollars over budget. Pity the poor taxpayers in that city.

Or consider Dell, the large computer manufacturer that spent over $50 million for a computer software program that promised to provide instant access to all the information that managers would need to run their business. They tried and tried to make the system work to their customized requirements. Finally they gave up and abandoned a project in which they had more than $50 million invested!

If you want to avoid similar mistakes, you want to be clear on some things before you commit to a project:

- The goals, including the need for the project and the measurable benefits to the stakeholders and users

- The scope

- The time needed to carry out the project

- A rough estimate of resources and costs

Doing this work up front gives your project more credibility and manageability.

Clear Project Goals Make Sense to Everyone

Goals are the heart, mission, and purpose for initiating a project. Put most simply, goals are what you hope to achieve at the end of the project. But the Dell story illustrates some important concepts to know about setting appropriate goals for your projects—set realistic goals or you probably will not be able to reach them. Here is some additional advice regarding setting project goals:

- Any project you undertake must make sense in terms of an overall goal that benefits people in some way. If a project doesn't have a benefit for someone, why bother? Another way to look at this is to make sure the goals for the project specify how completing the project will make things better than they would be without the project. You should be able to clearly describe the outcomes and benefits to stakeholders and end-users.

- Project goals must be carefully thought out; even the most obvious questions should be considered to make sure the idea is really as good as people think it is.

- Project goals should provide the criteria you need to evaluate your success in completing a project. These criteria include measures of the time, costs, and resources required to achieve your desired outcomes.

- The project goals need to be reviewed with the core team, and consensus must be reached before you move into the next phase of the project.

Words from the Wise

It concerns us to know the purpose we seek in life, for then, like archers aiming at a definite mark, we shall be more likely to attain what we want.

—Aristotle

Of course, you can use project management techniques on projects with inappropriate goals and still accomplish something, but you may fail to do anything useful. For example, one of the biggest complaints about information technology projects is that they are perceived as a waste of time by the end-users. Often, the IT department is totally baffled by such claims. In a software application project (as a typical example) they point out, usually quite correctly, that the software works just as advertised. The problem often centers on the fact that people don't know how to use the software to get their job done. As a result, the software rapidly becomes "shelfware" because it never gets off the shelf! Was the project a success? Maybe from a technical point of view, you could argue that it was. However, from a practical point of view, it was a failure. If your key stakeholders don't like the product you have given them, then the project is a failure regardless of whether it works or not.

The Primary Goals of Every Project

Every project has three primary goals:

- To create something (such as a product, procedure, organization, building, or other deliverable)

- To complete it within a specific budgetary framework

- To finish it within an agreed-upon schedule

Beyond these goals are the other goals that must be specified and that actually define the project. For example, it's not enough to have the goal of building a mid-priced sports car. A more appropriate set of goals would be to build a mid-priced, convertible sports car that will ...

- Use both gas and electric power.

- Be of a quality comparable to the Volvo C70.

- Sell for 10 percent less than all comparable cars.

- Offer specific features to meet competitive demand, such as antilock brakes, a geo-navigational system, onboard Internet access, and an electrically powered convertible top.

- Be available for the 2006 sales year.

- Be manufactured by the factory in Japan but designed by the engineers in the United States.

To differentiate primary goals from other project goals, these other goals are often referred to as "objectives" in other books—but "goals" and "objectives" are really different words for the same thing. Whether they're called goals or objectives, they should meet the criteria outlined in the following section.

> **Risk Management** _____
>
> Taking over someone else's goals can be difficult. If you aren't in on the goal-setting process, carefully review the goals before you assume the project. Make sure the goals are complete and well-formed. If they are off base, ask to review and revise them with the key stakeholders. If you're not given that opportunity, consider looking elsewhere. It's better to decline the offer to be responsible for an ill-defined project than to be blamed for it later.

Six Criteria for Setting Great Goals

As you and the key project stakeholders begin setting goals, you should be aware that there are six general criteria that most project goals should meet to ensure that the project will accomplish something of perceived value.

If you write goals for your projects that always meet these six criteria, you'll be working on projects with a purpose.

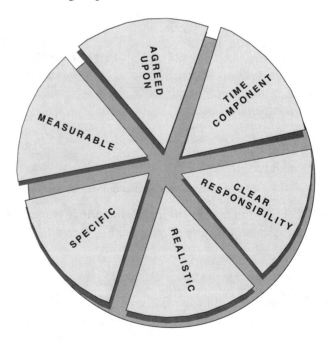

Criterion 1: Goals Must Be Specific

Your goals are adequately clear if another, equally competent manager can take over your responsibilities and guide the project to completion. If your goals meet this criterion, you're pointed in the right direction. Ask co-workers to read your goals and determine what has been stated and what the project will look like when it's done. Confused, surprising, or conflicting responses mean more refinement is required.

Criterion 2: Goals Must Be Realistic

Your goals must be possible or at least be within the realm of possibility. For example, if you have a project to implement a software application that costs $5.7 million and you only have $2 million available in cash and credit, you obviously have little chance of getting the project done. In this case, perhaps you should consider a preliminary project to build up your cash reserves before you draw up plans for the installation.

Criterion 3: Goals Must Have a Time Component

Projects must have a definite finish date, or they may never be completed. Projects with no terminus never terminate, so to speak. Projects with unrealistically short dates blow up like an overloaded fuse. We had an energy company as a client that needed to overhaul the trading software they used to maximize their power generation assets. When the project was launched in January, the original target was for completion in October, a pretty aggressive target, but doable. Suddenly, in February, the deadline was moved up to an April launch! That project was doomed to failure no matter what the project manager and the project team did!

Criterion 4: Goals Must Be Measurable

You must be able to measure your success at meeting your goals, whether you use a computer program such as Microsoft Project or a chart full of colored push-pins tacked up on the wall. These results are called *deliverables*—the results of the project. Quality is a vital part of this criterion.

Projects can have interim deliverables that don't reflect the final product. For example, you might need to build a model of the strip mall that you are building (the finished product) early in the project cycle so that more work can be completed later on. The strip mall itself is the final deliverable, but the model may be a deliverable for the design phase of the project.

Project Lingo

Deliverables are the clearly defined results, goods, or services produced during the project or at its outcome.

Deliverables, like projects, are evaluated not only by the fact that something is produced but by their quality as well. Don't confuse *quality* with *grade*. Quality is how well the product satisfies the needs of the customer. Grade is the number of features a product may have. For example, a new software product may be of high quality because it doesn't have bugs or problems. However, it may be of low grade because it only has a limited number of features compared to other competitive products. Low quality will always be a problem. Judging the grade that a customer wants, and is willing to pay for, is quite another issue. Determining, and then delivering, both the quality and grade of the finished product is a key element in defining the scope of your project.

Project Lingo

Quality is defined by PMI as the "totality of characteristics of (the finished product) that bear on its ability to satisfy stated or implied needs." **Grade** is "a category or rank given (to products) having the same functional use but with different characteristics."

Criterion 5: Goals Must Be Agreed Upon

At the onset of a project, you as the project manager and the other initiators of the project (your boss, for example, or the customer or the steering committee in the case of All-Star Cable) must agree on the goals before you take any further steps toward planning the project. If you don't reach consensus, there's no point in beginning the project; it's doomed from the start because the stakeholders can't agree on the outcomes that will make the project a success. In a large project that crosses many departments or other organizations, gaining consensus can be a long and thankless process. (Refer to the section "Seeing Eye to Eye" later in this chapter.)

Eventually, all the team members as well as the stakeholders must agree to support the project goals if you're going to manage the project effectively. Without consensus on the goals, the project faces a bumpy road to completion. Remember that *consensus* doesn't mean that everyone gets what they want—it means they will support the goals of the project as defined. Projects started with misunderstood goals often have team members working at cross-purposes or occasionally duplicating each other's efforts.

Criterion 6: Responsibility for Achieving the Goals Must Be Identified

Although you, the project manager, bear the brunt of responsibility for the overall success of the project, others may be responsible for pieces of the goals. Like agreeing on the goals, the people responsible for the goals must be identified and be willing to accept responsibility before the project proceeds further. (See the following role description of the project sponsor as an example.)

Once you identify all the major players who will be making decisions and contributing major pieces to the project, it is best to get them to sign off up front. For example, if the All-Star Cable project is going to choose and implement a new piece of software to allow the billing department to input customer requests for changes in services, you need to get an agreement from your accounting group, and the Information Technology group that will be tasked to support the new software once it is installed.

Establishing Goals Step-by-Step

It's easy to establish goals for your project. In fact, it's so easy that you'll find yourself with more goals than you can handle. (You'll have time to develop goals for specific activities later in the planning cycle.)

Here's how to establish good overall project goals:

1. Make a list of the project's goals. At this point, don't rule anything out. Just make a list and check it twice.

2. Study the list and zap anything that has no direct bearing on the project.

3. Eliminate anything that is really a step in meeting the goals and is not a goal for the end result of the project.

   You should now have a "pure" list of project goals. It's now time for the final step in goal setting.

4. Study the list again. Make sure each goal meets all the relevant six criteria. Now determine whether all these goals are doable within one project. Look for goals that really belong to a separate project or are not directly germane to the project at hand. Cross them out. Leaving them in your current project confuses team members and eats resources you need for this project to succeed.

   If the items you yanked from the list are important, you should consider alerting your management to them so they can decide what, if any, action to take. This may require explanation on your part as to why you can't take on the extra work and how each item really deserves a project world of its own.

> **Time Is Money**
>
> Another key to establishing your goals is to consider what the project *will not* do. Often, in setting our goals, we think about what we want the final product to do. However, a valuable exercise will be to list what it will not do, too.

Successful projects must meet their goals with a minimum of changes and without disturbing the main workflow of the organization. If a project derails for one reason or another, additional resources may be used in an attempt to meet dates. This can cause serious organizational problems as other important work is put aside to accommodate the problem project. Your task is to run the project as smoothly as possible with no requirement for additional time, bodies, or money that interferes with other projects or day-to-day operations.

The best goals are spelled out in writing. Written goals are a powerful consensus builder, especially in a large, complex, or multilayered project. When you and other decision makers need to make changes to a project, the goals help you decide whether each change fits the confines of the goals. If it doesn't, the change may be unnecessary or detrimental to the project. It may indicate that a problem needs further research, which could require approval from other teams' managers and possibly senior management or whoever is paying the bill.

> **Project Lingo**
>
> The **statement of work** (SOW—nice acronym, huh?) is an integrated set of purposes, goal descriptions, resource requirements, conflicts, assumptions, and authorities that define a project and accompany the evolving master project plan during its development throughout the project.

The goals document (usually a part of the *statement of work*, which you'll learn about later in this chapter) becomes the vehicle for discussion and consensus building. In its agreed-upon form, it gives you the framework to proceed with detailed planning of the project.

Project Scope

No, it's not a mouthwash development project. The scope is the size of the project. When looking at any project, you always look at its scope. Some project managers specialize solely in projects of a certain scope, considering small ones to be too petty for their talents or massive ones to be too long-lived or problematic to get involved.

Project scope can include one or more of the following considerations:

- ◆ How much is to be achieved in the project?

- ◆ What is the project window? (When must it be started and when should it be completed?)

- ◆ What resources are required (the usual: money, people, supplies, equipment)?

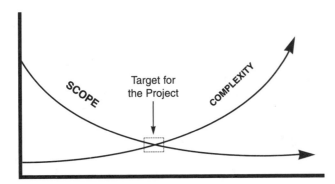

As scope "width" increases, the project has fewer tasks. As it decreases, more projects may spin off. Where the lines meet in this simple model is the ideal point—a balance of complexity versus simplicity.

With the exception of the simplest projects, squeezing the scope often spins off additional subprojects. Making it too broad adds complexity because too many disparate elements must be managed simultaneously. The project scope for assembling a marketing plan for a minor new product is much smaller than for building an attack jet. As a project manager might explain, "It's a small-scope project."

When establishing a new project, the scope must be clearly defined and agreed upon, just like the goals for the project. It's the scope that defines the assumptions for making all the cost, schedule, and resource projections in your planning. The scope established for a project puts some boundaries on the planning process and the deliverables. In defining scope, the specific outcomes or deliverables of the project should be delineated along with those activities and deliverables outside the scope of the project.

Scope "creep" is the process of adding work to a project, little by little, until the original schedule and cost estimates are completely meaningless. Always make sure that any creep in the SOW or project plan is agreed to in writing—along with the accompanying schedule and budget changes.

Putting It Down in Writing: The Statement of Work

The statement of work (SOW) is a formal project management document that establishes expectations and agreements about the project. It is not a contract, but a tool for clarifying responsibilities and working relationships among project stakeholders.

The audience for a SOW includes all the project stakeholders including the customer. When a project is produced for the company alone (the customer and the project team work for the same company), the SOW is the only project agreement required. When outside customers are involved, both a contract and a SOW are advisable because the SOW specifies project details typically outside the scope of a contract and the contract specifies legal agreements outside the scope of the SOW. In some cases, a SOW will be referred to in the contract as the official definition of the work to be completed.

Time Is Money

The terms *project charter* and *statement of work* (SOW) are often used interchangeably. Many companies use the term "charter" to refer to the document that is actually the SOW. That's okay as long as you understand the difference. The charter is a written document that allows the project manager to begin the project and apply money and people to it. This is the way the Project Management Institute (PMI) uses the term. The SOW, on the other hand, is the formal project definition document that describes in detail the products or services that will be delivered from the project. Both uses of the term "charter" will likely continue; just be clear on how the word is used within your organization and your customer's organization.

The Components of the SOW

A SOW lists and defines the goals, constraints, scope, communication guidelines, and success criteria for a project. The initial SOW, once written, becomes a document subject to negotiation and modification by the stakeholders. When the SOW is finally approved, it becomes the "official rules" for the project.

In size, the SOW can range from a one- or two-page memo on a small project to a 100-page document of understandings for a major technical endeavor.

The usual minimum content of a SOW includes the following:

- **The purpose statement:** The basic question of "Why are we doing this project?" should be clearly answered in this section. In addition, the business case for the project is referenced but not necessarily detailed. (If a detailed business case for a project is required, this typically is done in a separate document, often called a cost-benefit analysis.)

- **The scope statement:** The scope statement clearly defines what the project will and won't do. The relationship of the project to other priorities or business endeavors should be mentioned here as well, especially when the project is a subproject of a much larger project.

- **The project deliverables:** This section defines what the project is supposed to produce. This helps focus the team on producing outcomes. The intermediate deliverables as well as the final deliverables should be listed by name. For example, "scale model" is an intermediate deliverable on the way to a final deliverable of "a completely built refinery." Even regular status reports, change requests, and other reports should be specified as part of the deliverables of the project, along with the frequency and audience for each report. It's important for the project management deliverables as well as the project deliverables to be written into the SOW; this ensures that the basic communications within the project are clearly understood.

- **The goals and objectives:** This section defines the criteria for success. Not only will the on-time and within-budget criteria be specified, all the other goals that were created for the project should be listed here. Some of the goals may include those that protect the customer's business ("We will install the software without disrupting current operations.") or that measure specific outcomes ("New customer sales will increase by 25 percent within four months of introducing the new e-commerce website.").

- **The cost and schedule estimates:** This section provides the rough but well-researched estimates of both the cost and the schedule for the project. The questions of "How was the budget arrived at?" and "How was the deadline determined?" should be answered in this section. On large projects, most of the complete project planning process might need to be completed to produce adequate numbers. In other cases, reasonable budgets and schedules will be set with specific variances that will be detailed further in the next stages of project planning. In either case, the rule is to set realistic expectations for project stakeholders; thus, the figures must be reasonable if not yet set in stone.

- **The list of stakeholders:** This is the section in which all the key influencers, managers, and sponsors for a project should be introduced. At a minimum, the names and roles of the steering committee, project manager, key project team members, the sponsor, managers with an interest in the project, and the customer contacts should be identified.

- **The chain of command:** This section defines who reports to whom on this project. A project organization chart is required here. Another useful tool is the written responsibility matrix—the table that defines the important roles and responsibilities on a project. This section of the SOW is particularly important because projects often cross organizational boundaries; thus, projects have their own reporting structure that is outside the functional reporting structure of the overall organization. If project roles and reporting requirements aren't defined and agreed to in the SOW, conflicts about decision-making roles and authority may derail a project midcourse.

- **Assumptions and agreements:** Any assumptions that limit the project or agreements that form the basis of interactions should be detailed here. Don't leave anything out that could affect the future management of the project. If you want the project to be considered a success, all "side" or "off-line" agreements must be agreed to in the SOW. This is the section in which to document them.

CAUTION

Risk Management

Too many goals and objectives are like too many cooks in the kitchen—they spoil the broth. When considering a project, look for tasks or sets of tasks that should really remain as separate projects. Split them off as such. A word of warning: Management may attempt to add objectives to your project that don't belong there in order to meet other political agendas. Make sure this doesn't happen.

♦ **The communication plan:** This section details the basic reports that will be produced and any meetings that will be held during the detailed planning phase of the project. At this point, the frequency and audience of the status reports and basic meetings for the project planning phase should be specified. On large projects, a more detailed communication plan will likely be produced later in the planning cycle or during the project implementation phase(s). These later communication plans will add more information about the author, content, and frequency of reports to be produced and meetings to be held during the later phases of the project. On small projects, these more detailed communication plans probably won't be required if the SOW is sufficiently detailed.

Seeing Eye-to-Eye

We've used the term *consensus* several times in this book already, and we will continue to mention it throughout this book. Gaining consensus is the all-important process of getting honest buy-in from the people involved that all aspects of the project are understood and agreed upon. Further, consensus implies that people chosen for certain roles will accept them and that the goals are smart (meaning they're specific, measurable, agreed upon, realistic, and timely). Before you proceed with the project, consensus must be reached on the SOW. Give the stakeholders plenty of time to give their input. It may take multiple meetings and multiple iterations of the SOW to get it right.

Once the SOW is agreed upon by all the key stakeholders, the final step in initial consensus is getting signed agreement on the SOW from the stakeholders. The signatures provide evidence that everyone agreed to the project as defined in the SOW. At this point, the SOW establishes the baseline for the detailed planning activities and establishes a detailed schedule and budget for the project.

As time goes on in the project, the SOW will likely need to be amended and agreed to again. Making changes to the SOW becomes an important way to manage stakeholders throughout the project life cycle. The SOW at the end of a large project might be quite different from the SOW you agree to at the beginning of the endeavor. The difference is not important. The only things that matter are that everyone has been informed and all changes have been agreed to by key stakeholders—and always in writing. Thus, consensus building will be an ongoing activity during the project, especially when project changes are necessary. You'll learn more about consensus building and change management in Part 5.

Defining the SOW at All-Star Cable

In putting together the SOW for the project, the project manager and the project team determined that the purpose of the project was to allow the company to expand its business by entering a new service line that no competitors had, and open that new market. For the project's scope, they decided that they would initially target their existing customers as the primary audience for this service. Also, they decided to use a film library from an outside source since they didn't want to maintain a library of movie titles, and outsourcing would allow them to change titles more frequently. Also, they decided not to offer "adult" videos as part of the potential titles to the customers since such offerings might offend many of their existing customers.

Their goals were to get 70 percent of their existing customers to order Movies-on-Demand before moving to target new customers. They also targeted a return on investment of 15 percent with a payback of 5 years. As for assumptions, the project team assumed that they could use the existing cable system to deliver the movies and that it would not require a complete re-tooling of the system. In their communication plan, they wanted to pay particular attention to their customers and the Southside Civic Association.

The Least You Need to Know

- Goals (also called objectives by some project managers) consist of specific, measurable, agreed-upon, realistic, and timely aims.

- Your goals for a project should include completing it on time, within budget and using available resources, and achieving the desired quality of end product or result.

- Goals require clear, concise writing so that project participants understand each one.

- When planning a project, its size (scope) must be specified and agreed upon by the stakeholders.

- The statement of work (SOW) should be written and approved to document the goals, scope, deliverables, cost and schedule estimates, stakeholder roles, chain of command, and communication guidelines for a project.

- The SOW becomes the basis for the rest of the formal, detailed project plan and is a tool for managing stakeholders throughout the project.

Chapter 8

Managing Risks and Constraints

In This Chapter

◆ Understanding that risk involves uncertainty and loss

◆ Dealing with risky business projects

◆ Constraints that bind you

◆ Managing risks and constraints

A good project manager measures risks in advance. Even with clear goals, you need to establish the probability that something will go wrong and keep you from completing the project successfully. On a small project, this step may only take a few moments to ponder, but on larger projects, risk assessment can be a complete project in its own right. The goal of the risk and constraint analysis is to establish the feasibility of the project within the economy, politics, laws, and organizational structure that limit your business. This risk and constraint analysis establishes whether the project goals you just defined in Chapter 7 are feasible. These risks and constraints should also be documented in the statement of work (SOW) you just learned about.

A project that moves beyond the initiation phase without taking into account risks and constraints, including the organizational and business risks, will be buffeted by the internal and external forces surrounding and will be more likely to fail. Bad weather? A delay. Your main supplier goes bankrupt? A delay. A strike? A delay. Waffling among senior management? A delay and maybe even project termination! Maybe even your job … well, we won't say it. You get the idea.

The Three Types of Risk

As you might assume, the kinds of risks you'll encounter varies with the project. Team members may fail at their tasks, sunspots may blow away your satellite uplink in the middle of an important transmission, and the concrete rebar used in your new corporate headquarters may turn to rust about one month after installation.

Ultimately, all the risks in a project boil down to these:

- **The known risks.** These are the risks that you can identify after reviewing the project definition within the context of the business and/or technical environment. You must draw on your experience and that of the stakeholders in defining risks of this nature.

- **The predictable risks.** These are risks that might occur. They also are anticipated risks based on work with other similar projects. These risks have to do with things such as staff turnover or economic changes that can have an anticipated impact. Instinct, rather than concrete evidence, tells us to be wary of these risks.

- **The unpredictable risks.** These are the things that go bump in the night or the "stuff that just happens" beyond the control of the project manager or team. You simply can't predict everything!

Risk Areas

Risks can be further broken down into areas that may have an impact on delivery of the defined product or service. The primary among these include:

- **Funding:** You may not get the full amount of capital that your project needs.

- **Time:** You may find that things are taking longer than originally planned. Thus, you risk running out of time.

- **Staffing:** As work on the project begins, you might realize that you can't find the right staff in the marketplace or don't have the requisite experience or skill set available in the company to meet the project objectives.

- **Customer relations:** If your customer doesn't have the time to work with the project team and assist in defining the attributes of the solution to project problems, you risk having a dissatisfied customer as the project proceeds.

- **Project size and/or complexity:** The project is large or complex to the point of taxing the ability to complete it on time or within budget. There are just too many factors to attempt to control, especially given the time or budget restrictions.

- **Overall structure:** As a result of political decisions, responsibility is fractured between competing work groups or organizations.

- **External factors:** There are external risk factors outside of your control such as new government regulations or shifting technologies.

Don't Forget the Business Risks

Business risks also may have an impact on the acceptance of a product or service. These risks include the following:

- **Market acceptance:** The product is a good one, but customers won't want to buy it.

- **Time-to-market:** It will be a good product, customers will want it, but only if you can deliver it six months earlier than projected.

- **Incompatible product fit:** It will be a good product, customers will want it, but due to the cost of producing it, customers won't be able to afford it.

- **Difficult-to-sell:** It's a great product, but who's going to sell it? It will be too expensive for retail outlets but won't cost enough to provide dealers with incentives for selling it.

- **Loss of political support:** If a project loses support from executive management, the whole project could be jeopardized. This might happen when a new manager is brought on board. This also could mean loss of financial support.

The Ultimate Risk: Acts of God

As humans, we can do little to prevent acts of God from affecting projects, but we can take steps to avoid the most likely. Don't build precision models in San Francisco under concrete freeway ramps, for example, and avoid vibration-sensitive experiments near the runways of Dallas-Fort Worth airport.

Otherwise, with this in mind, your project should be insured. It's the best, well, insurance against hurricanes, floods, earthquakes, and other unpredictable acts of God. (Check the policy to verify that such events are covered and are not exclusively prohibited, as is common in most commercial policies.)

Taking Risks Stage by Stage

Risk can occur during any phase of a projects life cycle, but there are some common ones at each stage. Let's take a look at them.

Risks During the Project Definition Phase:

- ◆ Unavailable subject matter experts
- ◆ Poor definition of problem
- ◆ No feasibility study
- ◆ Unclear objectives
- ◆ No buy-in from the organization

Risks During the Project Planning Phase:

- ◆ No risk management plan
- ◆ Spotty planning
- ◆ Underdeveloped requirements and specifications
- ◆ Unclear statement of work
- ◆ No management support
- ◆ Poor role definition
- ◆ Inexperienced team

Risks During the Project Execution Phase:

- ◆ Changes in scope
- ◆ Changes in schedule
- ◆ No control systems in place
- ◆ Unskilled labor
- ◆ Material availability

- Strikes

- Weather

- Regulatory requirements

Risks During the Project Close-Out Phase:

- Unacceptable to customer

- Poor requirements fit

- As-built changes

- Budget problems

So how can you address these potential pitfalls? Here are some ideas:

- Identify potential problems early in the planning cycle (the proactive approach) and provide input into management decisions regarding resource allocation.

- Involve personnel at all levels of the project, focus their attention on a shared project (or product) vision, and provide a mechanism for achieving it.

- Avoid the problem by eliminating the cause of the threat. For example, if I feel a significant risk might be the loss of a key team member during the project, I could avoid that problem by simply finding someone else to fill that role.

- Use a mitigation strategy that reduces the impact of the risk by reducing the probability of the risk occurring. Using the same example above, I might add another person to my team who has similar knowledge and experience so that if I end up losing a key team member, I have someone who is capable of stepping in to fill the role.

- Use a retention strategy. This simply means that you accept the risk as possible and you will develop a plan for dealing with it if it occurs. This usually occurs for risks that you and the project team think are relatively unlikely to occur.

The Basics of Risk Management

You can reduce the risks on your project through risk management. Some folks even refer to project management as "the practice of risk management." Here are the steps we use on our projects:

1. All risk management starts with identifying the risks. We do this by making a list of the risks and describing their potential impact on the project. Identifying risks involves careful analysis. Assume that anything can go wrong. Learn from past projects. The failures of the past are often the best source of risk-control information. You can also anticipate problems by looking at critical relationships or resources in the project and anticipating what could occur if these change. It also helps to look at deliverables from different points of view, including those of the staff, subcontractors, vendors, suppliers, service providers, management, and customers. You should also evaluate the environment, labor practices, and the availability of raw materials or technologies.

> **Project Lingo**
>
> In **basic risk management,** you plan for the possibility that a problem will occur by estimating the probability that the problem will arise during the project, evaluating the impact if the problem does arise, and preparing solutions in advance.

2. Analyze the probability that the risk will occur and the potential impact of the risk. First, assign a number on a scale from 1 (lowest impact), 3 (medium impact) to 5 (highest impact) to quantify the potential impact of the risk to your project. Next, determine how likely you think it is that this event will occur and use the same 1 to 5 scale.

3. Determine the overall severity or importance of the risk. We do this by multiplying the probability number by the impact number (each on a scale of 1 to 5) to come up with a measure of severity.

4. Determine which risks are the most important for further action. We usually establish a "risk threshold" that determines all those that are high in both impact and likelihood get the most attention (a 25). Risks with less severity than this are considered for further analysis. You can use whatever number seems appropriate for your industry or situation; the key is to come up with a risk threshold that establishes the risks that require further attention throughout the project.

5. Document a response plan for the risks. This plan should be approved by the project sponsor as part of the SOW or project plan. You have four basic options for dealing with the risks on your list:

   ◆ Accept the risk. This means you intend to do nothing special at this point. If and when the risk emerges, the team will deal with it. This is an appropriate strategy when the consequences for the risk are cheaper than a program to eliminate or reduce the risk.

◆ Avoid the risk. This means you'll delete the part of the project that contains the risk or break the project into smaller subprojects that reduce the risk overall. Be aware that reducing or avoiding the risk in this way may also change the business case for the project. Sometimes you'll want to take on more risk to earn more return. This option is similar to the sentiment of "no pain, no gain" in the athletic world.

◆ Monitor the risk and develop a contingency plan in case the risk becomes imminent. If the best offense is a good defense, then when you encounter problems, having a contingency plan in place is vital to ensure continued success of the project. Developing contingency plans for key risks is one of the most important aspects of risk management. These contingencies are alternative plans and strategies to be put into place when necessary, often referred to as "Plan B." The whole concept of contingency planning is based on the assumption that you can develop more effective and efficient scenarios if you do so proactively—before things happen—rather than reactively when you are under the stress of a slipping schedule or a cash shortage.

◆ Transfer the risk. Insurance is the most obvious, although often expensive, way of transferring risk. The risk is effectively transferred to the insurance company for risks including theft, fire, and floods. Another way of transferring risk involves hiring someone else to implement a part of the project. For example, with a fixed-price contract with a vendor, you transfer the risk of cost increases to the vendor. Of course, fixed price contracts aren't always possible—but when they are, they can reduce a substantial amount of budgetary risk on a project.

Risk Management Worksheet						
Type of Risk	Jeopardy	Description of the Risk	Expectation of the Risk (1 to5)	Impact of the Risk (1 to 5)	Severity of the Risk (Expectation X Impact)	Contingencies Plan of Action
Critical Resource Delay	Budget, schedule	Crane not available due to other project	3	5	15	Increase funding for lease from another vendor
Permit delay	Schedule	Building permit not approved	2	4	8	Focus on the task, not additional contingency required
Project staffing	Schedule, resources	Can't hire enough carpenters	1	3	3	Not necessary to monitor; low risk

Use a form like this one to analyze and respond to the risks in your projects.

Remember that risk management and response planning are ongoing processes. You must regularly reevaluate. Every project encounters problems neither planned for nor desired, and they require some type of resolution or action before the project can continue. Depending on the size and type of problem, various resources may be required to solve it. Note that, in some cases, no action is required! Project managers get to live long, productive lives by properly recognizing which is which.

Keep a Weather Eye

Ultimately, the key to managing risk is to be aware of everything that can negatively affect the project. Be suspicious. Look for problems. Persistence in analysis reveals risk, and new risks bring new plans for dealing with them. Although risk management starts at the beginning of the project by identifying the problems and constraints that are known, it will continue as you identify and contend with the unanticipated sources of risk that inevitably emerge until the project is finished.

Constraints vs. Risks

Constraints, unlike risks, can be identified in advance. Constraints are the real-world limits on the possibilities for your projects. A typical constraint is budget. You will only receive a certain amount of money to finish the project and to get more you'll likely have to lobby long and hard. If you ignore the constraints in defining your project, the project will fail in some way. Your job as project manager is to make sure you understand the constraints of your project and work within their limits.

Constraints to Consider

Project constraints, along with risks, are a major factor when establishing the project plan and when the project is underway. You may want to add a roof to the new baseball stadium you are building, but you may be constrained to assembling little more than a simple field with two sets of bleachers. The constraints that bring a grandiose project down to earth include answers to questions like these:

◆ How much money is really available and when?

◆ By when must the project be completed?

◆ What inside resources are required?

◆ What outside resources are required and can you afford them?

- ◆ Can you get consensus among project members, executives, and stakeholders that the project is important and deserves your time and effort?

- ◆ What are you willing to settle for that will still meet your needs?

- ◆ Is there a way to do it using less expensive or fewer resources? (If there is, your problem may be solved.)

The process of answering these questions permanently grounds some projects as the real world intrudes on what's really little more than an energetic pipe dream. Constraints are a modicum of reality. Use them as a tool to fine-tune a project as well as to brush off grandiose suggestions.

Words from the Wise

Laws and regulations can be constraints, sometimes acting in strange ways. For example, a project might be planned to implement a new accounting procedure to meet new laws or regulations. In that case, the constraint is that, if the project is not completed by that date, the organization might be breaking some law. So perhaps the scope might be pared back in other ways: for example, deciding to implement a manual procedure first and then later integrate it into computerized systems.

—James MacIntyre, project management expert

Project constraints are quite broad. Similar to the restrictions every manager faces when confronted with any task, constraints, like risks, must be identified beforehand or an expensive project may hit the skids (along with its manager) after bogging down in an avoidable quagmire.

Constraint 1: The Budget

The budget is both a constraint and a risk. Most projects suck up money faster than you may realize. Whether you're opening a new sales office or developing a new product, the budget will constrain your efforts. Most organizations will also charge your project budget for the employees you borrow and any company-provided services you may require. Depending on the charge-back service, you may find it less expensive to bring in outsiders because you can choose exactly the skill set you require without the corporate baggage that comes with insiders from some organizations. You should be aware of the danger of agreeing to a budget to please the boss, management, or the customer when you know in advance the funds will be inadequate. See Chapter 15 for more information on project budgeting.

Constraint 2: The Schedule

Time waits for no one, especially not the manager of a faltering project built around impossible dates. In addition to being a risk for failure, the schedule is always a constraint, even if a project's due date is not that critical. If it rambles on after the predicted end date, the budget will expand, and team members may be pulled off to handle other responsibilities. Missing an end date may cause serious marketing consequences. A new but late-to-market product may arrive at the market window only to find it closed and firmly locked.

Constraint 3: The People

We'll explain how to deal with people conflicts in Chapter 23. For now, keep in mind that people's skills, as well as their conflicts, are always a project manager's most pressing concern. You can argue for more money and time, but it's the people who really make the project. If the right ones aren't available or are unaffordable, you will have to make do with the team that's available—no matter how inexperienced. The availability of the right people is both a risk to anticipate and a constraint that must be dealt with as the project proceeds.

> **Time Is Money**
>
> A project that has more than one manager controlling it is likely to be unsuccessful no matter how hard you work. Pass on such opportunities unless you can (politely) demand that you have only one boss running you and the project. On the other hand, many projects require the approval of managers in more than one department. Your skill as a project manager may be measured by your ability to form a schedule and budget that they agree on. Just make sure you're the one to control things after consensus is achieved.

Constraint 4: The Real World

Once a project is underway, reality has an ugly habit of settling in. Inadequate budgets, impossible schedules, and team members with more spirit than skills make for a project that's late, underfunded, and difficult to complete. Getting a project underway is like breaking in a new car. It takes time to get all the parts accustomed to working with each other. On a project, this synchronization may require fine-tuning. Some people may not get along with their supervisors, or a brilliant engineer may quit and join a competitive company. Communication is the best vehicle for keeping the engine fine-tuned. The first milestone, positioned at about 10 percent of the project (5 percent on large projects), is the time to review relationships, progress, and the effects that the actual project is having on your workforce, the project budget, and the schedule.

Constraint 5: Facilities and Equipment

Every project assumes that required equipment will be available within the project's time. Whether it's a 20-ton grader, an electron microscope, or a simple freight elevator, the right tools must be available for their period in the spotlight. Just like people, equipment resources are key to completion. If a project slips its dates, that critical piece of equipment might be tied up on another project somewhere else.

The constraints for your project should be well-documented in the SOW as part of the scope statement (refer to the preceding chapter for more information on the SOW). These constraints limit what can be done in the project.

Look at the Upside and the Downside

Although motivational speakers may try to convince you otherwise, looking at the downside of a project is the best way to anticipate events that might slow down or even kill the project. Because you, as project manager, are directly responsible for the success or failure of your project, you must look at both the positive and negative sides of the equation before making a commitment to the project. It could be a relatively risk-free venture, or you could be handed the task of captaining the equivalent of the maiden voyage of the Titanic.

Words from the Wise

There is much to be said of failure. It is more interesting than success.

—Max Beerbohm, one of Britain's foremost caricaturists and writer

Risky Business

As project manager, you're responsible for all aspects of the project including those that, while a part of the project, are largely out of your control. Projects may involve risks in any one of a hundred areas beyond your direct control, but as project manager, the finger of responsibility will point directly at you.

Identifying risks and constraints beforehand provides you with time to mitigate those that can be fixed or to notify the stakeholders (both verbally and in writing) that the project may be in jeopardy before it even begins. A critical analysis of the project is crucial to get it off to an acceptable and workable start. It is not unheard of for a would-be project manager to be handed a project that has languished for a period of time because no one in his or her right mind would touch it. This is especially typical of a new employee handed an obvious boondoggle. Although the people delegating the job may congratulate the person on getting off to a good start with an important piece of work, once the poor soul has left the room, they sigh with relief, all pleased with themselves that somebody was foolish enough to take on the work.

Going into a project with a "We can do anything" attitude may support team spirit at the onset, but when things come unglued and reality sets in, your team will become frustrated, management will complain, and you will kick yourself for not fixing the up-front problems up front. Plus, budget and schedule problems will blow any possibility of getting things done within the constraints of the original plan, and this means asking for more time and more money. You need to learn to communicate and negotiate change (see Chapters 24 and 25).

If you're lucky, you'll get a new lease on life and resources to revive and revise the project. If not, you'll have to read Chapter 28 to learn how to bring such a project quickly to its termination—it's not the most pleasant process in project management, although we must admit we've been forced to that stage once or twice through the years.

The Least You Need to Know

- ◆ Project risks and constraints are known roadblocks that should be accounted for before the project is underway.

- ◆ Remember that you won't be able to predict everything that might happen. However, that does not absolve you of your responsibility to analyze and plan for risks.

- ◆ The impossible remains impossible no matter how enthusiastic your team.

- ◆ Focus on the most likely risks and plan for dealing with them in advance. The best defense against "losing your head" is to have a plan for dealing with it!

- ◆ The risk management process can help you identify, quantify, and ultimately reduce the risks (problems) that may affect your project.

Part 3

The Project Planning Phase

Congratulations! You've made it through the definition steps, have reviewed the project for potential risks, and have identified a core team to work with you. Now you can start planning the key elements for successful projects, the activities, schedule, and budget.

The plan is a roadmap for your project that helps you guide the work from start to finish. It not only details the work that will be done, but it also serves as a tool for communicating with both stakeholders and the project team.

In addition to the goals and objectives for your project, the risks and constraints, and the core project team that you identified, there are three standard components in most project plans: the work breakdown structure (WBS)—which may or may not be put into a network diagram or some other charting format—the schedule, and the budget. Even a plan for the simplest project should contain these three parts. In this section, you'll learn how to put them together as a complete plan for projects both large and small.

Chapter 9

The Breakdown of Tasks: What Really Needs to Be Done?

In This Chapter

- ◆ Starting at the top and working down to the details
- ◆ Why you should break a project into work packages
- ◆ Subprojects as milestones and milestones as groups of tasks
- ◆ Understanding the work breakdown structure (WBS)
- ◆ The right WBS levels for your project
- ◆ Measuring the quality of task completion

Project managers use a tool called a work breakdown structure, or WBS, to break larger activities, also sometimes referred to as milestones, into individual components. It's only after you've established the milestones for a project that the real work breakdown begins: putting together a work breakdown structure (WBS).

Breaking Your Project Into Bite-Sized Pieces

A work breakdown structure (WBS) is a hierarchical chart used to organize the activities required in a project into related areas. It often takes the form of a tree diagram or an outline. The completed WBS can be used for budgeting and personnel-selection purposes as well as scheduling and network diagramming.

In a WBS, a project is broken down into the following levels:

- The total project
- Subprojects if the project is a complicated one
- Milestones that summarize the completion of an important set of work packages or the completion of an important event in a project such as a subproject (which is just a smaller portion of the overall project)
- Major activities—also called summary tasks
- Work packages (also sometimes called tasks, activities, or work elements)

You can have as many subprojects, milestones, and major activities, and work packages in your WBS as befit your needs.

As a project manager, the levels in your WBS will help you control work at each level. An appropriately organized WBS can help identify the right time to ask and answer resource and staffing questions.

The Work Breakdown Structure and Your Project

The WBS is the document that organizes and summarizes the work necessary to complete the project. Every WBS starts with a summary of high-level project areas and milestones. In All-Star Cable, those areas are Storage, Related Systems, Interfaces, Applications, and Reports. For most larger projects, however, the activities you list for a project should be organized into some kind of hierarchy (which you'll learn about here) and then translated into a network diagram (explained in Chapter 10). The complete WBS ultimately will include a schedule (see Chapters 13 and 14), and a list of resources required to complete each task (see Chapter 11).

The WBS you create should be able to help you do all of the following:

- Identify the major parts of the project so that all the work needing to be done is clearly indicated.
- Organize the work in the most logical sequence so the work packages can be efficiently scheduled.

- Identify work packages that need to be assigned to various team members.

- Identify the resources necessary to complete each work package so a budget can be developed.

- Communicate the work to be done in an unambiguous way so that team members understand their assigned jobs and responsibilities for completing the project.

- Organize related work packages using logical milestones.

Your WBS is the underpinning of a successful project because the need for resources and the schedule come from WBS and the way you sequence activity. On larger projects, the WBS will likely undergo several revisions before you get it right. If you are new to project management, you should have the core team members or other key stakeholders review the completed WBS and sequences to ensure that they include all the work necessary to get things done.

> **Along the Critical Path**
>
> Organization is crucial in the work breakdown structure. On a large project, related areas should be organized into milestones or subprojects. This makes it easier to visualize the overall project without getting into the details.

> **Time Is Money**
>
> When you believe you have a credible draft of a WBS, put it away for a while and then revisit it. This gives you a chance to get an objective view of the various parts. You might see something you forgot to consider, or you might notice a better way to organize the work.

An outline-style WBS for All-Star Cable follows. We've also included a tree diagram for another project, just to give you an idea of what they look like. The outline method works best for projects that have too many layers to conveniently lay out in the tree format.

Outline Style WBS for All-Star Cable

All-Star Cable Company MOD Project
    Start Project
    Storage
        Design Data Model
        Load Data
        Write Stored Procedures
    Related Systems
        Analyze System
        Design new related system

continues

continued

Construct new billing system

Test new system

Billing system test accepted

Implement new billing system

Interfaces

Customer GUI

Design new customer GUI interface

Test customer GUI with application

Obtain customer GUI approvals

Customer GUI approved

Build Prototype

Move customer GUI into production

Employee Interface

Design Employee Interface

Build Employee Interface

Build employee interface prototype

Test employee interface with users

User acceptance obtained

Move employee interface into production

Applications

Design full application requirements

Submit RFP for OTS S/W

Evaluate S/W

Decide to make or build

Make/build decision made

Purchase SW

Install S/W

Test SW (unit)

Test S/W (System)

S/W accepted

Move S/W into production

Reports

Analyze information needs

Design reports

Modify existing reports database

Test with test files

Full Scale systems testing in production

FSD Test Completion

Project Management
      Planning
      Communication
      Project Tracking and Reporting
      Closeout Activities
Finish Project

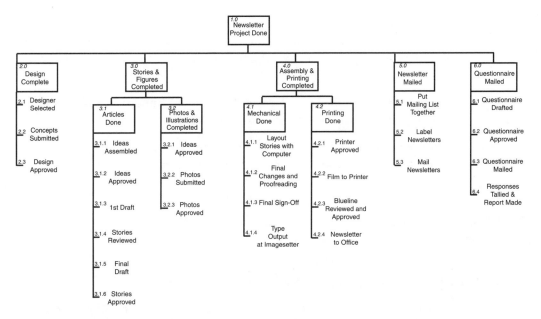

A sample tree diagram for another project.

You can choose to focus on whatever level of the project is germane to your current management needs. However, the smallest unit in your WBS should be the smallest unit of work you must track in your project—this is the work package. It is only the work package level that is actually assigned an time estimate and a cost—everything else in the WBS is simply an organizational tool for summarizing how the work packages combine to complete components of the project.

The lowest level in your WBS should not reach the level of absurdity, but you should track everything that could affect something else in the plan. While doing this, you must remember that not everything in life can be planned down to the minute; if it could, nothing would ever go wrong. You'll need to make your best guess about the detail and sequence of most project tasks.

Organizing the WBS

There's no magic formula for organizing a WBS. In the All-Star Cable example, the WBS is based on the category of tasks. Alternately, you could base it on any of the following (and I'm sure you can think of other ways, too):

◆ **Functional or technological disciplines.** What is required in each phase of the project? Schedule the machine tool operators separately from the marketing specialists.

◆ **Organizational structure.** In a clearly divided organization or a cooperating set of separate organizations, establish the WBS according to reporting structure. If outside vendors are involved, they can be included in this kind of planning.

◆ **Physical location.** Working with separate facilities? Build the WBS based on the geographical locations instead of the people.

◆ **Systems and subsystems.** If there is clear demarcation between several aspects of a project, the WBS can be assembled to reflect this.

You can use the "wrap-up" approach as well. In a wrap-up, you start at the bottom, listing each element, and work up. Each layer as you move up contains a wrap-up of all the elements of the layer underneath it.

There are a few other suggestions for creating a WBS that you might want to consider. They are especially important for assembling a complex WBS:

◆ Each element of work should be assigned to only one level of effort. Never repeat an element in another part of the tree or outline.

◆ Narrative must accompany the WBS. You may want to label each box or line with a number that references a page in an overview narrative document to provide more detail than "Get CEO approval for expansion plan." Software tools such as Microsoft Project will allow you to attach "notes" to as many tasks as you would like.

◆ Related work packages should be clearly identified in the WBS. A great way to show the linkage is through color—related tasks have the same color.

◆ At all levels, the WBS should provide measurable deliverables for each aspect of the project. There are deliverables for the project itself, such as the cable box for All-Star Cable, and there are deliverables for work packages, such as building the drop-down screen menu that the customer will see on their TV set.

◆ Assemble the WBS in a format that allows changes if and when the project shifts slightly in direction. Computers are ideal, but a carefully protected whiteboard (wrap it loosely with plastic wrap) can fill the bill for a simple project. Lots of sticky notes can be used as well so that things are easy to move around as you make changes.

Along the Critical Path

When maintaining a WBS for a large project, you need version control in place. This means that each version, no matter how preliminary or final, should be date- and time-stamped. That way, older plans can be relegated to the file, and everyone works only with the most current document. Even if you work on a computer and don't print all versions of the WBS, each iteration should be saved separately by date so you can be sure you're using the latest and greatest plan. Also, the older versions should be saved in an archive file, either in hard copy or electronically, so they can be used to track project history and to serve as a learning tool to evaluate what (if anything) went wrong.

Five Steps to the Work Breakdown Structure

You must complete five steps to develop a WBS that meets all of its goals:

1. Break the work into independent work packages that can be sequenced, assigned, scheduled, and monitored.

2. Define the work packages at a level of detail appropriate for the length and complexity of the project.

3. Integrate the work packages into a total system with a beginning and an end. This may involve combining tasks into milestones (also called subprojects).

4. Present the work packages in a format that can be easily communicated to people assigned to complete them during the project. Remember that each work package should have a deliverable and a time for completing that deliverable.

5. Verify that completion of the work packages will result in attainment of all the project goals and objectives.

For most large projects, assembling and organizing a WBS takes time, but a carefully assembled WBS goes a long way toward streamlining a project after the work begins.

Criteria for Ensuring Quality Work

As you develop the WBS, you need to have some way of determining whether a *task* is done and that it was done correctly. You can do this through establishing measurable quality levels based on the standards in your industry. You can also do this by establishing standard quality checklists and formal testing procedures, which are often done on engineering projects. Peer reviews or stakeholder acceptance reviews can also be used to ensure quality. In a peer review you ask colleagues who are not a part of the project to examine the project plan and the deliverables produced to date to provide you and the project team with suggestions for improvement.

One way to document these criteria is to develop an outline of the WBS with the quality criteria and review process noted next to each appropriate work package or milestone. Completion and evaluation criteria improve the clarity of the WBS and will ultimately improve the quality of the project plan. This is important because it's a lot cheaper to fix a problem or task description during the planning stage than during implementation.

Work packages are important elements for ensuring quality. Work packages are useful in the following ways:

Project Lingo

In project management,

A **task** is defined as a generic term for work that is the lowest level of effort in any project.

A **work package** is the lowest level of the work breakdown structure and always has a completed deliverable associated with it.

- ◆ *Work packages* are a way of modularizing the project into manageable segments. Thus, tracking the progress of work packages is a way to assess and control the work done on a project.

- ◆ By breaking work into work packages, you can determine the skills you need to complete the work on a project, and you can quantify how many people will be required to do the work.

- ◆ Work packages allow you to communicate the work that needs to be done to other team members without getting into too much detail.

- ◆ Breaking the work into work packages ensures that all the work sequences are identified and understood.

The bottom line is this: Work packages help you organize the hundreds of small work activities, or tasks, that go into completing a project. Without work packages, the amount of work to track would make your head spin. You would have no way to keep track of things or prioritize work.

Work Packages: What Exactly Are They?

Each work package represents the lowest level of project activity that has both time and cost associated with it. Also, a work package should have a unique deliverable associated with it that, as project manager, you will know whether or not it is completed.

A work package for our All-Star Cable case study might be the development of a high-level diagram of the proposed architecture for delivering Movies-on-Demand. As project manager, if that diagram is due to you in two weeks, you will know if the work is completed or not. That's what we mean by a unique deliverable.

Including too many elements in the WBS amounts to micromanaging in the extreme, which will probably miff your staff; they might think you're attempting to manage their lives as well as the project—an impossible and thankless task.

> **CAUTION**
>
> **Risk Management**
>
> Don't forget to put the project management tasks into the WBS. These tasks take time, too. These tasks might be grouped under a summary task called "managing the project," which would include time for developing reports, holding meetings, and gaining approvals from stakeholders.

Give Yourself Plenty of Time

Building a WBS for a complex project takes time. The WBS is a way to take the requirements that the stakeholder gave us (from Chapter 5) and turn it into the work that will need to be completed for the project to be delivered. Work is listed so the overall amount of work can be assessed and the work can be sequenced in the most logical fashion. A list of activities can be short and simple or long and detailed, depending on the size and goals of the project. Don't try to sequence the tasks or estimate time and budget during WBS definition. Those steps come later (see Chapters 10 through 15). Finally, don't try to do it all yourself, unless you are working on the project all by yourself. Enlist the members of your project team to help you think through all the work that will be required.

The WBS makes communication among core project team members easier. And, as mentioned (nay, harped on) throughout this book, forgetting to list an important task can have a very negative effect on the project's bottom line and its schedule. Therefore, it's a good idea to have the members of your project team help you in developing the WBS. Generally, you have chosen them for their knowledge and experience, so rely on that expertise to build the WBS. As project manager, you may take the high-level pass at the various activities, but rely on people who are more experienced in particular areas to finish it. You will be glad you did. The WBS should account for the production of every deliverable on the statement of work (SOW) that was approved for the project. Use the goals and deliverables in the SOW as a starting point for developing the tasks.

Defining Your Deliverables

Developing work-sense (something like horse-sense) takes time. "Do I lump all these procedures into one work package? Or are they actually two, five, or nine separate ones?" Correctly defining the level of effort in a project provides an easier way to control the project and keep it in the groove.

Most project managers use the 8/80 rule for determining whether an activity qualifies as a work package. That rule states that any work package that takes less than one day to complete (8 hours) is probably too small and you should consider combining it with something else. One the other end of the spectrum, if a work package takes longer than two weeks (80 hours), it is probably too large and you should consider breaking into smaller work packages.

Another way to judge the lowest-level task you should accommodate in your WBS is to consider budget or time criteria. The lowest-level task should require at least .25 to 2 percent of the total budget or project time. You also can use segments, such as half or full days, to define the smallest task levels. These approaches may appear initially imprecise, but they establish a general guideline for the lowest-level tasks in your project.

A third option is to use the reporting period rule to determine the work packages. That rules states that no work package should be longer than a standard reporting period. Thus, if you make weekly status reports, no work package should be longer than a week in length. This helps eliminate work package statuses that are 73 percent or 38 percent done; work packages will only be reported as started (50 percent done), not started, or complete (100 percent). If a work package using this rule is started and is on the not-complete list for more than two reporting periods, there is a problem to solve.

When you start building the WBS, you will need to consider all of the deliverables that will be required, including any drawings, designs, documents, and schematics, for example. Here are some other tips regarding your project's deliverables:

◆ A deliverable should be unambiguous. The "design the button layout on the hand-held remote control" task is much clearer than the "design the TV control system" task, which may be really five to ten separate work packages. The latter is so unclear that you can't schedule it because there are too many elements; team members won't know where one work package starts or stops. ("Do we complete the remote control and the TV's receiver side of the system as well as the power controls? Or do we just do the remote control?") But the "design the TV control system" task could be a milestone—one that includes tasks for the remote control, primary power system, and television receiver.

♦ All work within the same work package should occur within a sequential or parallel time frame without gaps for possible other work in between. Thus, "framing and plumbing the bathroom" is not a well-formed work package in your bathroom remodeling project because plumbing the bathroom is not necessarily related to framing the bathroom—and other tasks, such as adding insulation, also could come after the framing task. It's better to define the tasks as separate work packages, "framing" and "plumbing," in the project plan rather than to risk confusion about the sequence or priority of events. Also, don't confuse work packages with milestones, which are a significant event within the project such as the completion of a major deliverable.

♦ A work package should only include related work elements. When washing your car, for example, the work package "get soapy water" wouldn't fit with "polish the car" because there's no relationship between the procedures and they occur at different times in the project cycle. (At least they do when I wash my car!) Therefore, a work package called "get soapy water and polish the car" is not a well-formed work package because it involves unlike steps.

> **Project Lingo**
>
> An **element of work** (also known as an activity) is an activity required to complete a project that's too small to be elevated to the rank of work package. Elements of work are the steps to complete a work package. Remember, work packages are tracked in the plan, but elements and activities are not; elements and activities still need to be accounted for, however, in the overall time allocated for the work packages.

Sometimes it is easier to write a listing of the work packages that may need to be done and then work on rolling them up into the WBS. Use a brainstorming technique to capture all the information and then develop a more detailed diagram to see how they will inter-relate to each other.

Over and Over Again

If you manage projects in which many of the same kinds of work packages are duplicated over and over again, you may want to create a standard template for these common tasks. This technique is used often in construction and engineering, where the time to complete a standard operation has been established and proven over time.

Criteria for Ensuring Quality Work

As you develop the WBS, you need to have some way of determining whether a task is done and that it was done correctly. You can do this through establishing measurable quality levels based on the standards in your industry. You can also do this by establishing standard quality checklists and formal testing procedures, which are often done on engineering projects. Peer reviews or stakeholder acceptance reviews can also be used to ensure quality. In a peer review you ask colleagues who are not a part of the project to examine the project plan and the deliverables produced to date to provide you and the project team with suggestions for improvement.

One way to document these criteria is to develop an outline of the WBS with the quality criteria and review process noted next to each appropriate task or milestone. Completion and evaluation criteria improve the clarity of the WBS and will ultimately improve the quality of the project plan. This is important because it's a lot cheaper to fix a problem or task description during the planning stage than during implementation.

So that's a wrap! Now you know how the work breaks down in your project. You've taken all the goals of the project that were developed in the SOW and have broken them into specific work packages. But that's just one important step in planning. Now, let's take a look at sequencing the work in a network diagram.

The Least You Need to Know

- ◆ A single task is a cohesive work package with a unique, measurable deliverable that can be monitored and tracked.

- ◆ A work breakdown structure (WBS) organizes the tasks of a project into hierarchies and milestones.

- ◆ Milestones divide the project into logical, measurable segments. When all the milestones are completed, the project should be done.

- ◆ Once you create a complete task list and WBS, you can plan the schedule and resources for the project.

- ◆ Criteria for measuring the quality and completion of tasks should be built into the WBS and the project plan.

Chapter 10

The Network Diagram: A Map for Your Project

In This Chapter

- ◆ The network diagram—your project's roadmap
- ◆ Why network diagrams are a lot of work but a good idea
- ◆ Symbols and conventions in network diagramming
- ◆ Five steps to create a network diagram
- ◆ Major network diagramming systems

You may be thinking that this is going to be the cool chapter in which you get to use networks and computers to plan and control your project from the depths of cyberspace. Forget it. Even though you could put information about your project plans and status on the Net to keep team members up-to-date, when most project managers talk about the network, they're not talking about an information superhighway or even a slow road.

The network, in project management terms, is a tried and proven way to organize and sequence the activities of a project. Anything but the simplest project should have a network diagram. Yes, the network diagram is a road-map of sorts, but you won't find mondo sites on weird cults by following the links like you would on the web—you'll just get your project done a lot easier. In fact, you don't even need a computer to create a network diagram (but it sure helps on big projects).

In this chapter, you'll learn how to create a network diagram by hand using pencil and paper, although we mention how computers can help throughout the text. In Chapter 30, we talk a lot more about the computer tools you can use to do the same thing (and do it a lot faster). It's important that you understand how to create your own network diagram before you start letting the computer do your thinking for you. For small projects, doing it by hand is often easier and faster. (Don't tell our friends at Microsoft and Intel about this heresy—they think everything is better and faster with a computer.)

What's a Network Diagram?

The *network diagram* shows the path of the project, lists starting and completion dates, and names the responsible party for each task. For people not already familiar with your project, such as management and new team members, the network diagram explains at a glance (well, it might take more than a glance) how the work on the project goes together. Remember the peer or stakeholder reviews we talked about at the end of the last chapter? Network diagrams can help there, too!

Project Lingo

A **network diagram** is the logical representation of activities that defines the sequence of work in a project. A network for a simple project might consist of one or two pages. On a large project, several network diagrams might exist: one for the overall project based on the project milestones and one for each subproject that leads to the completion of a milestone.

If properly sequenced, a network diagram will …

◆ Show the sequences and relationships among activities necessary to complete a project.

◆ Identify relationships among milestones in the project that can be used for monitoring progress and completion.

◆ Show the interrelationships of activities in different parts of the work breakdown structure (WBS) hierarchy.

◆ Establish a vehicle for scheduling activities (covered in Chapters 11 and 12).

◆ Help reduce uncertainty in the project by breaking it into many small phases that have been analyzed and sequenced in advance of starting the work.

If you put the network diagram on a wall where the whole project team can see it (especially your boss) and then use a bright color to mark off the activities as they are completed, the network diagram can be a powerful way to communicate what has been done on the project and what remains to be accomplished. Of course, if the project gets stalled and the activities don't get done, it also can be a sure way to let people know you're in trouble. (Hopefully, this won't happen to you.)

Why Do I Need a Network Diagram?

For simple projects of fewer than 30 activities, the list of activities is often all you need to schedule a project. If you're the only person working on a small project, you'll likely complete the work one activity after the other until the project gets done. If this is the case, simply list the activities in your project in the proper order, and you can move on to Chapters 11 and 12 right now to learn about project scheduling.

If your project involves more than one person or more than a handful of activities, the sequence of activities is probably not a simple matter of working on one activity after another. Project work also happens in parallel because people may be working on different activities at the same time. To make things more complicated, the activities may be related to other activities that depend on them. All these relationships and interdependencies can be tough to figure out in your head—and impossible to understand from a list of activities that must be completed. This is why you need a network diagram: to help you understand how the work should really go together. Only then can you develop a somewhat reliable schedule for your project.

The WBS and the Network Diagram

A WBS is a great first step in identifying the work packages in a project. However, WBS representations don't graphically display the sequencing relationships between various parts of the project. A WBS only shows the hierarchical relationships between work on the project—you can't schedule a hierarchy as easily as a sequence. Therefore, it cannot be used to create a schedule or to coordinate work done by different people or resources unless all the activities in a project are sequential (and they rarely are).

Project Lingo

A **Gantt chart** is a special bar chart that lists activities on the left side of the chart; dates are listed across the top, and activity duration is as a date-based horizontal bar running across the page.

Complex *Gantt charts* can display relationships among the activities, but these are best produced by computer programs. Network diagrams are an easier way to identify and plan sequences.

Network diagrams reveal the workflow, not just the work. Networks are usually drawn from left to right with lines drawn between activities to indicate the precedence among activities in the project. Arrowheads are placed on the lines to indicate the direction of the workflow through time.

Although it is possible to create a network diagram for a small project without first developing a WBS, there are some limitations to network diagramming that make this undesirable. Network diagrams simply sequence the work activities and identify their relationships in time. Networks are not as good as a WBS at demonstrating hierarchical relationships (milestones) in a project, but they can be used to demonstrate the sequence of activities and relationships among activities in different milestones in the WBS. So it's customary to complete your network diagrams after the WBS.

In addition, a network diagram is awkward for managing budgets and personnel assignments. A WBS is awkward for scheduling. Thus, the use of both a WBS and a network diagram provide a powerful combination for managing and controlling your project.

Two central concepts must be understood before a network diagram can be created for a project: the concept of precedence and the concept of concurrent (or parallel) activities.

Precedence Relationships in a Project Network

Precedence defines the sequencing order and how activities—called work elements—are related to one another in the plan. If one activity must be completed before the next activity can be started, the first one has precedence over the second. In the All-Star Cable project, for example, the development of the Graphic User Interface (GUI) must be completed before it can be tested. In a network diagram, this precedence is illustrated by drawing one activity to the left of the other. There is other precedence in the project as well. For instance, we must build the employee interface prototype before we can test it with the user groups.

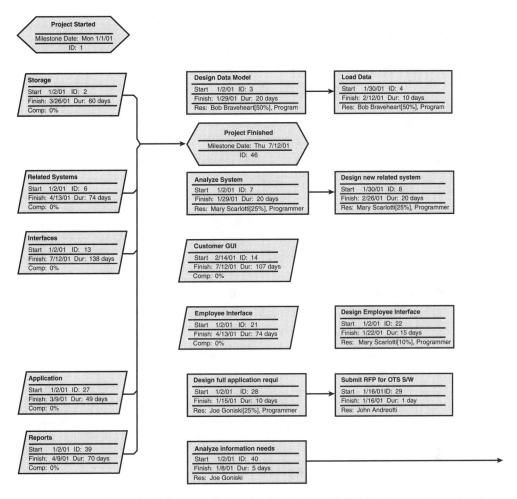

This is just a small portion of the network diagram for All-Star Cable's Movies-on-Demand project.

Although some activities must precede others, many activities can be started at the same time as other activities. This leads to the other important diagramming concept: parallel activities. Many project activities can be worked on in parallel as long as suitable resources are available. For example, it is possible to begin working on the data storage model for All-Star Cable at the same time that others are working on the interfaces and application development activities within the project. However, both of these take precedence over the reporting activities within the project. In a network diagram, it is possible to identify parallel activities by drawing them in parallel to each other in the same plane. These activities may also be called simultaneous or concurrent activities as well as parallel activities.

The concepts of precedence and simultaneous work are important because the relationships between activities ultimately will establish the basis for scheduling a project. (You will learn about this in Chapters 11 and 12.) That's why network diagrams are often called precedence diagrams. Adjusting the parallel activities and the precedence alters the time and resources required to complete a project. The goal in developing the network diagram is to identify activities that can occur in a parallel manner and to specify the precedence that exists among the activities. This leads to the development of an optimum sequence of activities for scheduling purposes.

It can also help to determine if "crashing" or "fast tracking" the project make sense. Crashing is a term that project managers use when they want to compress the time to catch up on the project schedule by adding more people, if the budget will allow it. Fast tracking is when a project manager determines that there are activities that can be done in parallel without compromising the project. In each of these instances, the activities may not have been planned that way, but the network diagram allows the project manager to see that crashing or fast tracking is an option.

> **Project Lingo**
>
> When one activity in the project must be completed before another activity can be started, the first activity is said to have **precedence** over the other.

> **Time Is Money**
>
> If an activity doesn't have a clear precedent (that is, if it's unrelated to any activities performed previously), it can stand alone with an arrow pointing to it from the Start Project task. Such activities might have significant float (explained in Chapter 12) and can provide you with additional scheduling flexibility.

How It Works: Symbols and Conventions

We have found that simple is better in most project management situations. Therefore, the network diagramming techniques we recommend are simple ones. Still, in every networking method, specific symbols used in the charts can seem complicated if you're new to the idea of a network diagram. But stay with us. The system we recommend is based on a simplification of a diagramming technique called precedence diagramming. If you work through the steps, you'll see that it isn't as difficult as it looks at first glance. It's really just lots of lines and boxes—and most people learn to draw those in kindergarten.

Boxes hold the description of each task. Lines connect the activities to one another, as you can see in the diagram in the following section. The activities are laid out horizontally from left to right to coincide with the time sequence in which the activities will be completed. Groups of activities that lead to specific deliverables are identified by boxes with rounded corners. These mark the milestones in the chart.

Network diagrams are really a simple matter of linking activities in boxes with lines. Just put the activities in the right order, draw lines between them, and you have a network diagram. You can easily do this with Post-It Notes on a dry-erase board if need be. Then, if something changes, it is very simple to erase and rearrange.

Diagramming the Relationships

So that everyone who uses network diagrams can figure out what's going on, there are a number of basic conventions (rules) in putting activities into a network diagram. Here are some of them:

- The defined sequences of activities are represented by placing activities in horizontal order from left to right in the network.

- Activities that can happen at the same time are shown in columns. These are called parallel activities because the work can happen at the same time as other work in different rows.

- The precedence between activities and milestones is shown by drawing lines from activity to activity, indicating that the activity on the left must be completed before the activity on the right can begin. The activity that must be completed first is called the precedent task. The activity that starts after the precedent activity is called the dependent task. That's why the network diagram is said to reveal the dependencies among activities. (Getting pretty technical? Don't worry. This is as hard as it gets.)

- Lines among activities can cross the rows to show how activities in the various sequences relate to each other.

Other relationships among activities also should be clearly explained in a network diagram. Here are some of them:

- One activity may depend on the completion of multiple activities or milestones. The precedence for all of these activities must be shown by drawing lines from the precedent activities to the dependent task.

- An activity may start independently of some activities but still be dependent on others. Lines are only drawn between activities with dependency.

- An activity without a precedent activity or milestone can logically be started at any time after the initial "Start Project" activity because it has no other dependent relationships. Put such an activity in its own row.

Standard conventions for network diagrams.

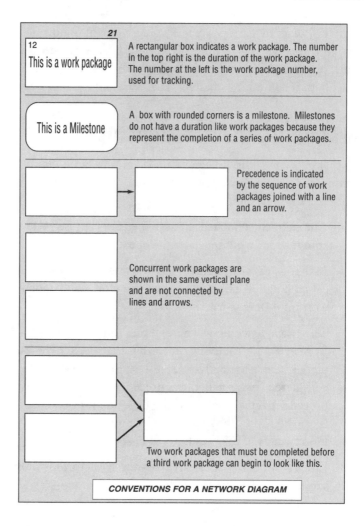

A rectangular box indicates a work package. The number in the top right is the duration of the work package. The number at the left is the work package number, used for tracking.

A box with rounded corners is a milestone. Milestones do not have a duration like work packages because they represent the completion of a series of work packages.

Precedence is indicated by the sequence of work packages joined with a line and an arrow.

Concurrent work packages are shown in the same vertical plane and are not connected by lines and arrows.

Two work packages that must be completed before a third work package can begin to look like this.

CONVENTIONS FOR A NETWORK DIAGRAM

If you look at the complete network diagram earlier in this chapter, you can see most of these conventions put into action. You'll also notice that it's pretty easy to figure out what's going on when you follow the rules.

Five Steps to Create a Network Diagram

By convention, most network diagrams start with a box labeled "Start Project" and end with a box labeled "Project Finished." All you have to do is fill in the activities in between. But as you may have guessed, there's probably more to it than that. Actually, there are five steps (explained in the next sections) that you can follow to produce a network diagram for any project. Before you start, however, get a whole lot of sticky note packages because you will need to change things as you go. These tools can help as you try to figure out the sequences and relationships.

Don't expect to get things right the first time. Network diagramming takes practice. Even after you get it all put together, you should have some other folks from the project review your efforts. Now, with all that in mind, the following sections describe the steps to follow.

Words from the Wise

"Begin at the beginning," the King said gravely, "and go until you come to the end; then stop."

—Lewis Carroll, *Alice's Adventures in Wonderland* (1865)

Step 1: List the Activities Using the WBS

You have already learned how to create a WBS (refer to Chapter 9). For a network diagram, each activity should have a unique identifying number or other code. (As you begin, don't worry if you don't have them numbered yet, just remember that you will need to number them later.) A network diagram will lay out the work packages or individual activity levels in your WBS. Higher WBS levels will be identified as milestones (see step 3).

Step 2: Establish the Interrelationships Between Activities

To determine the sequences and precedence to be diagrammed for the activities, ask the following questions about each activity:

♦ What activities must precede this task? That is, what other activities must be completed before this one can be started?

♦ What activities follow this task? That is, what activities cannot be started until this activity is complete?

♦ What activities can take place concurrently with this one? Or more simply, what activities can be worked on while this one is being completed?

The precedence and dependencies should be noted in a simple list. Some of the precedence won't become apparent until step 4, however, when you actually draw the activities and link them. If you don't identify all the precedence now, it's fine. Just list them as you discover them to form a record. This list of activity numbers and their precedence is especially useful if you use computerized project management programs such as Microsoft Project.

Step 3: Identify the Milestones That You Want to Specify

Milestones summarize a sequence of activities or specify a key accomplishment during the project (refer to Chapter 9). Milestones are not activities. Milestones do not take effort; they are just convenient markers for summarizing work that has been performed to that point on the network diagram. The top levels in the WBS are a good source of milestones for the project. Milestones have defined precedence and sequences. You can draw a network of only milestones, or you can combine milestones with activities to display a complete project—or you can leave the milestones out of your project altogether (recommended only on small projects).

> **Time Is Money**
>
> When establishing a network diagram using a program such as Microsoft Project, before using the software's demand for start, duration, and finish dates, take some time to roughly diagram the basic network on paper. This will help you understand the basic precedence and will assist you in building the chart correctly once you begin the computer entry procedure.

Step 4: Lay Out the Activities and Milestones as a Network

Some experienced project managers start from the last activity in the project and work backward when charting the project. In his book, *Seven Habits of Successful People*, Stephen Covey calls it "begin with the end in mind." Many people find it easier to identify preceding activities than successive ones. However, there are many arguments for starting with the first activity and working forward because this is how the work will actually be done. The outcome is the same—the approach used is a matter of preference.

Step 5: Review the Logic of the Network

The network review process is important because it is through adapting sequences and precedence that an optimum order of project activities can be identified. To review the logic of the network, look at each activity and each connection and ask yourself the following questions:

- Are the activities properly sequenced?
- Is all necessary precedence identified?

◆ Is there any precedence that isn't really required? That is, are there activities that can be completed concurrently (in parallel) that are incorrectly shown as sequences?

◆ Are all of the activities really necessary?

◆ Are any activities missing?

◆ Does the completion of the activities in the network represent the accomplishment of everything necessary to meet the project goals that have been specified?

Along the Critical Path

To make activities and sequences easier to find in your network, be sure to identify each activity and milestone with unique numbers or other identification labels. In computerized project management programs, activities are always numbered as well as being identified by activity description. The same method of identification or numbering used in the WBS is usually appropriate; however, it is common in networks to skip numbers between activities to allow flexibility in the network when requirements for new or different activities may become apparent later in the project. For example, instead of numbering activities as 1, 2, 3, and so on, it might be better to number activities as 10, 20, 30, 40, and so on. Then, when you need to add new activities between activity 10 and activity 20, you can number them 10.1 and 10.2 without disturbing the logical numbering sequence of the original activities. The numbering system should be flexible because projects almost always have changes that need to be represented in the network.

The sequences of activities you put in your network are not absolute. Experienced project managers often revise and adjust the networks until they are optimized. People often find when they begin mapping precedence that activities have been left out of the WBS. Add these new activities and make sure to note them in the appropriate places in the WBS. The network and the WBS should always match. In reverse, if you find that some activities are redundant, remove them from both documents.

Be careful not to sequence activities in an arbitrary order. Just because you've always done something a certain way does not mean it's the best way to do it. Try to look at the network

Risk Management

If an activity defined in the WBS doesn't seem to fit in the network diagram, this usually means it's out of place. The activity could be too small to include in the network diagram, or it could be too large and require further breakdown into more elemental activities. If you change an activity's status, make the change in your WBS so that it and the network diagram match.

from a new point of view; find better ways to get the work done. A network diagram provides a great opportunity to do this. Can the activities be sequenced differently for better use of resources? Can some activities be split into two or more activities to make the organization of work more flexible? It is usually a good idea to have objective outsiders review the sequences, in addition to the project team, to avoid bias in the sequence of work. Sometimes a person outside the politics of a project can identify a better way to complete the work.

Complex Time Relationships for Critical Projects

The optimum way to represent precedence in projects isn't always a simple matter of completing one activity and then starting another (called a finish-to-start precedence). Your precedence diagrams also can specify complex timing relationships between activities. By overlapping activities in the diagram and using arrows to represent specific timing, relationships can be shown in which activities must be started at a certain point after another activity is started. This is especially important in complex projects. For example, using precedence diagramming techniques, you can show the following complex task-sequencing requirements:

- An activity that should start at the same time as another activity because they're logically related. For example, in All-Star Cable, the project team could be gathering reporting requirements for Movies-on-Demand at the same time they are taking an inventory of the existing reports that All-Star used in pay-per-view. Overlapping activities like this reduces the total project duration.

- An activity that must be completed at least five days before another can begin. For example, the pouring of foundation of a house must be done five days before the walls are framed to allow the cement to cure.

- An activity that must finish before another activity can finish. For example, the planning of a product can start before the design approvals are started, but the planning cannot be completed until the design approvals are done.

> **Time Is Money**
>
> For the most accurate scheduling, advanced concepts in network and precedence diagramming are available. They are especially useful for construction and engineering projects.

> **Project Lingo**
>
> **Lead** is the amount of time that precedes the start of work on another activity. **Lag** is the amount of time after one activity is started or finished before the next activity can be started or finished.

For most simple business projects, it isn't necessary to define these types of complex *lead* and *lag* times at the activity level. Simple precedence relationships (finish-to-start relationships) are adequate for all but the most complex scientific and construction projects. The terms are mentioned here, however, because they are often referred to in computerized project management systems or in other project management literature. You should know what the terms mean even if you don't use them. As a project manager, it's a matter of pride (and being well-informed). These advanced techniques can also come in handy when you need to adjust activities to meet a deadline.

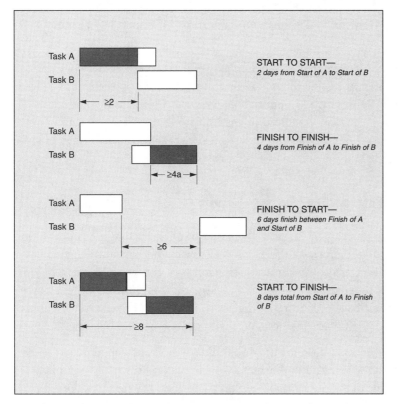

Complex precedence diagramming conventions for showing lead and lag times between activities.

When Is Enough Enough?

Goals and constraints establish the scope for your project. (You learned about this in Chapter 7.) In creating a network, as in creating the WBS, the project goals and scope establish the level of detail for defining the work that must be completed. Even so, the question arises in developing every network as to how many activities should be included. There are no hard and fast rules, but the experiences of early project management practitioners revealed that, after a certain point, the marginal return in control offered by more detail is far outweighed by the additional work required to develop and maintain the network. At some point in every plan, more detail becomes a negative rather than a positive attribute. The best advice is to use your judgment.

What About Huge Projects?

Some giant networks for major construction or engineering projects may have 25,000 or more activities that really need to be tracked. It obviously is impossible for any one person to understand all the relationships between these 25,000 individual activities—and the network diagram would take up an entire wall or more of a large conference room.

One way to make such a large network more manageable is to create network diagrams for each major subproject or milestone of a project based on the WBS. These milestones can then be summarized in another diagram. If there are dependencies between the milestones, they can be noted in the milestone network. This approach also allows people responsible for specific milestones within a project to be responsible for a detailed network of his or her own subproject.

When Is a Network a Waste of Time?

The more complex a project is, the greater the value of network diagram in developing a schedule and a budget. Though there is a cost associated with implementing network management of a project using network diagrams, this cost is relatively low when compared to the potential advantages. Typically, the cost in time and money for implementing a network-based planning system is somewhere between .1 to 1 percent of the total project—the percentage gets smaller as the project becomes larger.

Most studies indicate a significantly lower probability of cost and schedule overruns when network diagrams are used. In a business world concerned with profitability and performance, this seems like a pretty good reason to employ the network technique for organizing and scheduling work—it reduces the risk of going over budget or running late.

Three Major Network Methods and Others You May Encounter

We've discussed the basic precedence diagram because we think it is the easiest, most effective networking diagram for most small to mid-size projects—the projects most people manage in everyday business. But even if it's just to impress your boss by using nifty acronyms, you should know that related systems of network diagramming and scheduling techniques are used in industry today.

The two most common forms of networking systems are the Performance Evaluation and Review Technique (PERT) and the Critical Path Method (CPM). The techniques are similar in principal to what you've already learned. The differences lie in how the projects display information and deal with scheduling uncertainties. And given that these techniques were developed by engineers for engineering projects, a lot more symbols are used to represent the relationships between activities in a network.

Until PERT/CPM techniques were developed, simple Gantt charts or other bar charts were the best tools available to represent project sequences. Gantt charts show a graphic representation of work on a time scale. You will learn more about Gantt charts as a useful way to represent the overall project schedule in Chapter 11. Gantt charts are really just timelines that show activities in parallel. The complex versions produced by today's project management software can even show the dependencies between activities represented in networks, work in progress, and comparisons between the current status and the planned status (baseline) of the project.

Along the Critical Path

One of the pioneering efforts to show the interrelationships among activities on a project was undertaken by the science management team of Morgan R. Walker and James E. Kelly in the mid-1950s at the E. I. Du Pont Company. Their joint efforts resulted in the Kelly-Walker network technique. However, in later publications of their work, they referred to the method as the Critical Path Method. Du Pont tested the CPM method in the construction of a major chemical plant and in several maintenance projects that were completed by the middle of 1958. It is claimed that Du Pont credited more than $1 million in savings to this technique in the first year it was used. (And remember, that was in 1958 dollars!)

During the same period, the management scientists of the Special Projects Office of the U.S. Navy, along with the firms of Lockheed and Booz, Allen, and Hamilton, developed a similar network system called PERT, which stands for Program Evaluation and Review Technique. The system was developed to help coordinate more than 3,000 people involved in the development of the Polaris missile. The use of PERT is credited with reducing the time required to complete the project by two years.

CPM is often cited as better for construction-type projects. It is argued that PERT is more appropriate for software-oriented projects. For that reason, the project manager for Movies on Demand has decided to use the PERT method for establishing the schedule.

The primary reason for this is the different approaches the two systems use for scheduling, not because of the networks, which are largely the same in terms of sequencing possibilities. In CPM, one time estimate is used for creating the schedule; PERT uses a more complex system based on three time estimates that are used to determine the most probable time for completion.

This more complex time-estimating approach is deemed by some to be more appropriate for research projects with high degrees of uncertainty and risk. For most general business projects, these differences are not critical, and some people call all network systems by the name PERT/CPM because of their similarities.

Circles or Boxes? Who Cares?

Okay, this next part is for people who just want to know more about the PERT/CPM differences. It might get a bit technical—you can opt out now if you just want to get your project plan done. See you in the next chapter.

Still with us? Curious? Glutton for punishment? Well, in any case, here's the scoop on PERT and CPM.

Traditionally, PERT/CPM networks use circles and arrows to describe work in a project. The two systems use the same basic diagramming conventions you've already learned as a way to link activities, except they refer to activities as "activities" and milestones as "events." These two concepts, activities and events, are central to the traditional PERT/CPM diagrams. An activity is a specific project activity that requires resources and time to complete. An event is a specific end state for one or more activities that occurs at a specific point in time. An event occurs as a result of completing one or more activities.

AOA and AON

There are two methods of representing activities and events in PERT/CPM networks: activity on arrow (AOA), also called activity on arc, and activity on node (AON). The method used is largely a matter of preference. In AOA, the arrows are the activities, and the circles (called "nodes" in PERT/CPM) are the events. In the AON method, the activities are the circles, and the lines demonstrate the precedence between activities. Some of the traditional ways of diagramming activities in a PERT/CPM chart are shown in the following diagram.

Simple precedence networks using boxes, as shown here, are really just another version of an AON PERT/CPM network. We think the boxes are a lot easier to use. (Bet you do too at this point.) We've found that most mid-size business projects are easier to describe and understand using the boxes than by creating complex number, circle, and arc networks. In fact, most computerized project management programs now offer boxes to replace the circle/arc format.

PERT/CPM activities.

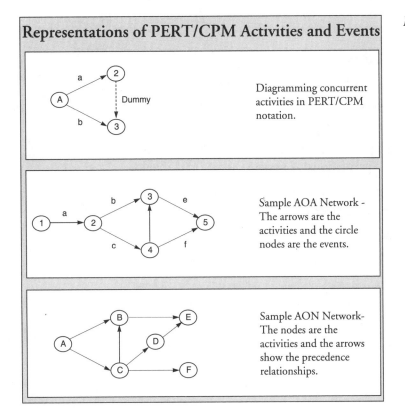

Representations of PERT/CPM Activities and Events

Diagramming concurrent activities in PERT/CPM notation.

Sample AOA Network - The arrows are the activities and the circle nodes are the events.

Sample AON Network- The nodes are the activities and the arrows show the precedence relationships.

We're glad you made it through all this because it's important for an informed project manager like you to be familiar with some of the other diagramming options in project management. As you get more experience, you might want to experiment with these other diagramming techniques for your networks. (We suggest you get a comprehensive book on PERT/CPM techniques before you do.)

Tried and True Networks

Over the years, with the advances in computer software, some of the representational techniques in PERT/CPM and precedence diagramming have been improved or modified and expanded. Still, the simplicity of the original system has withstood the tests of time and application, and no truly substantive changes have been made in the original methods.

In Chapters 11 and 12, you'll learn how to turn your network diagram into a schedule you can be proud (and confident) to present to management for approval.

The Least You Need to Know

◆ The network diagram isn't always necessary for small projects, but it's a good tool for most projects to establish the order of steps and the relationships among the various activities in a project.

◆ As a project manager, you predict the future. The tough part is making the future match your predictions! A network diagram can help.

◆ The task-in-box diagramming method is supported by most project management software and is relatively easy to use.

Chapter 11

Project Start to Finish— Establishing the Time to Get Things Done

In This Chapter

- ◆ The importance of accurate scheduling
- ◆ Building estimates from experience
- ◆ Four ways to correctly estimate tasks
- ◆ Schedule inflation and how to avoid it
- ◆ The confidence factor in scheduling

As you would assume from reading earlier chapters in this book, the schedule is intertwined with the work breakdown structure (WBS), the network diagram, and eventually, the budget. Change one and you invariably influence the others. We have separated the schedule and the budget in the next few chapters, but in reality, you should work on both at the same time. The schedule and the budget work together to float a project or sink it.

The Schedule or the Budget: Which Is First?

Some naive project managers are inclined to start with the budget first, but we don't recommend it. Because time is money, the schedule will affect the final budget in many ways. That's why we talk about scheduling first. The best project managers establish the schedule before finalizing the budget, even if everyone thinks they're nuts. It's best to try to determine how much time is really required to complete a project before you let your (lack of) money get in the way of your thinking.

The experienced project manager can look at an activity, understand what's required, and provide a reasonably realistic guesstimate of the time requirement as if pulling the number from the air. You will get to that point someday with the help of this book and with a few projects under your belt. But until you get that experience, you can establish a reasonable schedule using this and the subsequent chapter's advice as a procedural guide. And maybe more important, in the following pages, you also will learn how to deal with external pressures (such as bosses and customers) that demand unrealistic dates. No matter what your manager says, you can't build Rome in a day.

Building a schedule also verifies the project's viability. If, when assembling the schedule, time is not on your side, you may need to work out an extension with management or an increase in resources. Working on the schedule might also reveal missing activities. Remember: It's all interrelated, so expect to adjust the network diagram, WBS, and budget as you adapt the schedule.

The Schedule Synchronizes the Project

Accurate, realistic, and workable scheduling is what makes a project tick. The schedule shows who is doing what and when they are supposed to be doing it. Scheduling involves converting the well-organized and sequenced tasks in your WBS and network diagram—as well as the list of resources and vendors you will develop in Chapters 15—into an achievable timetable with start dates, finish dates, and assigned responsibilities for each activity.

The steps in creating a schedule are carried out sequentially, as follows:

1. Establishing the scheduling assumptions. From earlier chapters, you already know why it's important to clarify goals and objectives before the project plan reaches its final stages. For the same reasons, it's important to specify scheduling assumptions before the schedule is completed. Answering the following questions should help in this process. We've also included a simple worksheet (see Chapter 12) that will assist you in determining the assumptions germane to your project.

◆ Are there a fixed number of resources (remember that resources mean the people, time, technology, and money) to be used on the project? Or can you add them to meet the schedule priorities?

◆ Is there an absolute date by which the project must be completed so that it doesn't become worthless? (An example would be designing a new trade show booth for the big July show. If the booth is a no-show, then the time and money used to design and build it as well as the cost of the trade show floor space gets flushed down the toilet.)

◆ Can the completion date be negotiated based on a realistic schedule of when all the deliverables (goals) can be met?

◆ Will people work standard workdays or will overtime be allowed or expected? Watch for holidays and expect to pay extra for having people work on Christmas Day!

◆ Are all resources currently trained and available? Or will your project require hiring additional people and acquiring new equipment? If training or hiring is required, it should be scheduled.

Here are some examples of assumptions for our All-Star Cable example: A network expert from the organization will be available from August through October; new cable boxes for Movies-on-Demand will be operational as planned by January 25; there will be no major changes in procedures for billing within the next six months. Assumptions protect the project from being severely impacted by planned change in other parts of the organization, change that the project manager may not be aware of. Assumptions can also reveal risks and limitations, and then enable you to build contingencies for them into your plan.

Large projects require that you document your assumptions in writing. That way, you are less likely to forget something. Also, when you review those plans with your project sponsor or the project steering committee, they may alert you to incorrect assumptions that you are making. Simple projects don't always require documentation of the assumptions, but you should have a verbal agreement on them among your team and outside resources.

Time Is Money

Even though it takes a woman nine months to have a baby, two women can't have a baby in half that time!

2. Estimating the number of resources, the activity effort, and the work package duration (the time to complete each activity on the network diagram) based on the

resources you have on hand or can afford. Remember that these estimates are all constrained by your personnel and equipment resources. The more resources, the less time required, in most but not all cases. Here you need to estimate the duration of a activity over a number of days.

Sometimes duration and effort are the same. If it takes seven hours of effort for a secretary to stuff envelopes during the course of one day, then the effort is one workday, and the duration of the work package is one workday. Sometimes duration and effort are very different. It may take only four hours of meeting time to get the building inspector's approval of a building's wiring, but these meetings happen over a period of two weeks. Thus, the effort for getting the wiring approved is four hours, but the duration of the work package is two weeks.

It is important to know both the effort (also called labor estimates) and the duration required to complete a work package to create both an accurate schedule and a detailed budget for a project. It's also important to know that you can often, but not always, shorten the duration of an activity by adding more people to complete the labor. Thus, estimating the number of people and resources that will perform an activity is an important consideration in estimating duration.

Project Lingo

Duration is the time, usually in days, that it takes to complete the *entire* project, from starting the first task to finishing the last one. Effort is the time it takes, usually in days or months, to complete an activity or work package.

Duration stands out in project management terms because the accumulated duration of activities along the critical path in the project plan directly affects all the subsequent activities in the project. (You'll learn about the critical path in Chapter 12.) It is the duration (the total time span, usually noted as a number of days) of the activities that, when added together, establish the time required to complete the project.

3. Determining calendar dates for each activity and creating a master schedule. For a complex project network, you also will need to determine the critical path and float for each activity on the project. (You'll learn how to do this in Chapter 12.)

4. Adjusting the individual resource assignments as necessary to optimize the schedule. This is called the resource-leveling phase. (You'll learn about this in Chapter 12.)

5. Charting the final schedule. (Note: In most cases, all of these scheduling steps are easier with a computer program unless the project is very small.)

Estimating Time: Your Best Guess at Effort and Duration

Of all the steps in scheduling, estimating the duration of tasks is the most important. Unfortunately, this is like trying to predict the future. You can only guess, but there are better ways to guess than others. Without accurate activity duration estimates, the entire plan and project might crumble around you.

When estimating the duration of activities, there are five options you can use to make the estimates (guesses) as good as possible:

- ◆ Ask the people who will actually do the work, but have them estimate the work they'll be doing—not the duration. For example, in our all All-Star Cable case study, the project manager has asked the project team to estimate the time it will take to interview the potential vendors for the equipment needed, and they told the manager that they would need about two hours per vendor. However, he knows that it will take a good deal of time to schedule the interviews and evaluate the information gleaned during them. So with three vendors, the interviews might take one or two days (level of effort), but the activity will likely take nearly one month to complete (the duration). You'll have to extrapolate the durations based on the workload, other commitments, and the project member's experience with similar activities.

- ◆ Get an objective expert's opinion (for example, from someone who isn't working on the project). This is usually called a Rule of Thumb.

- ◆ Find a similar task in a completed project plan to see how long it took to get done. This is called an analogous estimate.

- ◆ When you know the relationship between a certain activity and time, use that estimate. For example, most programmers can tell you how many lines of code they can develop per hour or per day. This is called a parametric estimate.

- ◆ Make your best educated guess. This is the last resort when you're under pressure, so make sure the guess is more educated than it is arbitrary. If possible, instead of guessing, try the preceding options instead.

Who You Gonna Call?

To get reliable estimates on the duration of tasks and the effort required, you will likely need to ask other people about the time it will take them to get things done (unless you're completing the entire project on your own, of course). The following sections describe some of the people you can ask to help determine the task duration and the effort estimates for your schedule.

Representative Team Members for Each Part of the Project

Seek out the most experienced team members who will be completing work on your project. Hopefully, these are the people we talked about in Chapter 6. If they have worked on similar projects in the past, they can use what are called historical estimates, how much time it took them last time. Again, ask them for the level of effort, not the duration. Some team members will pad their estimates a little or a lot, and some will be overconfident about their abilities to accomplish miracles. You must adjust the duration in the final plan to account for these idiosyncrasies if you want to come up with the optimum schedule.

It's often useful to sit down with all the team members to estimate activity durations. Even if nothing useful (to you) comes of the sessions, they still serve to build team relationships and to give you a better understanding of the project from the team members' points of view. It's also an excellent technique for assembling a rough-cut schedule in a hurry.

Outside Vendors and Service Agencies

You must get estimates directly from any outside service providers and consultants who will work on your project. Never estimate their time for them. You can negotiate their estimates, but if you dictate a vendor's schedule without their input, you'll never get the schedule you demand. You should politely request a written estimate that fixes the cost and commits them to a schedule (unless the project runs off the rails or changes in scope, of course). Shop price! Shop time!

Experienced Managers or Experts

People in your organization who have handled similar projects can provide excellent advice and can study cost estimates for problems. They also might be able to provide exact estimates if a project they worked on had elements common to yours. Or they may be much more experienced project managers and be willing to help. If no such experts exist within your company, you could get advice from a consultant or a colleague in another company who can help verify your work and duration estimates.

Management and Other Project Stakeholders

If you want your managers and stakeholders (such as the steering committee members) to buy into your schedule, you need to give them an opportunity to help plan the schedule (or at least review it before you submit the project plan for approval). By bringing stakeholders into the process, they'll see that you will efficiently use your time and wisely spend their money. Their involvement will assist you in getting the final plan approved because they'll already have a grasp on the realities of the schedule.

Weighing the Risk

After getting information on the labor requirements and activity durations from various sources, you'll need to use your judgment to determine the duration you'll actually assign to the schedule. Each of these durations will have a risk associated with it. It's often useful to come up with a best-case schedule and a worst-case schedule based on these risks. For example, the project manager for Movies-on-Demand may estimate it will take the team one month to develop the prototype for the Graphical User Interface (GUI) for the home buyer. However, if the project manager only has one person with the skills to complete the design, there is risk. What if the developer gets sick? Or gets into an automobile accident and is hospitalized for a while? These are the kinds of risks that the project manager must always plan for.

Best Case and Worst Case—Compromising Between the Two

In estimating every activity, assume that the actual time required will fall somewhere between flawless execution and major disaster. The best approach is to establish a compromise between the two. Some project management methodologies, such as PERT (refer to Chapter 10), provide the mechanics for estimating all three. These include ...

- The optimistic estimate. Everything goes like clockwork and without problems.

- The most likely estimate. A few problems crop up, and normal delays compromise the optimistic estimate.

- The pessimistic estimate. Allowances are made for many elements to go wrong, substantially delaying or jeopardizing the activity. The pessimistic estimate assumes that the project is going ahead. A complete disaster could still occur that would sink the project's timetable and budget.

Ultimately, these three estimates will be used in combination with each other to come up with a "most likely" schedule based on your confidence in the estimates. Sometimes people just go with the pessimistic estimate; other times, the realistic estimate wins out. If you use the optimistic estimate, you're just looking for trouble.

Many managers of large, high-risk, big-money projects use these estimates and feed into a formula to determine the most likely duration. The approach that's best for you will depend on the project, your experience with similar work, and your organization's culture.

Along the Critical Path

In the standard PERT methodology, the accepted algorithm for coming up with the "most likely" estimate of a task's duration is:

Expected duration = [OD + 4(MLD) + PD] ÷ 6

OD = Optimistic duration

MLD = Most likely duration

PD = Pessimistic duration

The Confidence Factor

Just how reliable are your estimates? You might be comfortable with the timetable for delivery of a photocopier and other office equipment to a new company headquarters but be unsure how long it will take to complete the electrical wiring for the building. You're even more uncertain about the task to design a new logo, which takes lots of creativity and political approvals.

For the duration of each activity on your list, you'll have varying degrees of confidence. The tasks with the highest degree of confidence are usually those you've performed previously or those you'll do yourself. The tasks you aren't sure of usually are those with which you have either no direct experience or very little.

The degree of confidence is also influenced by the complexity (or simplicity) of the task and how much the task is dependent on the completion of preceding (and possibly complex) tasks.

Remember that if you do the estimates alone, your team members may not buy into them. You might create and sell a schedule to management that team members cannot support (or deliver). Make sure team members are involved in task estimating.

If many of the estimates have low confidence associated with them, move your schedule dates toward the worst-case scenario. If most of the estimates are high confidence, a schedule closer to the best-case estimate is the best choice. The more complex (and interdependent) the tasks, the more you might want to lean toward a worst-case scenario.

As you develop your schedule, be sure to evaluate the dependencies that your project has on other projects for success. For example, if the project manager for All-Star Cable knows that the Information Systems department is developing and rolling out a high accessibility network, and that the Movies-on-Demand system will require that network in order to work, then there is a risk that the IS people will not complete their project on time, or that it might not work as advertised. The MOD project manager will need to build some contingency into the project plan to cover that risk (if possible).

If you do add a little protection to your schedule for risky tasks, never make your padded time estimates too obvious. This tactic won't win you any popularity contests with management. Such obvious protection schemes will have management sniffing through the entire project for inflationary tactics at all levels including in the budget. Ultimately, you'll lose not only credibility, but the real resources and time you need to get things done.

If your schedule starts looking like it will take too long to get things done, try adding more people or resources to the plan. This impacts the budget, however, and some tasks could suffer from the too-many-cooks-in-the-kitchen syndrome. Just having more people doesn't always mean you'll get things done faster. More people always has unforeseen costs in management time and coordination, so make sure that adding people is really a good solution to adjusting the schedule.

> **CAUTION**
>
> ## Risk Management
>
> Don't pad the schedule just to cover your uncertainties. Too much padding is as bad as agreeing to complete the impossible in no time at all. A little padding (called contingency planning) is standard practice in all project plans because no one can foresee the future, but padding adds expenses and time to your project. Most experienced project managers will include a 10 to 15 percent contingency in the budget to cover unexpected delays to the schedule.

> ## Time Is Money
>
> Scheduling a large project to the hour from the beginning of the project would produce silly schedules and mounds of useless paper. On the other hand, inadequate schedule detail at the beginning of a small project might leave team members thinking they have more time to get things done than they really have. It takes practice—you'll get the hang of it.

Details, Details ...

After estimating the task duration and making a judgment on the estimates, you must decide on the level of detail you want to put in the initial schedule. Usually, the scheduling level should relate to the levels in your WBS or network diagram. For example, you can probably schedule a small project down to the day on the first go-around, but you won't be able to schedule a megaproject any finer than by the month or week.

For planning purposes, the schedule may be produced at the weekly or monthly level. As work on the project proceeds, you can schedule the work at finer levels. Many large projects are scheduled phase by phase instead of scheduling the entire project from the beginning.

Applying Calendars to a Resource

Every resource will have dates and times when it will be available for use on your project. These dates and times are called the "calendar" for that resource. For people resources, you need to create calendars that include their work hours, workdays, holidays, and vacation days.

Risk Management

Don't forget holidays and vacation time when scheduling project duration. One project manager thought he was going to get a lot accomplished between December 10 and the end of the year. Unfortunately, several people on his project team had vacation time coming and took the last three weeks of the year off! Also, if you are working on an project with an international team, remember to check on the dates of holidays in those countries and schedule accordingly.

You also need to specify how many overtime hours will be allowed, if any. Sometimes you may want to assign a different person to a task based on his or her calendar availability instead of paying overtime.

For equipment resources, you need to indicate any special restrictions on availability. For example, if you only have one electron microscope available and it is being used by three different research projects, you'll need to specify when this resource will be available for your project (or vice versa, you'll need to tell the other projects when you'll need it—if your project has priority, that is.) As you develop the schedule for tasks, you'll need to take the calendar into consideration as you write out the dates.

On a complex project, dealing with the calendars of all the resources can get very complex. Thank heavens for computerized project management programs that enable you to define calendars for all the resources including working days, hours, and nonworking periods such as holidays and vacations. The computer can then do the complex scheduling for you.

Putting It Down on Paper

Once the assumptions for the schedule (that is, the number of people and the activity sequences) and the activity effort is nailed down, you can begin assembling a reasonable schedule. For a simple project with few dependencies, you can simply list activity effort. For more complex projects, use the WBS and the network diagram to schedule your project. You'll need to note the labor for the activities as well as their effort as you work on the schedule. You may find that you need to adjust effort, but not in a way that will affect the actual labor needed to complete an activity.

Scheduling with a network diagram is conceptually simple. Plug in the estimated activity effort for each activity on the network and then add their efforts to get the total time required to complete the project. Just lay the days out on a calendar and—voilà!—you have a schedule. To show you how it's done, we've provided the following example of a network diagram with task duration and dates added.

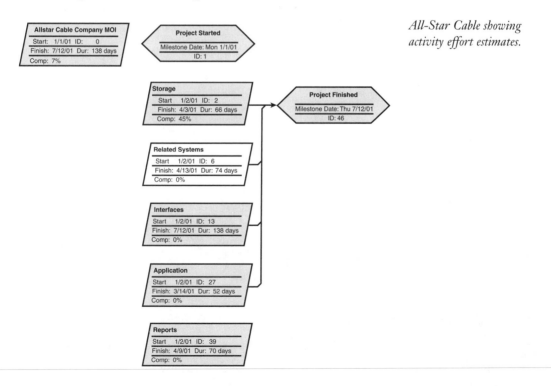

All-Star Cable showing activity effort estimates.

Of course, nothing is ever as simple as it sounds. You need to take into account work-days, holidays, vacations, parallel tasks, and other special circumstances. That's why scheduling a large project is easier with a software program designed for the job. (See Chapter 30 for more information about project management computer programs.) You'll also need to level the resource utilization on a large project if you're overworking some of the resources (or underworking others). You'll learn more about making these schedule adjustments in the next chapter.

Schedule Charting Pros and Cons

There are several schedule-charting formats you should be aware of. The trick is choosing the format that best suits your project. Here are some of your options for displaying the schedule:

- **Calendar charts.** Annotated calendars can be extremely useful for keeping track of schedules for many small projects. Multiple projects or different team member tasks can be entered in various colors on the calendar. Calendars are a good communication tool when displayed in a central location where many team members can see the dates. Large display calendars with reusable, washable surfaces are available at many business supply stores for this purpose.

- **Gantt charts.** Gantt charts are best used as a visual overview of project time-lines; however, they should not substitute for a network diagram or master schedule listing. Gantt charts can be very useful in initial schedule planning, for simple projects, or for individual timelines on a complex project involving many people. These charts also are good for comparing project progress to the original schedule.

- **Milestone schedules.** Milestones can be assigned to summarize major paths on a network (more on this in Chapter 15). Milestones also can be used to chart an overall project schedule. A milestone schedule doesn't have enough information to help you manage a project, but it can be useful for communicating an overall schedule on a large project to upper management or other people who need an overview of the project without task details.

More on Gantt Charts

Simple Gantt charts—sometimes referred to as project timelines—are the most commonly used scheduling charts in business because they're easy to produce and easy to understand. Gantt charts, named after Henry Gantt who developed them in the early

1900s, ordinarily have a list of dates at the top and a list of tasks down the left side. A line on the Gantt chart shows the date each task begins and ends based on its precedence and duration.

The level of scheduling detail you display in your Gantt charts will be determined by the time periods you use on the top: daily, weekly, monthly, or whatever is appropriate for your project. If a project takes a year or more to complete, you may want to use a monthly or weekly Gantt chart. If your project takes 30 days or fewer, a daily Gantt chart will provide more useful information. Gantt charts are most effective if you can present the whole chart on one document such as on 8½" by 14" or 11" by 17" paper.

In a Gantt chart like the one included here, you can see the activities and their numbers to the left of the activities. The small icons let the project manager know that there are additional notes attached to those activities. To the right of the activity, you will see the names of the people who will be working on that activity. The percentages indicate the percentage of their time that will be devoted to that activity. This chart comes from Microsoft Project and illustrates All-Star Cable Movies-on-Demand.

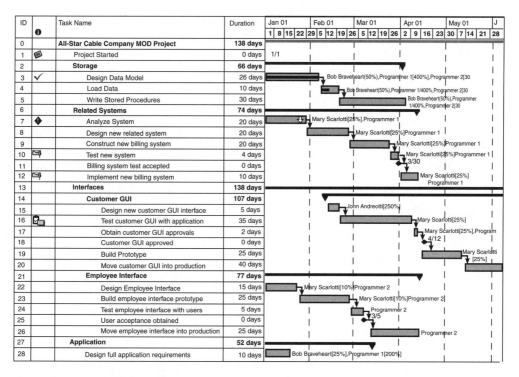

Gantt charts are useful for envisioning the entire project through time.

Simple Gantt charts don't show the interrelationships among tasks. You need a network diagram for this or a project management program that produces complex Gantt charts that indicate summary activities and relationships between them. Also, a Gantt chart alone may not provide enough detail to communicate schedules to individual team members in a complex project. For this, you'll want a project list that includes work package assignments and schedule dates.

Scheduling on the Network Diagram

In addition to creating a Gantt chart, some people like to annotate the schedule dates directly on the network diagram. Although this is a good reference tool for reviewing the entire project, it is awkward to use as a working schedule when assigning responsibilities to individual team members. Therefore, you should use a schedule listing in addition to the network diagram to display and communicate the schedule details.

Time Is Money

As project manager, you need to be able to create a personal timetable for each individual on the project team. Each individual working on the project also needs to be able to relate his or her personal timetable to the master schedule.

Another schedule format that is seen more frequently, thanks to computer programs, is the time-scaled network. This combines the timeline approach of the traditional Gantt chart with the precedence relationships of the network diagram.

Of course, many variations of schedule formats can be used to accommodate individual preferences. No matter what variant you use, however, it is important to include the following key information: task descriptions, start dates, expected finish dates, and assigned people. It should also be easy to read and interpret.

Revisions and the Schedule

Assume that your schedule (and every other aspect of your plan) will require several revisions. As feedback arrives from both team members and outside resources, you might redraft the task estimates and dates several times until you come up with a workable, approvable timeline (schedule) for the project.

Learning Takes Time

Even in the most routine jobs, some time is required for learning the procedures in the new company and adapting to the new work environment. This also is true of some consultants who must become familiar with your company's way of doing business before they can get down to work. When you schedule a project, allow for these various training and development requirements. You might even want to identify training activities as specific tasks in your WBS or network.

The Heat Is On

Instead of caving in to unrealistic pressure, you need to be comfortable with estimating the time each task will require. Unfortunately, no one will make it easy for you. Team members may pull a date or time block (hours required) out of a hat at the same time senior management wants the work completed the day before yesterday. Every project is a rush. With that in mind, how do you, as project manager, avoid succumbing to unrealistic expectations and unrealistic goals? Assuming that the people commissioning the project are somewhat rational human beings, your best tool is the schedule. Think of it as a game. Management will constantly challenge costs, time, and resources. You must make them believe—through a well-documented schedule and plan—that your estimates are realistic and not unduly padded.

Risk Management

If you must share your preliminary drafts of the plan with management, stamp "DRAFT" or "INCOMPLETE" in bright red letters on each page. That way, you won't be held to the shifting sands of an unfinished plan by senior managers who assume that an early version of the project plan is final.

Team Member Estimate Errors

Chances are, you're counting on the core team members and experts to provide the best and most accurate scheduling estimates possible. But rather than carefully thinking through the process for which they are responsible, some members of the team might simply choose a number and feed that into your plan. If it's unrealistic, you're stuck with it.

To avoid this problem, insist that your project team use a method like PERT to reach their estimate. And be sure that you know which method they are using and you are comfortable that the estimate is reasonably accurate and defensible.

Make sure the estimators consider elapsed time in the duration estimates. For example, if their task is to evaluate a new software package, they need to build in time to order it, install it, test it, and go through some conversations with support staff. What looks like four days of effort (32 hours) could result in a 12-day duration when all the "dead" time between activities is accounted for. Have the team estimate both numbers—the effort and the duration. If they don't understand the difference, have a training session with them before they complete the estimates.

Along the Critical Path

A new technique we started using to cope with uncertainty in a schedule involves simply putting the "padding" for the project into a final task called "Schedule Contingency" with a duration that's based on a percentage of the total duration of the project. For most projects, a schedule contingency of 10 to 15 percent of the total duration should be adequate, with the larger percentages going to the longer projects. If you use this approach, you should keep the padding out of the individual task estimates—use the estimates you think will be most likely. This keeps the team focused on the real time they have to complete a task, not an inflated estimate. Then the "padding" at the end becomes a sort of savings account for contingencies that you can use as needed when real schedule changes are required. Using this "padding" account will still add cost to the project in most cases, but it won't mess up expectations about the delivery date you've promised to the stakeholders.

The Just-in-Time Strategy for Scheduling Resources

The just-in-time strategy for getting materials and supplies is credited to the Japanese, but the technique is now common practice worldwide. Just-in-time delivery depends on accurate scheduling and project coordination. With an accurate schedule in place, you can order just what you need and get it delivered exactly when you need it. This means that supplies, equipment, and even people arrive only when the project is ready for them.

By having goods delivered (or people hired) exactly when they're needed, you save money for storage, reduce up-front costs for ordering materials, and are assured that you don't have extra stuff on hand that is costing you extra money.

The key to making this approach work is, you guessed it, communication. Having a contract with suppliers that lets you adjust dates is the essence of just-in-time delivery. That way, you don't have to warehouse items from the supplier. You need to make just-in-time delivery a mandatory contract clause: no delivery until a written request is made and guaranteed delivery within a set number of days or hours after you put the order in. This type of requirement is necessary when you are working with a project that uses a large amount of physical materials, such as construction projects.

The window for just-in-time delivery must be agreed upon in advance; otherwise, the whole schedule falls apart. A temp agency hiring 20 people for your project will want enough time to hire the needed people, but you should notify them if the project goes late. The maker of 6,000 bicycle seats won't want to wait three extra months because the frames are coming in late from France. They'll want them out of the way and will expect payment as well. You, as project manager, must ensure that people and supplies arrive appropriately according to the original or revised schedule.

Dictate Doesn't Mean Doable

At some time, you'll be asked (actually told) to shorten the schedule—even though you know it's impossible to get the work done any faster. Before you cave in to dictate, sit down with everyone pressuring you and go over the schedule day by day, if necessary. Be friendly and cooperative and explain each task and the assumptions about your time allotments represented in the schedule. Bring in expert project managers or technical team members to explain the more opaque tasks.

Your goal for this process is to communicate why the project requires a certain amount of time. In a truly impossible situation, you might need someone senior to you (usually the project sponsor) to go to bat when others attempt to force an unworkable adjustment to the plan on your shoulders.

Now you're ready to learn about how to fine-tune a schedule to meet your stakeholders' objectives. You've only just begun to understand the scheduling complexities.

The Least You Need to Know

- Scheduling involves estimating the task durations for the project and plotting the dates on a calendar. You need to account for holidays, special events, and unknown circumstances.

- No schedule is ever perfect, but the goal is to make the best estimate possible. You do this by using your own judgment and the experience of others to help you make your estimates.

- A Gantt chart is an excellent tool for studying overall schedules, but it doesn't show the interdependencies among tasks shown on the network diagram. Thus, using both in a project plan is a good idea.

- Time estimates should be based on best-case/worst-case scenarios. Your degree of confidence in the accuracy of these estimates should dictate the ultimate schedule, which should be a compromise somewhere between the two extremes.

A Balanced Schedule and Critical Path to Success

In This Chapter

◆ Understanding the critical path

◆ All about float and slack in a project

◆ Important adjustments in complex project schedules

◆ Leveling the resource utilization

◆ Ways to adapt a project to meet a forced schedule

In Chapter 11, you learned the good news: Scheduling is a simple matter of estimating durations for tasks and then plotting the dates on a calendar. Now here's the bad news: Even using computer-based project management software, scheduling a complex project is, well, complex. Because an accurate schedule is essential to managing projects of all sizes, don't cut corners. You need to consider some of the complexities of scheduling before you finalize your project plan. That's what this chapter is all about—the complexities of project scheduling.

For complex projects, computers have a significant advantage over manual scheduling. Yes, you'll learn how to calculate the critical path and float in this chapter, but you should get a computer program to help on projects of more than 25 or 30 tasks (see Chapter 30). Then you can easily change and revise the schedule as you work through the issues and changes in a project.

Here is an example of the step-by-step scheduling process.

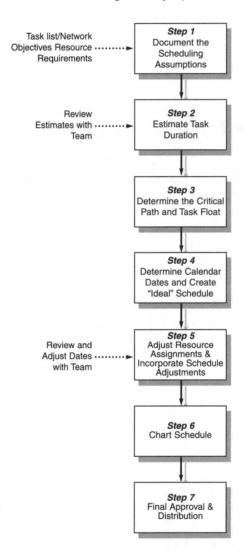

Task list/Network Objectives Resource Requirements ········►

Step 1
Document the Scheduling Assumptions

Review Estimates with Team ········►

Step 2
Estimate Task Duration

Step 3
Determine the Critical Path and Task Float

Step 4
Determine Calendar Dates and Create "Ideal" Schedule

Review and Adjust Dates with Team ········►

Step 5
Adjust Resource Assignments & Incorporate Schedule Adjustments

Step 6
Chart Schedule

Step 7
Final Approval & Distribution

How to Determine the Critical Path on Any Project

When you have determined task durations and are confident in your estimates, it's time to assemble a schedule using real dates. On a large/complex project, however, one more step remains in the way of assembling a working schedule. For projects with multiple parallel tasks and subprojects, you must determine a critical path to identify the time required to complete the project. (Most small projects with few tasks can skip this step.)

Scheduling Assumptions Worksheet

Project Name San Francisco Office Project   Date May 22

1. Are all the resources currently available for this project?
If no, list the resources required that are not available:
People   Leasing Agent Needs to Be Found

[ ] YES
[X] NO

Equipment

2. Is there a due date when the project absolutely must be complete?
If yes, enter date:

[ ] YES
[X] NO

Reason:

3. Will overtime be allowed?
If yes, how much?

[ ] YES
[X] NO

4. Are there any holidays or other breaks during this project?
If yes, list dates: July 4

[X] YES
[ ] NO

5. Have additional resources and people been approved for this project?

[X] YES
[ ] NO

6. Have the work schedules and availabilities of all resources been documented?

[X] YES
[ ] NO

Notes: Follow the Phildelphia Office Plan as Reference

Use a worksheet like this one to help detail the assumptions about the schedule for your project. Don't forget to refer to the statement of work (SOW) for additional scheduling criteria and constraints.

The critical path is a sequence of tasks that forms the longest duration of the project. If a task is delayed on the critical path, the project is delayed. For example, for All-Star Cable, if the cable boxes for the customers are delayed, the entire project will fall behind schedule.

Tasks not lying on the critical path are more flexible. You can delay printing the instructions for using the cable boxes as long as they arrive at the same time as the boxes themselves.

Adding together the duration of tasks on the critical path determines the total time the project will take. Because each task on the critical path must follow its predecessor in order, all tasks following a late task on the critical path will be late. Yes, the delay will hold up the entire project. That's why the critical path is, well, critical.

Not Just Floating Around

Tasks not on the critical path also must be completed. You can't build a house and ask someone to move in before the water and sewer are connected, but such tasks can occur later in the project's timeframe without substantially delaying other tasks downstream. This gives them a flexible start and finish date, which in project management lingo is called *float*.

Project Lingo _____

The amount of time that an activity may be delayed from its earliest possible start date without delaying the project finish date is called **float**. Float is also known as slack or slack time. Latest Possible Finish date − Earliest Possible Start − Duration = Total Float.

Basically, the equation calculates the latest date you can start given the duration that an activity will take and still finish on time for the next activity that need to start.

If the total float for a task equals zero, then that task is on the critical path. The amount of float is the amount of flexibility for starting a task.

The Different Views of Critical in Project Management

The term critical chain is used to describe a concept that is quite different from the schedule-based definition of tasks on the critical path. The concept of the critical chain is one of the ideas preferred by Dr. Eliyahu M. Goldratt's Theory of Constraints (TOC). The TOC states that any system has at least one constraint. Otherwise, it would be generating an infinite amount of output. Bearing this in mind, the TOC in project management is explained through use of the chain analogy: "A chain is only as strong as its weakest link."

If you look at your project as a chain in which each department, activity, or resource is a link in the chain, what constrains your project from achieving its goals? Only through identifying and focusing on the weakest link, the critical link in the chain, can substantial improvements be made. In other words, if the weakest link dictates the pace of an organization's ability to achieve its goal, it makes sense that attending to this critical link will allow the organization to achieve a substantial rate of throughput faster.

To illustrate how the TOC can be applied without getting into too much theoretical detail, the critical chain concept illustrates that project control and scheduling can be improved through identifying the critical links in the chain of a project and then focusing creatively on reducing these problems. The objective is to develop solutions of compromise based on fresh thinking that can help you continuously improve project performance through time. The performance is improved continuously because, as you fix one weakest link in the chain, a new weakest link emerges. Since project performance is never perfect, there will always be a weakest link to work on.

If you're interested in the application of the critical chain concept and the Theory of Constraints on project management, get a copy of Dr. Goldratt's books on the subject, including *The Goal*, *It's Not Luck*, and *Critical Chain*, or visit the Avraham Y. Goldratt Institute on the web at www.goldratt.com. An adequate presentation of TOC is beyond the scope of the book, but for people interested in continuous quality improvement, there's a lot of substance in Goldratt's work.

Establishing the Critical Path

The critical path is easy to determine in a project that has been documented with a good network diagram. Simply add each parallel path's tasks together, and the path requiring the most time to complete is the critical path. In the case of All-Star Cable, the building of the Interfaces takes 138 days. That makes it the critical path. Critical tasks—those on this path—not completed on time will delay the project unless you can make up the time further down the critical path or an on-the-path task finishes ahead of schedule. (Remember we mentioned "crashing" the project earlier.)

CAUTION

Risk Management

When its tasks go late, the critical path becomes the roadblock to project completion. That's why you should put extra effort into estimating these tasks. If you lack confidence in the task schedule or resource availability, delay the project until everything fits into place. If the project is already underway, put your best people on the tasks and focus your energies on catching up. Use the Critical Path Worksheet to calculate the critical path and float for the tasks on your project. If you have more tasks than will fit on a page, look into getting a computer program (see Chapter 30).

Critical Path: Myth or Reality?

The concept behind critical path is simple: If you delay a task on the critical path, the project is delayed. This seems to make perfect sense to most people new to project management. The path on the project has to go from beginning to end.

Unfortunately, as in all things involving people and plans, there are complexities. First, some tasks on the critical path may be less important than others. Some of the tasks may be there for mathematical reasons (which you'll learn about in a bit), not managerial priorities. For this reason, many managers also create a priority task list, which is a list of the most important tasks on the project. This managerial list of priority tasks, along with the mathematical list of tasks on the critical path, can be used to focus attention on the important work of the project.

Always remember that regardless of the mathematics of it—or the managerial importance—when you change task dependencies, duration estimates, and other network details, you need to reevaluate the critical path and reassess the schedule. There's no way around it. You can't change the sequences without impacting the schedule.

Use the Critical Path Worksheet to Calculate Path and Float

If you're new to project management, the calculation of the critical path initially sounds complicated. It's really simple, however, assuming you've done your homework by correctly listing, estimating duration, and assigning precedence to each task. If you're using a computer-based program, it will probably identify the critical path automatically. Otherwise, the steps are as follows:

Let's look at All-Star Cable and see how we can calculate the float in the project.

1. List the tasks and estimated activity durations on the worksheet. So for task #9, "Construct new billing system," let's say that the activity duration is 20 days.

2. Calculate the earliest starting date for each activity.

   In the case study, the earliest start for "Construct new billing system" becomes July 10. We know that because we have referenced the network diagram and we can see all the activity durations that immediately precede the beginning of that activity on the network diagram.

3. Calculate the earliest finish number for each task. In this case, we know that the earliest finish date is August 6.

Critical Path Worksheet
Project Name: All-Star Cable Movies-on-Demand

Task	Duration	Earliest Start	Earliest Finish	Latest Start	Latest Finish	Total Float
Design data model	26 days	5/15	6/19	8/25	9/29	72
Load data	10 days	6/20	7/3	9/30	10/13	72
Write stored procedures	30 days	7/4	8/14	10/14	11/24	72
Analyze system	20 days	5/15	6/11	8/13	9/9	64
Design new related system	20 days	6/12	7/9	9/10	10/7	64
Construct new billing system	20 days	7/10	8/6	10/8	11/4	64
Test new system	4 days	8/7	8/12	11/5	11/10	64
Implement new billing system	10 days	8/13	8/26	11/11	11/24	64
Design new customer GUI interface	5 days	6/27	7/3	6/27	7/3	0
Test new customer GUI with application	35 days	7/4	8/21	7/4	8/21	0
Obtain customer GUI approvals	2 days	8/22	8/25	8/22	8/25	0
Build prototype	25 days	8/26	9/29	8/26	9/29	0
Move customer GUI into production	40 days	9/30	11/24	9/30	11/24	0
Design employee interface	15 days	5/15	6/4	6/19	7/9	25
Build employee interface prototype	25 days	6/5	7/9	9/9	10/13	68
Test employee interface with users	5 days	7/10	7/16	10/14	10/20	68
Move employee interface into production	25 days	7/28	8/29	10/21	11/24	61
Design full application requirements	10 days	5/15	5/28	5/15	5/28	0
Submit RFP for OTS S/W	1 day	5/29	5/29	5/29	5/29	0
Evaluate S/W	10 days	5/30	6/12	5/30	6/12	0
Decide to make or build	3 days	6/13	6/17	6/13	6/17	0
Purchase S/W	2 days	6/18	6/19	6/18	6/19	0
Install S/W	5 days	6/20	6/26	6/20	6/26	0
Test S/W (unit)	5 days	6/27	7/3	9/22	9/26	61
Test S/W (system)	5 days	7/4	7/10	9/29	10/3	61
Move S/W into production	11 days	7/11	7/25	10/6	10/20	61
Analyze information needs	5 days	5/15	5/21	7/3	7/9	35
Design reports	25 days	5/15	6/18	6/5	7/9	15
Modify existing reports database	5 days	6/19	6/25	11/5	11/11	99
Test with test files	5 days	6/26	7/2	11/12	11/18	99
Test full scale system in production	4 days	7/3	7/8	11/19	11/24	99

4. Calculate the latest finish number for each task. This is often called the backward pass through the project schedule. The latest finish is the last day a task can be performed without changing the end date of the project. For this activity, notice that we cannot finish after November 4 without pushing the entire project past the deadline. You will need to know the activities that must precede this activity.

5. Determine the total float for each task. Total float is determined by the following calculation:

   Total float = Date of the latest finish − Date of the earliest start − duration. In this case, that calculation is November 4 minus July 10 minus the duration of the activity, which is 20 days. When we make that calculation, we discover that we have 64 days of float for this activity.

   The tasks with zero float are on the critical path. If you look at the activity labeled "Move customer GUI into production" you will notice that the earliest start and the latest start are exactly the same—so are the earliest finish and the latest finish. That means that this activity has no float available and has a zero in the float column. This activity must be done between those dates or the entire project schedule will be off.

Even if you use a computer to help you with your network diagrams and critical path calculations, it's important that you master the basic scheduling principles presented here. If you don't understand the basic principles of float, start dates, finish dates, and critical path, you won't understand how the computer derives the schedules it produces. And if you don't understand these concepts, you won't be able to appropriately modify the schedules to suit your project's priorities.

Normalizing the Schedule

You must review the schedule to determine whether the resources you assigned are actually available within each task's schedule window. Obviously, you need to start with the activities on the critical path (that have no float) and work the rest of the schedule from there. Move things around based on the float available to ensure that you don't overload someone and that others are fully utilized. After individual assignments are finalized and reviewed by the team, the schedule must be adjusted to accommodate any other necessary changes. It needs review and approval by senior management as well, as part of the project plan.

When you use the critical path in a project, the tasks that are not on the path (called noncritical) can be scheduled in a number of ways to accommodate various needs of the organization. Three strategies are as follows:

◆ Schedule all noncritical tasks at the earliest date possible. This offers a way to free up resources earlier for other projects or the later critical tasks.

◆ Schedule all noncritical tasks as late as possible. This shows how much work can be delayed without causing the critical tasks (and thus the project schedule) to slip.

◆ Schedule a subset of noncritical tasks. As milestones are met, complete the rest of the schedule. This gives the manager scheduling flexibility and a way to assign resources to critical activities without causing political problems.

Time Is Money

If one unique resource commands the premier place in the project, you must wrap your schedule around its availability. For example, you can find plenty of typists, and you can rent a crane from another company, but locating a qualified engineer who can handle fiber optic cables may limit your scheduling options.

When assigning people, the rules are simple:

◆ Make sure you know the specific availability of all the people (as much as humanly possible).

◆ Assign the best-suited available people to each task.

◆ Use equipment and people efficiently to ensure the smallest gaps in working schedules.

◆ Redo the schedule over and over until you get it balanced. (Get help in terms of experts or computer programs if it takes more than three tries.)

Loading Up and Leveling Out

Many ideal schedules forget to deal with conflicting availability of equipment, potential overuse of key people, and the needs of other projects and priorities. For example, the ideal employee to design the new employee interface may be unavailable the week you need him or her. If the task can't be rescheduled to accommodate his or her schedule, you'll have to choose someone else.

After working on your schedule, you will likely find that some team members have too much work—more than they can accomplish in a standard work week. Others may not have enough. The amount of work each team member or piece of equipment is assigned is called resource loading. As you would expect, it's easy to overwhelm important resources with an impossible workload while under-utilizing others.

To compensate for overloaded workers, scheduled work should be redistributed from people with too much responsibility to those folks not fully booked. This is called resource leveling. As you level resources, skills and availability must be considered. If Bob Braveheart, your computer network expert, has an unreasonable 64 hours of work scheduled per week, you can't redistribute the extra workload to three or four other team members who lack experience with computer networks. Instead, you need to acquire additional experienced resources and adjust the schedule and ultimately the budget to accommodate the necessary changes.

The Reallocation Questions

Before you reallocate and level the resource commitments, you need to ask yourself these questions:

♦ How many hours per day is each person or piece of equipment available? Can we expect employees to works 8 hours a day? They probably do—but all that time is not necessarily applied to the project. After all, they do have to go to the bathroom, take phone calls (some personal, most legitimate business calls), get coffee, talk to other project team members informally (sometimes personal, but more often it's discussion about work on the project), and talk to other employees in the company (sometimes personal, but frequently it's important networking with other team members or peers). As a manager, you should completely support these activities. Comfortable employees who feel they have control over their work life are that much more productive. As a manager, however, you also need to recognize that a work day usually consists of only about 6.5 hours of productive work time as a result.

♦ Is an assigned piece of equipment allocated to multiple projects for multiple project managers? Depending on shared resources is not an optimum state for a project manager, but frequently we have limited control over the resources we get on a project and have to take other priorities into consideration. Too many times in the past, we have had teams composed of individuals who have a minimal time allocation to another project. ("No more than a couple of hours a week, I promise.") Then, during project execution, we don't see him or her for a couple of weeks due to legitimate problems on the other project. ("Sorry, Sally is the only one who understands payroll, and we lost the ability to create payroll checks—we need her to help us figure out the problem.") Make sure you have a contingency plan built in for these people.

◆ Have you factored in time lost to anticipated interruptions? You can expect downtime due to weather, holidays, vacation and sick time, doctor's visits, and other personal requirements.

◆ Have you factored in sufficient time for administrative overhead? This means allowing time for company meetings, company travel time, completing time reports, completing weekly status reports, and project team meetings. This may also include reviewing team deliverables as well as internal reviews of prototypes or documents.

◆ Are you using people with specialized skill sets appropriately? Are team member assignments accurate in terms of matching skills and task requirements? Is there a need to reallocate these people or reassign work? Have you considered the productivity of the people as well as their relative skills?

◆ Are you scheduling people without appropriate skill sets? Frequently, we send team members out to be trained on a new skill and expect them to come back fully proficient in that skill. Depending on the skill, you should assume reduced productivity for a certain period of time to allow that person to become fully proficient after applying the new skills in the project environment. The period of time should be directly related to the complexity of the new skills.

◆ Have you planned for the time required to acquire additional people? Depending on the environment you work in, it will be more or less difficult to get the authorization to bring in additional staff regardless of whether they are full-time employees or temporary contract staff. In some organizations, that may take as little as a week or as long as two months. Our experience suggests you plan on an average of six weeks. Once you have the authorization, there is the time required for getting applicants, interviewing them, checking references, making an offer, and waiting for the prospective employees to finish commitments at their current place of employment. Then, once they do come on board, there will be the time required to get up-to-speed on what the project is about, the project's goals, and their job. If you're moving really fast in all of this, you can see why it would take six weeks to bring on a new project team member (on top of the time required to get the authorization). During all of this time, remember that your project is supposedly making progress.

Ready for Leveling Out

After making adjustments in response to all the preceding questions regarding people's schedules, you're ready to do the final leveling of resource commitments. One of the tools to help you do this is the resource histogram, a visual tool that allows you to chart resource task allocation for each period through the project. In the example, notice how the histograms chart the availability of the resource and the effort of that resource through the life of the project.

In weeks 1 and 6, the resource is overallocated but is underallocated in weeks 2 through 5. In this example, you would want to smooth out the peaks and valleys as best as you can by moving work packages out of period 1 into period 2 or 3 as time is available. You can move the activity within the available float for that activity (remember critical path?). You can extend the duration of a activity because you have available float. You also could reassign some or all of the work to underallocated people (if they have the right skills for the job—you'll have to refer to your skills inventory to do that).

The resource histogram can help you visualize resource utilization during phases of a project. Here you see that Dave is overallocated during week 1 and week 6.

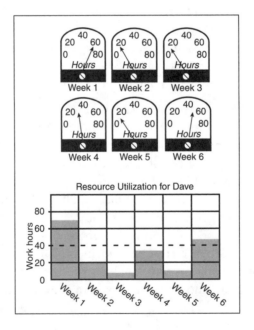

You can also use the leveling technique to smooth out the work allocation for a single department. Add up all of the department's project commitments. Identify the appropriate department workload. Visually demonstrate the difference between the department projection and the actual work in the department's work queue. Present this information to the department manager, who then has the ability to make the decisions as to what work should get done (and not done) or to approve the acquisition of additional resources.

Options for Adjusting the Schedule

In total, here are your options for reworking a schedule when you realize that no matter what you do, people will be overworked:

◆ Change the scope (size) of the project or add people, keeping in mind that more people and equipment will impact the budget. Obviously, this has to be done with approval of the steering committee of stakeholders.

◆ Give a work package more time or split it in two or more work packages, modifying who is responsible for completing them to make the process work. You can also adjust the basic finish-to-start precedence relationships (but only when appropriate) by adding lead or lag time to tasks that enable some of the work to occur in parallel. (Refer to Chapter 10 if you've forgotten how this works.)

◆ Move a task to a time when more people or equipment are free. This will mean calculating the entire schedule again to make sure the moved activity doesn't impact the critical path.

◆ Outsource the work. Remember that outsourcing work, while reducing work done by the implementation team, also adds new tasks for vendor management. Outsourcing also assumes that the vendor people have the right expertise and are available and uncommitted.

◆ Negotiate for additional time in the schedule with a later completion date and a budget increase. You'll obviously (we hope by now) need stakeholder agreement to do this. Don't negotiate the time required to complete the activities (these should be good numbers if you've done your homework). Instead, negotiate the balance among the time, resources, and results (goals) of the project.

◆ Reprioritize the goal and scope of the project. (Reduce the number of project deliverables and goals.) Again, this will depend on the consensus of your stakeholders.

◆ Deliver components of the project in a phased approach, thereby extending the total project schedule but still giving the customer acceptable products or services.

◆ Find people that are more productive (better trained, more experience). This choice may increase the budget, but you might get most of the added employee expense back in terms of increased productivity—if you choose wisely.

Adjusting a Schedule to Meet a Forced Deadline

Many projects have a forced or dictated deadline. A customer may need a project completed by a specific date. In our All-Star Cable case study, the president may need the project completed by the end of the year because he knows that a competitor is working on this same type of project and he wants to be the first into the marketplace with it.

Such a project should commence as early as possible in case unforeseen delays slow completion. If your careful scheduling shows that a project due date is impossible, you have three alternatives:

♦ Reduce the scope of the project.

♦ Add additional resources.

♦ Work out some way to extend the completion date (not always possible).

There are also projects with externally imposed finish dates that allow more than enough time to complete the project. Be wary of these because the time slips away faster than you think. At the beginning of these projects, there is actually no critical path at all because all the tasks have float.

> **Project Lingo**
>
> **Negative float** is the state at which all the float in a project is used up and any imposed or approved schedule dates are impossible to meet. In essence, a project with negative float is another description for a project that will come in late (unless you do something about it).

Unfortunately, when the float has been used up (on any project), a new form of float emerges: *negative float*. When there is negative float on a task, adjustments need to be made to keep the schedule in line with the critical path (and to ensure completion on the approved end date for the project). A project with negative float will have a new critical path that is longer than the approved schedule. If it isn't possible to make adjustments to realign the tasks to the schedule, you'll need to renegotiate the cost-schedule-results equilibrium with the key stakeholders.

Chart the Final Schedule and See if It Works

When the final schedule is in place and approved (along with the rest of the project plan), it should be distributed to all team members and posted in a common area so that team members can measure progress. This helps you maintain a healthy competitive attitude as the various team members rush to meet or exceed their scheduled delivery dates. At that point, you cease to be a project planner and take on your role as project manager. Of course, you still need a budget before you have an approved plan. With the schedule in hand, the budget should be no problem. Read on. It's time to play with the money. It's not just politicians who love to do that. We will discuss how to use the schedule for tracking in Chapter 23.

The Least You Need to Know

◆ Understanding the concept of critical path is important in keeping a project schedule on track.

◆ When assembling a project, you must document your assumptions. Can you assume that Grand Central Station will be deserted at noon for your restoration and painting project?

◆ Holidays slow projects because team members' minds may be on family matters rather than work.

◆ For noncritical tasks, there's float—the extra time between the earliest date a task must start and the latest date it is possible to start the task and still meet the rest of the project schedule.

Chapter 13

Budgeting and Cost Control Options for Your Project

In This Chapter

+ Common budgeting pitfalls

+ Avoid the classic budgeting mistakes

+ Begin with good estimates

+ Padding the budget against calamity

+ Controlling the purse strings

"Hey, how long do you think it will take to design the new GUI for Movies-on-Demand?"

"If you mean how long before we can have the GUI into production, I'd guess about six months."

"What do you mean, you guess. I need an estimate for the budget."

"Okay, I estimate it will take six months to put the GUI into production."

Unfortunately, this kind of dialogue goes on all the time as project managers work to build their budgets based on this type of estimate. It's no wonder so many projects run into trouble. However, there is a better way, and that's what this chapter is all about.

All budgets start with estimates, so that is where we want to begin this portion of the book.

How to Avoid the Classic Mistakes

These classic mistakes are ones that you (or a project manager friend) have probably made. The idea is to not make them anymore.

♦ **Classic Mistake 1:** You are in the hallway when a senior manager stops you and asks for the estimated budget for the project you have just been assigned. Maybe it's their authority, or maybe they just caught you off-guard, but you feel compelled to answer. Suddenly you blurt out an answer that you realize was probably a mistake immediately—the reason? They are on their way to a meeting and that number will be used to talk about the budget. You can avoid that predicament by looking concerned and replying, "I wouldn't want to give you a bad number, so I am reluctant to offer a guess at this time." If that fails, do a quick calculation and factor in all the things that you can think of that will go wrong and calculate that number—then double it! But be prepared to be really wrong in the end.

Time Is Money

The conceptual budget process is as follows:
People + Resources + Time = Budget.

Risk Management

You must understand that, once a budget is established, it becomes sacrosanct. You are stuck with it. Changing an entrenched (note this word) project budget is like trying to modify the Ten Commandments—if you could find the original stones and do a little chisel (again, note the word) work.

♦ **Classic Mistake 2:** Developing a budget without completing your work breakdown structure to get the effort that will be required to complete the project. The answer is to wait until you complete your WBS, sometimes even down to the work package level, before you begin the budget process. Without understanding the time it will take and the people who will need to complete the work, estimating a budget is just pulling it out of thin air.

♦ **Classic Mistake 3:** Often project managers will pad the budget so that they have the money to bring the project in ahead of schedule and under budget. While that may sound good, an honest estimate that reflects the effort is the best strategy for developing your budgets. If you pad your budget regularly, management will realize you are padding and cut your funding because they don't respect the estimate that the budget is built upon. Better to be seen as an honest broker in the long run.

Three Levels of Accuracy for Estimating

There are three levels of accuracy in establishing your budget and they are applicable at different phases of the project:

♦ **Ballpark Estimate.** During the project definition phase, the ballpark estimate is only useful if you have the experience to have a true "gut-level" feel for what the entire project might cost while you are still defining it. For All-Star Cable's project manager, a ballpark estimate on the budget would only be a guess since this type of project had never been tried before.

♦ **Order of Magnitude.** During the project definition phase, you might recognize aspects of the project that are similar to a project that you had worked on before. If our project manager for All-Star Cable had worked on the pay-per-view system when the company put it in several years ago, for instance, he would know what that project cost and be able to calculate a rough order of magnitude for this project. You may hear some project managers use the term *parametric estimates* for this type of estimate.

♦ **Detailed Estimates.** This level of budgeting would occur in the project planning phase. During this phase, the project team is developing all the plans for the work that will need to be completed to bring Movies-on-Demand to the customers. The project manager then rolls-up all the estimated costs and develops a budget. For that reason, this technique is often called a "bottom-up" estimate by project managers.

> **Time Is Money**
>
> Complete accuracy requires the project manager to forecast the future and to be in control of all project variables—two requirements that will never be met. But good estimates can be sufficiently accurate to support good business decisions.
>
> —Eric Verzuh, *The Fast Forward MBA in Project Management*

Other Sources of Data for Building the Budget

Of course, the work that the project team is doing comprises a significant amount of the money that will be spent on the project. However, there will be other costs that you will need to estimate too.

◆ Internal labor costs are often left out or miscalculated by project managers. For All-Star Cable, the project manager is using company staff from accounting, IT, market research, marketing, and so on. All of those people must be accounted for in the budget for the project to really know what it will cost. Even though many of these people will be on salary, don't think of them as free. That would only be true if they had infinite hours to work, which of course they might object to. You must calculate their labor, and most project managers use either daily or monthly rates and generally calculate that rate including benefits.

◆ Internal equipment costs may also be considered—items like computers, photo-copiers, and printers are just a few examples. Depending on how the company wants the budget drawn up, you may need to also consider office space even if you are not renting it separately. For example, in our All-Star Cable case study, the project team is taking over space that is normally used by the accounting depart-ment. So the accounting manager wants additional budget money for space for her employees who will be relocated. That money must come from the MOD project.

◆ External labor and equipment may also need to be included in the data you col-lect. For example, if the All-Star Cable team will rent specialized equipment used to test cable boxes that the vendors are supplying, those costs will need to be folded into the estimates. Likewise, any contractors needed to supplement the team must also be factored into your estimates.

◆ Materials costs are an important consideration. Office supplies are a perfect exam-ple. People will need paper, pens, and a variety of other materials over the course of the project.

◆ One final consideration is travel. If project team members will need to travel to various sites, for any number of reasons, don't forget to estimate the cost of those trips including airlines, hotels, meals, and so on.

Direct and Indirect Costs

Before you put any numbers to paper, you must learn the difference between direct and indirect costs on a project. Your budget must account for both of these types of costs, although how this is done will vary from organization to organization.

Direct costs are those specifically required by the project. Indirect costs are those not specific to the project; their value can be shared among many projects. You'll need to find out (usually from the finance officer for your project or from the accounting department) how indirect costs are allocated for projects. Then you'll need to establish the appropriate line items for indirect costs as part of the overall budget.

Direct costs include the following:

- **Labor:** The cost of the people working on the project. Benefits for the employees may be charged as direct costs or as a percentage of all overhead for housing the employee (which might include the cost of facilities, benefits, and so on).

- **Supplies and raw materials:** The cost of materials consumed by the project.

- **Equipment:** The cost of tools and machinery.

- **Travel:** The cost of travel associated with the project.

- **Legal fees:** Direct legal expenses charged specifically for work on your project.

- **Training:** Training for project team members and for the project end users and customers during project installation or implementation.

- **Marketing/advertising:** The cost of project introductions, announcements, promotions, and public relations; these costs can be quite large on a project to introduce a new product.

Indirect costs include the following:

- **Facilities:** The physical location required for the project participants and shared resources, such as the company intranet or communications network. The exception is when facilities are purchased or leased specifically and exclusively for the use of the project.

- **Site-specific requirements:** State- or county-specific charges for business operations.

- **Management and administrative overhead:** This is the cost of paying for the managers and support staff (such as human resources people) used by your project but that don't directly report to you.

Indirect costs may be allocated on a percentage basis from some central accounting or management organization such as a corporate office or the department responsible for the project. Don't forget to include these costs because it could doom your project to budget overruns before it even starts.

There are other possible sources of data you will need to gather to accurately put together your estimates. Talk with your project team and your project sponsor to identify anything you may have forgotten.

Developing Budgeting Skills

How do you establish a budget? This is done task by task, step-by-step. Doing the budget for a small project, such as establishing an internal copy center, might take an afternoon. For large projects such as All-Star Cable's MOD system, a team might take a couple of months to bring expenses into line and to remember forgotten tasks.

The budget should help the project manager control the project; however, it's common for the project manager to find the budget controlling him or her. A realistic budget is central to keeping control of the project. It's okay to have one that's a little too conservative, but you can't turn lead into gold.

> **Time Is Money**
>
> "Money talks" is one of life's truisms. (We'll skip the second part—you already know the sentiment.) You'll find that this is especially true when you control a project budget of which outside providers want a share. Avoid taking money, gifts, or vacations of any kind on a vendor's tab. This keeps the bids on the level and the lawyers out of your life.

Building a Budget

The budgeting process can be intimidating to project managers. How much will it really cost? What if the price of pork bellies doubles on the Chicago Mercantile Exchange? How can I control an important staff member who demands a salary increase? What if I make a mistake? (If you see someone at the office with the shakes, it's probably because he or she either has recently given up coffee or is assembling a project budget for the first time.)

The process of building a budget should be an orderly one; otherwise, it's impossible to get reasonable numbers. You must thoroughly understand the components of each activity and then use the bottom-up method to cost out each one. Yes, you might make an error, underestimate (or overestimate), or blow it completely, but all you can do is try, using your best estimating capabilities. Even so, business conditions might change, the project might get bumped into a new direction, or a task might fail. So what you are making in your astute budgeting is a set of assumptions that might change. Rub a lucky rabbit's foot while remembering the following:

◆ Costs are tied to project goals. For All-Star Cable, the company is betting on Movies-on-Demand to be the next big growth engine for its revenues. It is literally betting the future on this project.

◆ Costs are tied to timeframes and schedules, and doing things faster usually costs more money. The estimates you developed in your work breakdown structure, coupled with the schedule you developed to complete the project are critical to this. If the steering committee wants the project done faster, it will undoubtedly cost more money. It's your job to estimate, to the best of your ability, how much more they are looking at.

◆ When establishing detailed estimates, the costs require expert input. With specific activities developed in the WBS and a schedule at the ready, ask the people who will be doing the work about their charges for time and materials (refer to Chapter 14). It's important for each contributor to understand exactly what you want. For example, if you want an estimate for doing systems testing on the new MOD billing system, get written estimates and make sure they match your requirements. If you are using vendors, use the *answer-back process* to make sure that you have a valid and complete estimate.

Project Lingo

If a process is highly technical, large, or complex in scale, ask for an answer back. In the **answer-back process,** the vendor takes your specs and builds a simple model that allows your experts to ensure that a clear understanding exists and that no significant parts or systems were neglected.

◆ **Other managers or experts.** People in your organization who have handled projects can provide excellent advice and study cost estimates for problems. They also might be able to provide exact estimates if a project they worked on had elements common to yours. Or they might be much more experienced project managers and be willing to help out.

Project Lingo

Vendors who are looking to work with you on a long-term basis on future jobs might bid the first job at a loss to blow away the competition and get the work. This is called **buying the job.**

◆ **Your managers or owners.** Although sometimes unhappy about a project's cost, they might be able to provide advice from their own years managing projects. Plus, by bringing them in early, they'll see that you're carefully covering your bases and are spending their money in an equitable manner. That observation will assist you in getting the final budget approved because management already will have a strong grasp on the realities of the project and its budget requirements—not to mention faith in you and your abilities. This concept is referred to as preselling the project budget.

Expert project managers estimate budgets accurately not because they have years of experience, but because they look at the budget and final costs of similar tasks on related projects. You can do it, too. If you completed a similar project in your company in the past, review the project close-out files and lessons learned to discover how that project was budgeted and how close it came to meeting that budget.

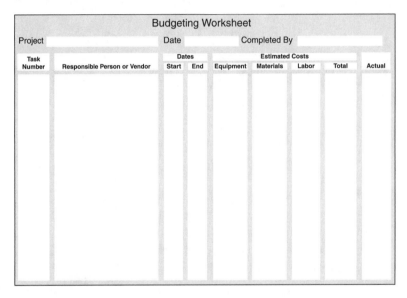

This worksheet can help you determine the costs associated with your project.

- ◆ **Purchasing department staff.** The purchasing department may or may not save you money. Purchasing is a department that may help you in your quest for success or may stand in your way at every turn. Use them if they've proved helpful in a timely manner in the past. Avoid or work around them if they are difficult to deal with. You might need permission from senior management to avoid working with them. This tactic is a slap in the face to the purchasing people. Don't expect to win any popularity contests with them next time you order a box of number two pencils.

- ◆ **Experts.** Completely lost? Request (probably expensive) a budget from someone with budgeting skills to assist you through a sticky project. Hire experts after carefully explaining their duties and setting a firm budget for their time. The best and least expensive experts are often people who have retired from a field after a lifetime of experience. You also can hire an expert project manager—not to take the reins but to review results and proffer advice.

◆ **Standard pricing guides.** Many government-regulated organizations and some private companies offer standard pricing in printed-guide format. Need to know how much Federal Express charges to move an elephant from Zoo A to Zoo B? Just look it up in the free user guide (assuming you have the current version!).

Once these cost estimates have been gleaned and carefully listed along with the names of the contributors, it's time to do a task budget roundup. In this process, you take all the estimates for Task A and combine them. (Use a worksheet like the one included in this chapter or enter the numbers in your project management software.) After you wrap up costs for all the tasks separately, you can add the total of the entire plan to ascertain the project's total cost. Costs that are not available because Joanna in research is out of town must be guesstimated with a large highlighter used to indicate that the total is possibly fictitious. With a computer, most unknown/unverified estimates can be indicated separately. Your manager and most stakeholders will want to see the budget in two formats—by cost center and by month—to assess cash flow and cost allocations. Some project managers will also want to present the budget by project milestones, WBS summary levels, or project phases.

Types of Budgeting Methods

There are two established methods for budgeting: top-down and bottom-up. Which is best for your project depends on your organization's standard approach to decision-making. Does management dictate most mandates? Or is the staff expected to produce ideas and decisions that percolate up to management for final analysis? Your answer to this question will determine the most likely budgeting approach for the project.

Bottom-Up Budgeting

In bottom-up budgeting, staff members get together and attempt to hammer out a budget from the task-level detail. As a group, they can speak frankly. One member might have a solution that's superior to another. It's also a good way to avoid missing a subtask. If one group member forgets it, another (hopefully) will remember it. This helps avoid budget-gobbling tasks appearing mid-project and throwing everything off down the line.

Time Is Money

Make an extra copy of a draft network diagram and write the budget for each task next to its box. In a glance, you will see where most of the money is being spent. Next, make sure that's where you should be spending the money.

Top-Down Budgeting

More difficult than bottom-up management, the top-down approach has senior managers estimating budgets from their experience and then allocating funds to lower-level managers for execution. Top-down budgeting works if managers carefully allocate costs and possess significant project management experience.

In many progressive organizations, a combination of top-down and bottom-up budgeting is used to ensure that the top-down numbers (which establish general expectations) are grounded in the reality of the workers' experience.

> **Time Is Money**
>
> Are you assembling a budget using a spreadsheet program such as Excel? Don't accept the final numbers without calculating them separately using a calculator. Otherwise, an error in an underlying formula might be invisible.

Phased Budgeting

Phased budgeting, like phased scheduling, can use either top-down or bottom-up estimates or both, but it estimates only one phase of the project at a time. There are costs associated with the project definition phase, the project planning phase, the project execution phase, and the project close-out phase. At each transition from one phase to the next, the budget is revised by the project manager and approved by the steering committee. On very large projects, this is a commonly employed methodology because it limits risk and uncertainty in the approved operational budget.

Refining the Budget

When the budget numbers are in, although subject to correction, the next step is to fine-tune the numbers. You might have to go through this process several times as new estimates arrive and are revised or as tasks enter the project that were forgotten or ignored in the initial estimating pass.

Here are the steps (all required) in refining the estimates:

1. **A rough cut.** This is a number pulled out of a hat, and it might have little to do with the final number. You may ask people to give you a number based on their experience. However, it's just a guess!

   Rough cuts should never become the actual budget numbers. This will kill a project manager and project faster than anything. Rough cuts are remembered as real budget quotations. Run like hell if you're asked to stop budgeting at this step.

2. **A second cut.** The resources required for each task estimate are reviewed carefully. These include the cost of labor, supplies and materials, equipment, overhead, and fix-priced bids from vendors (which account for all the vendor costs). This estimating process might demand the use of outside providers or might require more than one take as a complex subset of work is reliably broken down. You should also look at historical project costs to help guide your estimates. All estimating should involve the relevant stakeholders.

3. **Getting it right.** The third pass is the one in which you (and the team, of course) do the fine-tuning. For example, you might reveal that your initial $12,400 guesstimate is more realistic at $15,243.23. This process accomplishes two things: It turns guesstimates into something close to reality, and it provides an overall estimate of the project's real scope. This might not please the bill payer, but it must be done. Again, the relevant stakeholders need to be involved in these refined estimates.

4. **Wrapping it up.** If the budget appears to be workable (that is, affordable), it gets wrapped into the project plan while simultaneously heading for the steering committee for approval

5. **Presentation for approval.** At this point, the budget shouldn't be a surprise to anyone on the approval cycle because you have pre-sold the budget throughout the development process. Your complete draft for the budget is now ready for approval. Even though people have seen it before, they may still ask you to find ways to cut it, to modify the project, or to scrap the project as not worth the money (more common than you might think). If you're lucky, it gets approved right there. If not, continue to revise and present until you get consensus and signatures on the bottom line.

6. **Beware of the 10 percent solution.** The 10 percent solution is that all-too-common situation in which the steering committee arbitrarily cuts 10 percent from the budget because of hard times. There is no reason other than the feeling among stakeholders that they can cut the "fluff" out of the budget—a 10 percent padding they believe to be there. Most of the time, all this does is created chaos and could cause the quality or schedule to slip. Instead, revise your entire project plan to meet the new budget constraint and present a revised plan with a reduced scope.

Stuffing the Pillow with Money

Are you uncertain of the level of risk in a project? Want to provide a buffer of extra money? Add 10 to 100 percent to the budget to ensure completion and treat it as an insurance policy. *Padding* is a standard procedure in managing any project. There's no way that every risk can be fully calculated or anticipated. Everything from lightning blowing out your computer network to an outbreak of Legionnaire's disease might increase the budget as progress decreases. Padding, however, can get you into trouble; a small amount is reasonable and expected, but too much padding can distort the real requirements for a project.

Instead of over padding the budget, negotiate for the money you really need—or, as suggested above, adjust the project scope and objectives to be less expensive. Or use a technique like PERT, which we covered earlier in Chapter 10, that includes some of that padding as part of the calculation. Remember, it takes three estimates for effort, best case, worst case and most likely and calculates the effort using a formula. Formulas work wonders in establishing credibility.

Project Lingo

Padding means adding extra money to a budget for overruns. This is a standard project management tactic (also known as a contingency plan) used to mitigate unexpected cost overruns.

At the same time, you need to remember that it's often easier to get required money at the beginning of the project than to keep coming back for more because your estimates were bad.

Master Budget Control

Who holds the purse strings? You? Your management? A combination of both? Whatever the arrangement, you want as easy access to the money as possible. Work with your management to get signature authority for the project. That way, you can pay bills and purchase supplies in a timely manner. In another typical arrangement, you theoretically own the budget but must get multiple signatures from senior management each time you need to spend a chunk of it. This slows projects to a crawl because some members of the executive suite might be out of town and unable to sign. Besides, executives often let authorizations requiring their signatures sit in their in-boxes because they're too busy with their own projects.

Removing the Lid from the Pressure Cooker

Here are two techniques that won't make the problem go away but might at least ease the pressure:

◆ Get as much signing authority for yourself as possible; anywhere from $500 to $5,000 is appropriate. This allows you to pay the majority of expenses without the multiple-signature process.

♦ Establish (and closely monitor) a $500 petty-cash box. It's a resource for quick payoffs for small parts, day laborers, or taking the gang out for pizza after reaching a major milestone. All cash that comes from the box must be replaced with a receipt. Replenish the petty cash when it reaches the $100 level. Regularly count the remaining cash and receipts to ensure that no $20 bills have grown legs and walked out the door.

All in all, if you estimate carefully and document your assumptions thoroughly, you'll get a good budget approved—one that gives you enough money to get things done on time.

The Least You Need to Know

♦ Establishing a reliable budget is likely the most difficult task a project manager faces. Don't get caught in one of the classic estimating traps.

♦ Management personnel will rarely accept your budget as reasonable; they will attempt to squeeze money from it, even if it means putting the project at risk. You'll need to document why you projected the amount that you did and negotiate what you really need.

♦ Your budgeting skills will improve after successful completion of several projects.

♦ You want as much direct control of your budget as possible if you're going to be held accountable for the project outcome.

Chapter 14

Building a Winning Implementation Team

In This Chapter

- ◆ Determining exactly whom you need on your implementation team
- ◆ The importance of a well-chosen project team
- ◆ Matching required skills to available talent
- ◆ When training is an option
- ◆ How to choose outside team members

A single person doesn't win a baseball game—a team does. The same is true of projects. Thus, as in sports, project success depends largely on the right team members who support and complement each other. The ideal project implementation team completes the work on time and within budget with little micromanagement on your part. A weak or misaligned team requires substantial management on your part to limp past the finish line days, weeks, or for a major project, even years late. San Francisco's Bay Area Rapid Transit (BART) project and Los Angeles's unfortunate subway are prime examples of projects gone awry in part due to bumbling project teams as well as the ill winds of fate.

This chapter explains how to scope out required skills, assess current talent, and develop a list of people required to complete each task on your project. In addition, this chapter offers guidelines for filling the gap in people skills when adequately trained resources are not readily available.

You'll actually be doing most of your hiring after the plan is approved and you move into the project execution phase (that starts with Chapter 17), but you need to verify personnel costs and resource availability before the plan can be put into effect.

From Core Team to Complete Team

Remember, at this point, you are only planning the project staff and resources. You're probably already working with a subset of the project team, often called the core project team, which includes the managers, stakeholders, and key personnel. The core project team is the group you identified to help define and plan the project. (Do you remember doing this in Chapter 6?) But not all of the resources for your project can be identified during the project definition phase. You just don't have enough details about the project to know who and what you need until you have listed the tasks.

Words from the Wise

There is no substitute for talent. Industry and all the virtues are of no avail.

—Aldous Huxley

Only when you have the tasks and the work breakdown structure (WBS) in hand can you identify all the resources required to complete the project. The project sponsor and the core planning team may help you do this; however, it isn't until after the project plan is approved and the execution phase begins that you'll actually start working as a fully functioning project organization. (You'll learn how to organize the project team during the execution phases in Chapter 19.)

The Complete Implementation Team: The Worker Bees on the Project

The project implementation team includes the people who will actually do the work to develop the project deliverables. On almost any project, this team is made up of people with differing personalities, skills, ability, knowledge, and temperament. Your mission is to evaluate the project prior to choosing implementation personnel and to build an implementation team that takes advantage of each team member's skills without taxing their weaknesses.

Unfortunately, this isn't as easy as it sounds. Building the team and keeping it together are two of the most difficult tasks for any project manager. Whether through neglect or confusion, it's easy to let the team spirit slip away—and a spiritless project comes in with a bang and leaves with a whimper. Don't let this happen to you and your project! Even though we have spent a lot of time talking about activities, budgets, and schedules, your most important job will be managing the project team. Read this chapter and learn how to find the right people for your project to reap implementation success.

People First, Please

Even on a small or routine project, choosing the right people to successfully complete the work can be difficult, risky, and potentially time-consuming. The effort is worth it, however, because without people, the project will never happen—regardless of the cost and the availability of equipment and supplies. Thus, it's important to seriously consider the needs of personnel, even on the smallest project. People are, after all, the common denominator in making projects successful.

In any project, three major questions must be answered regarding the people used to complete the work on a project:

> ◆ What skills are required to complete the tasks on the project?

> ◆ Where will the people come from to complete the tasks?

> ◆ How should the people working on the project be organized?

Words from the Wise

A man's labor is not only his capital but his life. When it passes, it returns nevermore. To utilize it, to prevent its wasteful squandering, to enable the poor man to bank it up for use hereafter, this surely is one of the most urgent tasks before civilization.
—William Booth (1829–1912) Church minister and social reformer in the UK

The first two questions are the most important at this stage because the answers affect the number and cost of people required for the project. In Chapter 19, you'll learn a lot more about the organization of the project; however, some general thinking about the organization is necessary because the organization of the project can impact the need for supervisory personnel and other support people. It's a good idea to have some general organizational strategies while you're planning for resource requirements.

Matching Skills to Tasks on the WBS

The questions about the people skills you need for your project can be answered with confidence using a structured approach that starts with the project's WBS. For each task in the project, answer questions similar to the following:

- ◆ Is there a specific technical skill or combination of skills required to complete this task?

- ◆ How much experience should the person or people have to complete this activity? Does a person need to have specific experience doing this activity or can general experience be applied? If so, what general experience is required?

- ◆ Does this person have the knowledge, or education, required to fulfill the role that you need filled?

- ◆ In addition to technical skills, are any specific interpersonal skills required to complete this task effectively such as good written or verbal communication skills, diplomacy or negotiating skills, or management ability?

- ◆ How many of these skilled people will be needed for each task and how would they be organized by job title and job function?

List the skills and experience next to each WBS level or use a worksheet like the example shown for the All-Star Cable Movies-on-Demand project. With a form like the example shown here (often called a Skills Requirement Worksheet or Skills Matrix), you can list the actual skills you'll need to complete your project on a task-by-task or milestone basis.

Skills Requirement Worksheet
Project: All-Star Cable Movies-on-Demand
Produced by: H. Lieberum Date: 05/01/03

WBS	Tasks	Skills Required	Experience
2.0	Storage	Data management Data modeling	Oracle DB
6.0	Billing System	Accounting System development	Financial systems
13.0	Interfaces	Development and testing User interface with drop-down menus	Retail environment

More Questions About Whom to Choose

In addition to completing the Skills Requirement Worksheet, to decide on the team members you need, you'll also have to answer questions like these:

◆ If you could choose anyone you wanted for your team, who would these people be and why? (Hint: Your answers should involve both skills and personality for each person you choose.)

◆ Given the team that you actually get to work with, what levels of supervision will be required? You must be brutally honest here, especially if you're evaluating the skills of people who also happen to be friends or colleagues. Regardless of the talent involved, there's no sense in pretending that your team members will be self-sufficient if they won't be. Some people simply need more direction than others—and these people will need some of your time.

◆ Where will the people come from? Do you have the talent in your own department (assuming these people have the time to be assigned to your project) or must you hire outsiders or raid another department for talent? (You'll learn about many of the sources for obtaining people later in this chapter.) The source of the people will affect their cost and availability—maybe even the quality of their output. These are all things that will affect the schedule and budget you have yet to create and get approved.

Answering these questions will allow you to compare the talent required for the project to the people actually available. Are the people you need ready, willing, and able? If so, are they affordable? Will your project demand that already overburdened co-workers take on yet another responsibility? How much will outside resources, such as consultants, experts, and temporary labor, really cost?

Along the Critical Path

Free help! If your project is in any way civic minded, you can get volunteers to assist in the day-to-day operations and not pay them anything! Amazing as it may seem, there are a lot of people with time on their hands who will assist in any worthy cause. You might have to throw in lunch and a plaque or two, but many complex projects have been completed entirely with volunteer help. How can you find these people? Most large newspapers will run your plea for assistance at no cost or at a reduced charge. Treat these people well and you can have a helpful, dedicated staff on tap with a payroll that's close to nothing.

Wow! This whole thing is sure interrelated. That's why you need to put your thinking cap on while you're planning. The better you understand your choices, the better chance you'll have to make good ones.

Where Will the People Come From?

Staffing a project can be difficult because co-workers are already buried in their own work and hiring outsiders is expensive. Typically, your options are limited by people's availability and the cost of them. But an organization that wants or needs to complete a project must make staff available, even if it means pulling people off other projects or bringing in outside help. Staffing options include the following:

Words from the Wise

He is the best sailor who can steer within fewest points of the wind, and exact a motive power out of the greatest obstacles.

—Henry David Thoreau

- Using your own staff and other people from your department.

- Using staff from other departments.

- Contracting with consultants, outside vendors, or temporary agencies.

- Hiring and training new staff.

As with business options, each of these choices has an upside and a downside. Just working with unfamiliar faces can mean a few surprises. You might have to adjust the project to accommodate each personality and productivity level while keeping a wary eye on the project dollars and timing.

Your Own Staff and Other People from Your Department

The first step is to determine the skills you already have available to you. A staff skills inventory, which we discuss later in this chapter, is a useful document for this purpose. On it, you'll document all the relevant skills and experience of each person.

If staff members with appropriate skills exist in your department and aren't already (fully) committed to other projects, this is the easiest alternative. You have easy access to these people, you have a working knowledge of their strengths and weaknesses, and depending on your rank, you may have control over them.

However, don't kid yourself. If you use internal people, you will need to change their performance contracts to include the project goals. Think about it: If they have to choose between two competing tasks, they will choose the one they are getting paid for! If you want them to commit to the project in addition to their regular jobs, the project must show up on the performance evaluation and have a positive (or negative) impact on their year-end bonus. Otherwise, you will always lose this battle.

You may also want to set up two organization charts, one that shows them in their regular job, and a second one that shows them in the project organization. Visually, it sends a strong message. By that I mean that in the functional organization, for example Information Technology, we would see Bob Braveheart as a manager of infrastructure with seven people reporting to him. In the second organization chart for All-Star Cable, we see Bob as the team leader for infrastructure development that includes five people, including developers to database administrators. The people in IT know they need to listen to Bob because he is their boss. On the project team, the org chart shows Bob as the boss of the infrastructure development team.

If your project requires outside expertise, (either from inside or outside your organization), it will require time and money. Projects with high visibility can be problematic politically, too. If other departments see you utilizing vast amounts of resources on a single project, you may have to justify your resource use as other projects slip. Further, you may be considered hard to work with because you use only people from your own group when more experienced talent is known to exist elsewhere in the company or organization.

Staff from Other Departments

Working with others in your organization makes for good communication and camaraderie among those involved. In a large organization, this might get you the technical or specialized staff you need, or it might allow you to bring in competent people whom you watch with awe as they keep the team moving efficiently and effectively. For example, you might need a financial wizard from the finance department to track your budget and streamline purchase orders.

On the downside, the main difficulty you will encounter is convincing someone's manager to allow him or her to join your project. Down the line, you also might discover that your outside staff member is late on his or her tasks because his or her boss agreed to let him or her join your project without reducing his or her current workload. Negotiate carefully with line managers in advance to set the stage as much as possible. Don't assume anything here. Don't forget to include the cost and delays of the loss of key people at critical times in your risk analysis. It is a very common problem!

Contracting with Consultants and Temporary Agencies

Outsiders are always available—for a price. With careful selection, you can fully man a project with exactly the right mix of people. Hire them when you need them and let them go when they're done. This is a flexible arrangement in that you have no responsibility (other than paying the bill) to keep them on or even to provide office space because all but some temp agency employees will already have space of their own.

On the downside, outsiders can be expensive. The key to using outside consultants and temporary labor is to schedule their work carefully. The cost for a highly trained consultant priced at $125 per hour by his firm is mitigated if, with careful scheduling, he or she comes in, works using his or her own well-developed methodology, and leaves in five hours. But should the work fall behind, he or she may spend several hours, or even days, cooling his or her heels while the clock is running. He or she will become an expensive liability, regardless of his or her admirable skills and experience.

Along the Critical Path

Be careful of using the word "headcount" when you talk about additions to your project team. Headcount is the term used to describe the fixed number of internal employees approved to work in an organization or on a project. Hiring a new person "increases headcount." On many projects, using an outside consultant or other temporary worker only increases costs. Sometimes it's easier to increase costs than to raise headcount because headcount enlargement shifts the permanent overhead costs. Expenses for office space, furniture, tools, benefits, and even additional management time must be accounted for. Thus, if you need a person for a project and you don't have a job for that person after the project is done, it's usually easier, and in the long-run less expensive, to propose an outside team member than to propose additional headcount.

Choosing the consultants and service providers for a project can be a tough call. Experts, consultants, and even temporary labor can hide behind a salesperson's persona.

Good consultants are masters at selling themselves; otherwise, they would be out of business. Remember, just because someone proclaims him- or herself an expert doesn't necessarily mean he or she has a track record to back up the claim. Make sure the vendors you choose have been around the block a couple of times. Also, watch out for the "bait and switch." That is when a consulting group shows you experienced professionals for your project, but when the day comes to actually start, a group of inexperienced know-nothings shows up. You will spend time training them and constantly worry if they can keep up.

Words from the Wise

Knowing what you *cannot* do is more important than knowing what you can do. In fact, that's good taste.

—Lucille Ball

Even hiring low-level labor must be handled carefully. The temporary agency's polished salesperson may overwhelm you with smooth promises and glossy brochures, but eventually, you'll just need hard-working developers to write that code. Remember that the gloss and polish you paid extra for probably won't make any difference if you just need good code developers.

Because talk really is cheap, you must be careful of whomever you hire. Unfortunately, you won't really know what you have in hand until the person performs—or fails to perform. Check the person's references and get performance guarantees in the contract before you sign on the dotted line.

Hiring and Training New Staff

If the project is a long-term commitment or is ongoing with a finish date far enough out, you might find that adding to the headcount is the most expedient method for bringing in the manpower and expertise required. Of course, you noted the word "training" in the title of this section. You must be fully prepared with time and money to train your new bodies in everything from their task requirements to the culture of your organization. But adding new workers often brings a fresh point of view, takes some pressure off other staff members, and is an easy way to add a much needed skill set not available elsewhere in the company.

Be sure you understand the process for finding and securing new people before you begin this process. Note that you are treading into the territory usually reserved for Human Resources. Almost every company has documented guidelines to help you and copious rules that you must follow. And be sure to enlist the help of an experienced human resources manager before you make any decisions about who will be on your team and how much they'll be paid.

Headcount increases are enormously difficult to justify in most organizations, especially those furloughing long-time employees while you are looking to add. You may be told "no way" or be asked to take on an employee otherwise slated for a one-way trip out the back door. The latter could force you to choose someone with no appropriate skills for the task at hand. Avoid this potential nightmare by being very specific in your description of the job. If no one with a pink slip exactly fills the bill, you'll have an opportunity to choose from fresh stock.

If you don't have experience in hiring personnel, you should do some reading about this subject.

Individual Contributors vs. Team Players

Not everyone you hire will like being a part of the team or will be good at playing the role of a team player. Team players function like members of a baseball team: They work together and build on each other's strengths and accomplishments. They make for great project supervisors, and you'll see them having a beer with other team members after work on Fridays. But there are also the invaluable individual contributors in many projects.

Those with specialized creative skills, such as engineers, designers, writers, and (for lack of a better phrase) project visionaries, may appear to you and other team members as downright hostile. That's okay if their expertise is a must-have for the project. Although you should avoid mercurial personalities with no people skills whatsoever, a genius with a compelling vision might make the difference between a mediocre project and a great one. Just keep him or her out of supervisory roles wherever possible. Another approach is to assign them to tasks with little dependence on others. That way they won't need to interact too often. Or you may want to use them as a Subject Matter Expert that you only bring in at certain times to take advantage of their genius, but you don't have to supervise them, or follow them around sweeping up the mess they create.

You must structure the project team to work like a clock. Appropriate matches of worker to co-worker, manager to worker, and manager to manager are crucial. Assuming you are the team leader, you must also be comfortable working with the parties with which you have direct interaction.

In a long project, this team assembly becomes more important. Someone who gets along with a colleague for a five-week project may grate on the person's nerves during a project spanning a longer period of time. Conflicts are inevitable, but you should do your best to assemble a team that's prone to cooperation rather than discord.

Assigning People and Skills to a Job Description

"Go team!" "That's the spirit!" "Onward and upward." "Let's review the plan and make things happen." Most projects begin on these positive cries. As project manager, you should strive to sustain this positive "We can do it" attitude among the team members.

As you would assume, staffing and motivating a small, closely held project team is less complicated than building a finely honed organization for a major project. A really large project involves more risk and goes through large sums of money quickly. To help make your choices better than the luck of the draw, a skills inventory is required—along with the help of your human resources department if you have one.

For most projects, the staff assignment involves two steps: developing the job descriptions and then matching people to the jobs. You can create the description by writing out the individual competencies that you need, and then see how the overall team competencies would be filled out by the individuals you are considering. (Competencies are defined as having the right qualities or abilities.)

Along the Critical Path

If your skills analysis reveals that you need to employ more people, the company will likely have detailed hiring guidelines that include job description formats, pay scales, interviewing procedures, and reference requirements. Learn about these now before you have to start recruiting people. And don't forget to establish a good relationship with your human resources manager. This person can be a lifesaver when you need to get people on board in a short period of time.

Create a Skills Inventory

Before you decide whether to use existing staff, hire new people, or use outside vendors in your project to fill the job titles, you should develop a skills inventory of people in your own organization (see the sample skills inventory in this chapter). Such an inventory in a large organization often is maintained by the personnel or human resources department, although this normally lists only the technological skill levels and formal educational backgrounds of people in the company.

Managerial and communications skills should be listed if your information is credible, but only if you have direct experience working with a person or reliable feedback from people who have such experience.

Developing a skills inventory can be an informal process or part of a formal personnel review system. The end result of completing a skills inventory will be a listing of the technological, management, administrative, and human skills for each staff member in your organization. If you have a complete, up-to-date skills inventory, you can easily match the skills required on your project to the people who have those skills.

A skills inventory is something that must be kept up-to-date to be useful. It is also something that can be used for many projects, so developing a regular procedure for keeping it up-to-date is worth the effort. Skills inventories also can help you identify people for your project whom you might overlook if you rely on memory or intuition to establish your project team. A simple form can be used to create a skills inventory and cost analysis of people available for your project. We have provided an example in the next section.

Matching People to the Jobs

Using the skills inventory and your other personnel options, you need to identify someone to fill the shoes of the person you described in each job description.

Work in pencil! You might find that you can handle the project using people already on staff, or you might find that expensive (or maybe even cheap) outside resources are required because the time available simply won't allow you to train existing staff to do the job. At this point, it's a "We can do it" or an "It's too expensive" decision. The exercise of developing a skills inventory points out the degree of resource drain and quantifies the use of people not available on staff or in other departments.

Use a skills inventory like the one shown here to quantify the talent you already have available for your project.

Skills Inventory				
Produced by: Gail Murphy				**Date:** 12/17/01
Name:	**Category:**	**Current Job:**	**Skills:**	**Experience and/or Degrees:**
Fred Sands	Software Engineer 1A	Sr. Systems Analyst	-C++ -Oracle Database Programming -Human Resources Applications -Systems design using CASE	-BSEE Computer Science, UCLA -15 years in MIS, various positions
Sarah Wilkins	Software Engineer 2B	Application Programmer	-Java Certification -Some C++ -Web programming/HTML	-AA, CS Whittier College -3 years Web programming
Sam Garcia	Software Engineer 2A	Supervisor, Web Group	-Java -C++ -Perl -Web programming/HTML -XML -ASP -Management training	-BA, Sociology SJSU -MSCSE,1999 -4 years programming, 2 years on Web

Choose Me!

After you identify the jobs and pencil names into the inventory, you must move people around for the best fit. If there are too many question marks instead of names next to the job descriptions, you might need to take a longer look at the project and its scope. Maybe the project really isn't viable after all, or maybe you're trying to do something too ambitious with your existing talent pool.

If, after matching people to jobs, it still looks like you have the right talent available for the project, it's time to study the political ramifications of your choice of project team members. Also, you'll need to think about the location of the various people. Sometimes, all the people are in the same location, so it's easy. However, at times, you may have people scattered all over the country—or the world! Consider the political aspects of who to choose because you will need people from all the stakeholder groups to buy in. They are more likely to accept the project solutions if they have some of their people working on the project. Also, your boss may ask you to include someone on the project as a developmental opportunity for that person. He or she might need experience to grow into their next job. You might think of this as an imposition. However, what you may really have is a bargaining chip to gain further concessions on other aspects of the project.

> **Risk Management**
>
> There are times when an individual has a unique technical skill and must be given a supervisory or leadership role, regardless of how difficult this person is to work with. You (and the rest of the team) will just have to learn to work with the difficult personality to get the job done. This is one of the standard challenges project managers must handle with aplomb.

If you need to put a team together with resources from other departments, you need to answer these questions before you go any further:

- Who will you have to deal with in other parts of the organization to get approval for a prospective team member's participation? Is this politically workable?

- How much will outside services cost? Plop the Yellow Pages on your desk and make calls to get quotes. Would it be easier to use outside resources than to get approval to use the inside people?

- How much training is required for each team member? Is it worth it?

- Will team members come willingly or are you imposing your agenda on workers who would prefer to have no part in the project?

- Is another manager offering you a team member because he or she wants to get rid of the person? (This is called exporting the problem!)

What If You Need Someone Else?

Sometimes you don't have or can't find the person you really need to build your project team—even if you've done all the people-planning suggested in this chapter.

Other times, you'll find that the team simply isn't working out because the people aren't as skilled as you originally believed. In these situations, don't underestimate the role that training can play in solving your people needs. Also, it may take time for people who aren't used to working together to build a relationship toward maximum efficiency. In this situation, training can hasten the process (and possibly avoid conflicts).

When developing a team for a project, it may be possible to train or retrain existing people instead of hiring new ones. Existing employees are already familiar with the project policies and culture, a distinct advantage. Existing employees are also known quantities, so you avoid the risk of hiring someone who doesn't fit in. Besides, training people is often cheaper than hiring new employees when all the costs and time are added together. And if you encourage the development of existing staff, the entire organization will benefit from the resultant knowledge gain and the atmosphere of support and encouragement. If people are given an opportunity to advance, they are much more likely to be consistently productive and loyal. When considering training as an option to meeting organizational requirements, the following choices are available:

♦ Mentoring relationships with existing experts in the organization. Mentoring programs are excellent for developing management skills. Books on mentoring are available in the business sections of most well-stocked bookstores.

♦ Training programs are best for general technical training or basic skills training. But, because these programs can be costly, check their quality before you enroll people.

♦ Internal training programs developed by in-house specialists. These programs are good for company-specific technologies and procedures. Internal training programs may be time-consuming to produce, but if there is a continual need for new skills in specific topics, then a project to create these training programs is in order.

Call on Your Contacts and Supplier Networks, Too

If you will be working on many projects, build and maintain a network of contacts and suppliers as well as an inventory of your own organization's skills. If you will be producing different kinds of software projects, for example, interview a variety of temporary staffing companies in your area and become familiar with their pricing structures and quality of work.

Then, when a project comes up, you are ready with a list of people and vendors that can fill your project's needs. This extra time up front on your first project may pay off in later projects.

A Survival Resource After the Project Starts

Skills inventories and contact lists also are useful after the project starts. What happens if a key staff member assigned to your project quits or gets sick? Pull out your skills inventory to identify potential replacements. If you don't have a network diagram and skills inventory ready, you will waste valuable time trying to find someone who can take over for the lost resource, and the project may suffer delays or other problems as a result. This should always be part of your project risk plan.

Words from the Wise

"In order that people may be happy in their work, these three things are needed: they must be fit for it; they must not do too much of it; and they must have a sense of success in it—not a doubtful sense, such as needs some testimony of others for its confirmation, but a sure sense, or rather knowledge, that so much work has been done well, and fruitfully done, whatever the world may say or think about it.
—W. H. Auden

The Best of the Best: Making Your Selections

After you've considered your options and the talent available to you, create a list of possible people and vendors for each task on your list. This list should include the alternatives available. For large, complex projects, the alternatives should be ranked in priority order, and the strengths and weaknesses of each choice should be well understood. A worksheet like the one shown previously can be useful in identifying people and their strengths and weaknesses for a project team. (Guard your list closely and rarely share it with others!)

If you use a skills inventory, you will discover that there are almost no perfect matches of people and project requirements on your list. Because no one can perfectly fit your needs, the selection process usually involves trade-offs. For planning purposes, identify people with the closest match of required skills and ask yourself whether the skills deficiencies are workable. Can you use two people who complement each other's skills on the project? Can you make up for the lack of skills in other ways? The more critical the tasks, the more important the match of skill requirements to people becomes.

Sometimes You Have to Compromise

Obviously, you want the best people possible for your project, but even after making compromises and trade-offs, it's not always appropriate to use your first choice for every task, especially if another person's skills are adequate.

For example, if you were the project manager for All-Star Cable, you might have two people who could do the job of designing the new billing system. One of them has extensive experience in billing systems, but is relatively new to the company and you have not worked with them before. Another person does not have the experience of the first one, but you have worked with them before and you know what to expect if they join the team. So you will have to decide which trade-off you are willing to make—experience or familiarity? What will it be? Every choice involves risks and trade-offs.

Why is this so complex? Because people are involved. Things are almost never easy when people are involved, and they're never totally predictable. You'll have to make choices based on your own interpretation of the most important needs and your best guess of what you expect to happen with these people. It's the best you can do. With experience, you'll get closer to getting the right people for your jobs (but you'll still get surprises on occasion—that's why things never get boring in project management).

The Problem of Imposed Team Members

You won't always have the advantage of being able to choose and organize every member of the team for your project. The team and its structure may be imposed on you by other managers within your own organization. Sometimes people are selected because they are available and not because of their skills or talent. Imposed team members are common in every business for a variety of practical and not-so-practical reasons.

Before you decide that someone on your team is incompetent, give the person a chance. People can often do more than you think. Remember the self-fulfilling prophecy: If you believe people have talent, they will exhibit talent. If you believe they will fail, that's likely to happen. Be realistic about your team's ability, but don't charge the project with unnecessary negative energy before it even starts.

In dealing with imposed team members, there are a number of alternatives you can consider to make things work:

◆ Do the best you can with the people you have, but make sure resulting problems are documented as they occur (otherwise known as covering your rear end).

- If your team doesn't have all the skills necessary, build training into the project.

- If your team is not qualified in all required skills and training takes too long, consider hiring a consultant or an outside vendor to fill in the gaps (if you have the budget to do this).

- Compromise and negotiate for the team members you really need. Don't just complain—be constructive. If some of the team members are not appropriate, suggest a different team to the people who made the original selections. Always discuss the alternatives with the appropriate decision-makers. These people may be able to offer explanations for the staff selections that you never considered, making the choices more reasonable than you thought. If you have documented your own case with task requirements and skill inventories as suggested earlier in this book, a rational manager will usually listen. You may not get everyone you want, but if you identify the priorities, you might be able to negotiate for the people you really need.

  As an alternative, you may attempt to approach the manager with specific alternatives in mind and a convincing argument as to why your proposed changes would result in a more efficient project team that's better able to deliver the project on time and within budget.

- Suggest an alternative team-selection process for the next project. Although this may not help this time, it may be that the other managers never considered having you involved in the selection process. Explain the advantages of having the project manager involved and offer a structured approach to the staff-selection process. You may meet with political resistance if people are afraid of giving up their authority for making project decisions, but you can explain to your bosses that they can make the final selections—you just want to be involved.

Along the Critical Path

Don't forget to change your performance reward and recognition system to incorporate the success of the project into each and every person's evaluation criteria. Have an actual performance report that you will provide your team members at regular intervals, so that they will know how they are performing. And complete the deal with an actual handshake that says we both agree to the terms of the new performance contract.

Putting Your Best Foot Forward

Because there is no perfect project team, what do you do with the intangibly less-than-perfect set of players? First, try to avoid the imposed team whenever possible.

Always negotiate for the right team members, even when your choices must be approved and/or paid for by the stakeholders and managers who approve your project budget. Suggest alternatives and justify why your recommendations make economic sense. "Well, sir, Jenkins is an accomplished database administrator, but I'd rather see Biggles take the job. He can do it in half the time, according to the research I've done, and that saves the company money ..."

Second, whether the team is imposed or not, you should interview possible team members as if they were taking a new job. (They are unless the project is ongoing—and even then, if you are interviewing them, they're getting a new boss.) In the interview, try to get a reading on their enthusiasm for the project and ask for a resumé before the interview if you hadn't already done so. This gives you basic details on their backgrounds and interests so you can ask probing questions about specific skills.

Finally, when you find that you really are stuck with certain team members, training is almost always an alternative. Pair a novice team member with an experienced one. Working together to learn new skills has long been a standard educational practice. It usually works (unless the two team members kill each other in the process). If you match the two players appropriately, you might have the joy of watching an immature team member graduate to the status of important contributor once he or she sees how the "pros" do it.

There are many reasons why the project manager should be involved in personnel selection, such as becoming familiar with the strengths and weaknesses of the team as early as possible. This insight leads to better schedules and the development of monitoring and control systems that are geared toward the needs of the various staff abilities.

What About Next Time?

In a project-oriented workplace, it's rare that the same exact group of people works over and over again on the same kinds of projects. Projects usually bring unique groups of people together—groups of people from different departments or companies or points of view. Thus, it's important that you not be married to working with your favorite project members. You need to be willing to work with new people and be willing to take on different roles in other projects. It's all part of the project management style.

The Least You Need to Know

- Listing the skills required to complete each task on your project can help you identify the right people to put on your team.

- A skills inventory can help you identify both the talent you already have available and the talent you need to find.

- A comparison of project needs and people skills can help you match the right people to the right jobs on your project.

- If people don't have exactly the right skills, training is often a better option than hiring other people.

- Always negotiate for the best team members you can get. It's in the stakeholders' interest to see that you do.

- The choice of the implementation team is critical to project success, but sometimes you have to do the best you can with who you have available or who you're forced to use.

- You can guess what people can do for your project, but you'll never be sure until you work with them.

- Disparate personalities are standard in most projects, but disparity can be accommodated if you work at it. In most cases, it adds value to the project team in terms of ideas and flexibility.

Getting What You Need: Supplies, Equipment, and Other Stuff

In This Chapter

- ◆ Establishing exactly what you need
- ◆ Getting bids from outside vendors and suppliers
- ◆ Choosing the best vendors and suppliers
- ◆ Checking price and availability

After you have defined the tasks, established a basic network diagram, and selected the team members, you must create a list of nonhuman resources you'll need for your project. You have also determined your project schedule and budget, so you are ready to begin the process of procuring those additional items.

The Five Additional Resources You Need

As you proceed to figure out what you need to complete the project, you'll have to consider the five additional fundamental resources required to implement almost any project (We've already talked about people and money):

- ◆ Equipment
- ◆ Facilities
- ◆ Materials and supplies
- ◆ Information
- ◆ Technology

These are the five things that you and the core project team need to identify for the entire project. Ask yourself what resources are already available for the project. We often use a resource inventory to list everything available for the project (including equipment, facilities, and supplies).

As you begin to plan for procurement, you should consider a variety of inputs to help you. You will need to review the …

- ◆ Scope statement in your project charter
- ◆ Deliverables that you are responsible for
- ◆ Procurement policies within your company
- ◆ Market conditions for the equipment, supplies, and so on, that you need
- ◆ Constraints that were identified earlier in your planning process
- ◆ Assumptions that you made

After you (and the core planning team) take an inventory similar to the preceding section, you still need to know one more thing before you can complete your plan for project resources. That is:

- ◆ The estimated quality and output of people and equipment resources. This is important because it allows you to make a trade-off analysis between similar resources. If time is most important, choose the fastest resource. But if a slower resource really saves money in the long run, and if you have the time to spare in the project, then a slower but cheaper resource might be a better selection. If you don't make these estimates in advance, you won't be able to put the best budget and schedule together for your project.

Equipment and Supplies Worksheet

Task Numbers [   ]   Date Prepared: [   ]

Completed By [   ]

Required	Responsible Person or Vendor	How Much Is Needed?	When Is it Needed?	Check If Available
MATERIALS:				☐ ☐ ☐ ☐ ☐
EQUIPMENT:				☐ ☐ ☐ ☐
SUPPLIES:				☐ ☐ ☐ ☐
SPECIAL SERVICES:				☐ ☐ ☐
OTHER:				☐ ☐ ☐ ☐ ☐

An equipment and supplies worksheet like this one can be used to identify things that are needed and those that already are available for your project. Be specific. We usually list equipment and supplies based on the work packages in the WBS.

Planning for Outside Vendors, Contractors, and Suppliers

During the planning phase (where you are now), you need to determine a list of probable vendors, suppliers, and contractors for your project and get estimates of cost and availability. Before you talk to vendors, you need to be crystal clear about the materials, equipment, and/or work you want from them. This will come into play during negotiations, and a well-defined statement of work (SOW) is essential. Remember, the SOW work is a narrative description of the work to be accomplished. It includes the objectives of the project, a brief description of the work, any constraints along with the specifications and schedule. You'll usually make your final vendor selections based on these estimates after the plan is finally approved.

When you evaluate the need for vendors, consider doing a make-or-buy analysis. This is a technique for determining whether you can effectively produce the items you need internally within the company or whether your best alternative is to purchase what you need. Don't forget to include indirect costs when you begin this analysis. Often an internal source will look good until the indirect costs are factored into the equation. Also, keep in mind the overall perspective for the company and not just the project. For All-Star Cable, it might look like the resources for developing the cable box reside in-house. However, manufacturing several hundred thousand of them simply exceeds All-Star's capabilities will. It will be better to hire a company that specializes in them to make them for you.

You might also need people with special training or experience to provide input into the procurement process. For example, when we did a project on pipeline maintenance for a major energy company, we looked for people who could give us expert advice on turbine engines. We decided that we would talk with maintenance experts at a national airline on how they did the work on their turbine engines and see what we could apply to our project.

Determine What Kind of Contract to Use

Different types of contracts will entail different levels of risk. You will need to choose the right one for you. The three primary contact types are as follows:

- ◆ **Fixed price or lump-sum contracts** let you know how much you will pay for goods or services. It places much more risk on the seller's part, and therefore, most vendors will not enter into this type of agreement unless you provide them with a very clear and concise statement of work (SOW).

- ◆ With **cost-reimbursable contracts,** you pay the vendors for their costs, both direct and indirect, plus a fee over-and-above those costs that is the vendor's profit. This puts more risk on you as the buyer, and less on the seller, but it allows you to offer incentives to the vendor if they meet or exceed certain targets for the project.

- ◆ **Time-and-materials (T&M) contracts** are a combination of the fixed price and cost-reimbursable contracts and are often used for consultants or other personal services resources.

Words from the Wise

For art and science cannot exist but in minutely organized particulars.

—"Jerusalem" (1804–1820) William Blake, British poet

T&M contracts resemble the cost-reimbursable contracts in that they are typically open-ended since the full value will not be realized until the project is finished. However, they resemble a fixed price contract because you will negotiate fixed rates that you will pay for the services of different people (a senior programmer, for example).

Get an Estimate

No matter which type of contract you choose, you should ask for an estimated cost. You want to know that the estimates are good ones—and that the eventual commitments will be met. You should follow these guidelines for getting the best estimates for your project:

◆ Whenever possible, get written estimates from suppliers with whom you have extensive and positive experience.

◆ Make all providers (people, materials, and equipment suppliers) bid competitively. Get a minimum of three bids or more if you can. When you have trimmed the list down, ask the final two providers to present you with any revised estimates. When two companies know they are down to the wire with only one other competitor, they will often sharpen their pencils and give you an even more attractive estimate to capture your business.

Time Is Money

Save money by renting equipment required for the short term, whether it's a massive backhoe or a miniature electron microscope. Don't forget to get rental estimates for your plan.

◆ Consider out-of-town suppliers. What sells for $12,500 in Manhattan may go for $3,000 in Phoenix. (Be sure to take shipping and interstate tax requirements into account!)

Now you can get to the bottom line of working with outside suppliers. No estimate is set in stone unless you're working with a government provider or looking at a seller's market. (If you need 500 carpenters who already are busy rebuilding frame homes after a natural disaster, you'll have little negotiating power over the price of building your new corporate headquarters. Timing can be everything in a bidding situation.)

Negotiation is a fine art. There are many good books on the topic. Read a few. For a complete and free education, spend time at a flea market. Watch as expert negotiators go up against the most set-in-concrete pricing scheme and drive the prices down. Or even better, watch your organization's best salespeople at work. They wouldn't make those big salaries if they didn't know how to negotiate.

You need good estimates for your plans and good working relationships with your vendors to get these estimates. Work with suppliers, study the goods or services they sell, and check up on their reputations. Never let a powerfully persuasive salesperson push you into a commitment before the plan is approved. It may be harder to resist than you think when a honey-voiced merchant visits and applies rose-colored glasses to the top of your nose.

If you follow these simple steps, you'll get more accurate estimates from suppliers of all sorts of goods and services:

1. Get written estimates for your service, supply, material, and equipment needs. On large projects, you may want to put together a formal request for proposal (RFP) to attract the maximum number of potential suppliers. Advertise the RFP if that's what it takes to get good estimates and quality vendors. Offer detailed specifications of your project and its needs by return mail, fax, or e-mail. Vendors will assume bidding is competitive, although the words "Competitive Bid" stamped (in heavy red ink, of course) on the RFP will help get the point across.

2. Fully explain, demonstrate, and document your requirements for equipment, materials, and supplies for the estimate or in the RFP. Be as precise as the following sample bid request for professional services: "The Company expects the consultant to research and recommend billing technology that will satisfy the requirements listed in the statement of work and that will operate within the technical environment at All-Star Cable." In your RFP, ask the vendor to answer the following questions:

   ◆ What is your understanding of our need?

   ◆ What will be the overall or life-cycle cost? The definition of life-cycle cost is the purchase price plus cost to operate over a period of time.

   ◆ What are your technical capabilities to complete the work? Please give examples that illustrate these capabilities.

   ◆ What is your management approach and how will it be used to ensure the success of the project?

   ◆ What is your financial capacity to fulfill the terms of the agreement during the life of the contract?

Time Is Money

Keep in mind that, as you develop the rest of the plan, your resource choices will affect the quality, schedule, and budget for your project. If you aren't able to get the resources you planned to use, you'll have to adapt the objectives, schedule, and budget accordingly. It's a good idea to verify the availability of as many resources as possible before the project plan is approved.

3. Before you read a single proposal, sit down with your project team and develop the selection criteria. Determine if certain elements of your evaluation are worth more than others and develop a weighting system that takes those priorities into account. Also, consider developing certain minimum standards that any final vendor must meet to win the contract. You may be able to eliminate some vendors right away and not waste time on someone who wouldn't win against the competition anyway.

4. Make sure the vendors know that acceptance and performance clauses will be inserted in the final order for goods. This means that goods that don't meet specified standards will be returned and replaced at no cost to you. Also, make sure the vendor will be responsible for picking up the shipping tab for return freight if materials or supplies are inappropriate or substandard upon delivery. Include delivery requirements in the description of your needs. (Ordinary but unavailable materials have sunk more than one project.) These specifications must indicate when the goods must be delivered and to where; otherwise, the contract is void. If the company turns out to be a no-show, you're still in trouble project-wise, but at least you won't owe a bill for a shipment that arrives three weeks too late.

   Also make sure you find out how changes will be dealt with. All projects will change over time and you will need a clear process in place when you change the scope of work that you have asked a vendor to supply. It will also help when one, or more, of the stakeholders requests a change, because you will be able to explain to them how the price will change (increase) and any impact it will have on the schedule (delay).

5. When getting estimates from consultants or other service providers, ask for a formal proposal for their services. A formal proposal will tell you a great deal about a firm. Do they use "boilerplate" wording in response to your request. If so, it may mean they are not really familiar with your requirements, but are hoping to impress you with their credentials. You should be most interested in how they will work for you, not what they have done for others.

6. When hiring consultants or service providers, also ask for a description of their current workload. Many will boast about current projects without realizing that what you're looking for is a person with the time to take on your tasks. Although it's true that the busiest may be the best, when it comes to managing a project, you need adequate share-of-mind for your work and committed schedules from the vendors. Thus, a vendor who is a close second in quality but who has fewer commitments may be a better choice.

7. Check references, compare estimates, and use the estimate from the most likely choice of vendors for the rest of your planning purposes.

8. Hold a bidder conference to allow you to meet with several vendors at one time. A bidder conference is an invitation to all potential bidders to meet with you and some of your key team members. It will allow them to ask more detailed questions prior to submitting their proposals. Often, project managers will revise their RFP based on the questions they received during the bidder conference and then send it out to any vendors who are still interested in proposing on the contract.

Along the Critical Path

One way to get reliable bids and estimates is to have vendors develop their own WBS for their portions of the project, complete with the acceptance criteria and the list of resources to be used. Then they can assign individual costs to each task and resource in the WBS, just like you need to do for the rest of the project. This document can help you determine the quality of the estimate and the company's understanding of the work you want done.

The Ghost in the Machine

Sometimes you won't be given the opportunity to get estimates or to order resources without going through the purchasing department. This can be a relief—it takes the work out of your hands. But the purchasing department is the bane of projects (and project managers) more often than not.

If you're lucky, you'll find a professionally run organization with experienced purchasing agents who take the time to understand your needs and to handle your bid requests with aplomb. Be aware, however, that you may be faced with the uphill task of (literally) fighting with your organization's purchasing personnel to place an order.

The only way to know what you'll be up against during a project is to test the waters. Begin by ordering something simple such as a desk for a team member. The resulting cooperation of the purchasing department—or lack thereof—will let you know whether you need to add tasks to your project that read: "Work with purchasing to explain need, secure bid, and gain approvals to order desks."

Sadly, in our 25 years of experience with purchasing departments, many are run by bureaucrats who slow the estimating-buying cycle to a crawl as six signatures of approval are required to order a new lightbulb for an overhead projector. Too many purchasing departments work with favored vendors who make the purchasing process easy for the purchasing department but costly for your project. The department may choose vendors based on who buys the best lunch in town rather than price, timely delivery, and a workable approach to handling problems. Remember, it's not their project they're purchasing for—it's yours.

The best way to solve problems with a recalcitrant purchasing organization is to learn its procedures, follow its processes, and make friends in the department. If the department causes more problems than it solves, try to work around it when you can and learn to work within the process when you must. The test of the project manager's mettle is to make it all work, easy and hard.

Time Is Money

A database program on a personal computer can be used to maintain the equipment inventory for your project. The equipment categories can be assigned codes for easy sorting. Some of the more sophisticated project management programs allow you to include equipment inventories as part of the project data.

Don't Skimp on the Team's Needs

Your project demands the best equipment you can afford. Before you rent bargain Pentium I desktop computers for $9.95 each per week, consider your hard-working (and well-chosen) project team. With inferior equipment, less work will get done, and staff members might become alienated because they assume no one cares about their productivity. Is this saving money? We don't think so.

Give your people the best tools you can afford for the job. Provide them with modern equipment, a comfortable and safe place to work, and quality supplies as necessary. For special needs, ask project participants what they need and do your best to furnish that high-powered workstation or other specialized equipment if necessary. Obviously, people might ask for more than they really need, so give the choices some thought. Still, giving people the right tools is essential to completing a project on time and within budget. You need to sort out wants from requirements and then make sure your project gets all of the latter.

From the Plan to the Stuff

For planning purposes, getting the bids for people, supplies, materials, and equipment may be enough to finish the budget for your project. After the plan is approved and you have the go-ahead to proceed with the project, however, you'll have to choose the specific vendors you want to use.

At that point, you'll need to check references (if you haven't already), compare bids, verify delivery dates, and then choose the best vendor (probably in conjunction with the core project team). Then, by all means, get an attorney or the corporate legal counsel to draft the actual work agreements with any suppliers or outsider vendors. Require vendor signatures on the agreements before work commences or money is exchanged. All these procedures are part of the procurement process, and procurement is a major portion of your job as the project manager.

The Least You Need to Know

- After you have identified all the tasks for a project, you should identify the specific resource requirements for each task or milestone including people skills (see the next chapter), material requirements, information needs, and other resources.

- Before you get your project plan approved, make sure you've verified the cost estimates and availability for all the resources in your project. Otherwise, you can't put together a reasonable schedule or budget.

- Getting accurate estimates from suppliers of materials and equipment requires a clear description of your needs and a careful review of the vendors' capabilities.

- Establish a good relationship with the purchasing department and learn its procedures before you need to procure anything.

- You should always check out vendors before you sign a contract.

Chapter 16

Putting It All Together: The Approved Plan

In This Chapter

♦ Recalling the importance of planning in project management

♦ Putting the whole plan together

♦ Understanding why project plans fail

♦ Analyzing the risk in a plan

♦ Cross-checking the plan for accuracy

♦ Selling the plan to management and getting it approved

Okay, you've assembled a statement of work (SOW), a work breakdown structure (WBS), a network diagram, a schedule, a description of team requirements, and a budget. You understand the activities for the plan and the resources required. After all this effort, you may feel too tired to start working on the project, but don't throw in the towel. Besides, you haven't even finished the plan. You still need to integrate, evaluate, and get approval for the fruits of your planning labors. That's right: You need to get your plan approved before you can start working.

This chapter reminds you of all the good reasons for planning in the first place and provides advice for getting your project plan approved so you can get to work. Don't fret. D-Day is almost here! With an approved plan in hand, you'll be ready to start working on the project. Finally!

Reasons to Plan in the First Place

Sometimes people complain that plans take too much time. They would rather start working on the project than think about the plan. Some people think that plans are created only because other people want to see them. Your boss asks for a plan and you write one. The customers want a plan so you draft something to make them happy. Plans prepared slavishly rather than thoughtfully are a waste of time for the reader as well as the writer. Plans written only for the benefit of someone else rarely meet their goals of guiding the project to a successful conclusion.

If you're not going to take planning seriously, don't bother. Without a good plan, you're like a surgeon who decides to remove his or her appendix with a can opener. You'll likely get the offending organ out, but you'll also make a mess of things in the process.

A good plan can help avoid most problems (but not all). Even so, you should know that no amount of planning will make your project go exactly as planned. Your plan will go off course because of things you didn't know in advance—and every project will encounter some things that cause you to deviate from the plan. Remember that a project is unique so you will be learning as you go very often. Of course, you won't be able to think of everything. However, the better the plan, the more likely you'll get where you want to go. And the better you keep the plan up-to-date, the more likely you'll be able to make the best adjustments to keep the project on course.

Putting It All Together

The following diagram shows how all the pieces of the plan you've learned about in this book so far are interrelated. Ultimately, all of these pieces should be put together in an integrated document called "the plan."

The project planning documents are interrelated. If you make a change to one, you need to adapt the rest. If you don't keep the plan up-to-date, it doesn't matter how good the initial plan was. An out-of-date plan is a statement of what didn't happen—not a guide for the future.

The project planning documents are interrelated. If you make a change to one, you need to adapt the rest. If you don't keep the plan up-to-date, it doesn't matter how good the initial plan was. An out-of-date plan is a statement of what didn't happen— not a guide for the future. Project plans can vary from fairly simple documents that list the activity, budget, and resources on a single page with a cover memo to detailed books with overwhelmingly intricate levels of detail. Typically, the plan will include additional narrative and organizing information to help readers (and team members) understand how the entire project fits together. The complete project plan for a large project might include a table of contents like the following:

1. Executive Summary of the Project (or Project Overview)

2. Project Objectives

3. Project Assumptions and Risks

4. Project Milestones

5. Work Breakdown Structure (WBS)

6. Network Diagram

7. Resource Details

    Human Resources

    Equipment

    Materials and Supplies

8. Budget Details

9. Project Organization

10. Operating Procedures

11. Assessment and Review Standards

12. Contact Points and Information Sources (if relevant)

13. Project Approvals

There is no magic formula for the right level of detail in the plan. We use this rule of thumb in our own planning efforts: Never spend more time on the plan than it would take to fix the project if there were no plan. Thus, if your project is only a week in length, it doesn't make sense to spend two weeks on the plan. On the other hand, if your project involves hundreds of people and millions of dollars, you'll want to put detail in the plan that allows the myriad resources to be coordinated.

The project planning stage dominates almost one third of this book, but the actual time required to complete the plan (including the work plan, resource assignments, schedule, and budget) might only be a few hours for a very short project. It might take a month or more for a very large project. But it is the quality and thought that goes into a plan—not the time—that determines its value in the project management process. This is why it's so important to understand the issues in creating each component of the plan as we've explained them in previous chapters.

Now Write the Final Project Plan

When you have completed the SOW, a WBS, a network diagram, a resource list, a schedule, and a budget, you have all the elements necessary to put together the plan.

Draft the Final Project Plan Yourself and Have It Reviewed

Draft the final plan on your own if you have expertise in a project that makes you especially well-qualified to bring the major sections of the plan together. Also, if you are basing your project on a plan used successfully for a previous project, this approach can work because you can compare what your project planning team has done to an existing plan that has worked before.

Of course, once you've completed a draft of the plan, you should have it reviewed by qualified individuals before submitting it to the steering committee. If you don't, you might encounter the following problems:

- It is more difficult to identify errors in the logic of a network diagram or WBS.

- You might not identify missing activities or incomplete activities.

- You might not have all the information you need to create an accurate schedule or budget.

- It is often difficult to see your plan objectively when you do it yourself. When other people review it, they should be able to understand what you are doing, when you are doing it, and what it will cost.

- People might feel left out, and you've missed a great opportunity at building support for the project with others (including stakeholders).

Review the Plan with the Key Players

Getting the key players and stakeholders involved in reviewing the project plan may require one or more structured meetings and probably advance preparation by each of the team members. As you prepare for presenting the information to the steering committee, or whatever governance board will ultimately approve the project plan, put yourself in their place. What will they be interested in knowing? How can you best address their needs and concerns as you prepare to move into project execution? Who among your team members will they want to hear from, and question, about the project plan? After you have answered these questions, prepare your materials for the meeting.

As you prepare the written project plan, you will need to consider the following:

- How formal does the project plan need to be? In some groups, or for large, expensive projects, the project plan will need to be pretty formal—large notebooks with colored tabs and a Table of Contents. In other cases, the project plan can be done with PowerPoint slides and a few handouts.

- How does this group, or the key individual in the group, like to see information? For example, some people respond very well to charts, graphs, and models. Others need pages of written text with only the occasional diagram thrown in. Again, tailor the information to the audience that will be reviewing the plan.

◆ This can also be a test of how the steering committee will want to be briefed on the project as you progress, so pay attention to what they liked about your plan, and what they didn't like.

◆ Finally, try to determine how much detail you will need to provide. Sometimes a steering committee will not want a lot of detail. If that's the case, leave the details out of the plan but bring along any supporting information that you have prepared. That way, if you are asked a question, you can respond quickly without having to say "I'll have to get back to you with that."

No matter how careful you are in developing the plan, you will need to have the plan approved and reviewed by the appropriate people in your organization. Even after the plan is approved, as you bring new people into the project later in implementation, changes might be necessary if the new team members offer better or more appropriate alternatives for completing their assigned activities and reaching milestones. (When you start thinking about changing and modifying a network diagram with hundreds of activities during the life of a project and communicating these changes to multiple people, the rationale behind using computerized project management tools becomes apparent.)

From Plan to Approval

In the real world, the plan for a large project (or even a small one) will go through multiple versions on its way to approval. Sometimes the steering committee will tell the project team to go back and make changes. Don't think of that as a failure! These plans may be debated, discussed, enhanced, expanded, and revised several times until the project plan is complete and approved.

Risk Management

While you work on a plan, your project might change in relevance, and you might be plugging away at something currently as important as yesterday's newspaper. Avoid this problem by continually feeding progress reports to your project sponsor and other key stakeholders during planning. And learn to take the company's pulse on a regular basis to see how the political climate might be changing.

When the Planning Phase Terminates a Project

Of course, some projects collapse before the project plan gets approved. Here are some standard scenarios for projects that never make it out of the planning stage:

◆ **Inadequate planning.** You rush a plan together, and you haven't covered all your bases. If the stakeholders see the plan as inadequate, it's not going to get the go-ahead.

◆ **Incomplete plans.** You or your team provide uncertain estimates for scheduling and budgeting or fail to bring in the expertise to quantify the technical activity.

◆ **The mission of the organization changes during the planning process.** Many organizations change their priorities like people change clothes. A project must fit into the current political, economic, and business priorities of the company to gain approval. The truth is that many organizations are trying to react to a rapidly changing marketplace—this is more of a reality than a fault.

◆ **The project is no longer relevant, seems too risky, or has little chance of completion before the target date.** Who wants to support a project going down in flames in front of his or her management peers? After all, part of your work as project manager is to evaluate and present the feasibility of a project to stakeholders and senior management. You are helping management decide whether to proceed with the project as defined.

Sometimes the plan demonstrates to the stakeholders that the project is not viable. If you get stuck with one of these, just be happy that the project got stopped at the planning stage before you got stuck with trying to manage an impossible feat.

Other Issues That Can Sink a Plan

Upon integrating the various components of the project plan, you might find issues that have not been addressed in your other planning efforts. Not all of these are worthy of a activity in the plan, but if you ignore them or don't address them somewhere in the schedule, the project will suffer. Typical things that get left out of the plan (but shouldn't) include:

◆ **Space and facilities.** Do you have basic office, manufacturing, and sleeping accommodations arranged that are suitable for your team? Do these costs appear in the budget?

◆ **Transportation.** Should your team need transportation above and beyond normal commuting, you must locate effective transport and budget for it.

◆ **Permissions.** Do you require written or at least verbal permission to use specialized equipment, to trespass on private property, to cross international borders, or something similar?

◆ **Licenses, permits, and clearances.** Do you need official permission to use hazardous chemicals, to block access to a structure or roadway, to enter restricted government facilities, to move confidential equipment or materials, or something similar?

- ◆ **Insurance.** Are your team and other resources underwritten for accidents and infringements that might occur? If insurance is required, what existing policies protect you and how can you fill the gaps with additional coverage?

- ◆ **Weather.** How will the weather impact your plan? Can you hold the dates together if rain or snow delay construction, hinder delivery of materials and equipment, or impact team member performance?

- ◆ **Unavailable resources.** Is a strike possible within your organization or a major vendor? Is a key material in short supply? How will you address the problem and resolve it?

These are just some of the more common risk factors that might impact your project's timely completion. When reviewing your plan, you might find others that must also be addressed with contingency plans or specific activities and schedules.

Uncertainty and Risk—What Level Is Acceptable?

When you submit your plan for approval and discuss it in review meetings, the steering committee or stakeholders will judge the risk factors associated with each aspect of your plan.

Remember that activities with less than 50 percent certainty reflect a need for better planning or the assumption that the plan is more of a guideline than a real project plan. In many projects, pivotal points with low certainty become high risks. Designing a new appliance? What happens if, during a too-brief testing prior to production, the sample units catch fire and melt?

Most projects have potential weak points. You should study your plan to identify each one if you want to get the plan approved. If you don't want to be blamed for your failure to predict the future when things don't go as planned, be honest about the risks by documenting them in the plan and by coming up with ways to reduce them if possible.

The Reality Check Before Approval

Before submitting the plan for final approval, you need to perform one last *cross-check* of your planning efforts. This involves a line-by-line matching up of the WBS, schedule, budget, and network diagram, assuming you created these pieces. Computer-based planning software can help by finding impossible dates and durations on the critical path, missing network links (only if they're obvious), and missing activity data.

Even when you use a computer, however, you should check the logistics and flow of your project personally and by hand. Get your project planning team to help you with this effort.

Here are the steps for cross-checking a project plan:

1. From the network diagram, match the activities, durations, and dates to the scheduling worksheet.

2. From the network diagram, match the resources to the scheduling worksheet.

3. From the network diagram, match the activity to those shown in the WBS.

4. Verify the numbers on the budgeting worksheet and re-total them to make sure they match your existing estimate.

5. Study the activities on the critical path. Is the right path selected? Are there any activities that require more time? Have you separated the labor required from the duration on each activity?

6. Verify that the milestones (if you chose any) make sense as a means of summarizing the main activities in a project.

7. Check to see if the start and finish dates are still reasonable. Also verify that you have accounted for all holidays and vacations in the schedule.

Project Lingo

One of the best tests of completion, whether for the doors on an airliner or the workability of a project plan, is **cross-checking**. To cross-check a plan, one person lists a procedure and another verifies it. With two independent bodies carefully verifying the plan, chances for error greatly diminish.

Time Is Money

All steps of the plan should be run past your core team members before approval. The final fine-tuning of the project plan is no exception. After all, if you missed something, they might be able to fill in the gaps. If you've asked the impossible of a team member, you'll have an opportunity to hear about it before the work starts.

If you didn't assemble either a network diagram or a WBS, it's almost impossible to cross-check a project. Reread earlier chapters on why the components are important. If you're unwilling to prepare this level of detail in plans, whether formal or informal, consider another type of job. A plan is an absolute requirement of success in project management.

Checking It Twice

Inevitably, discrepancies will appear in the cross-checking process. As you might expect, larger projects tend to have more mistakes than smaller, simple ones. After finding the errors, you must modify the plan to correct them. If more than 3 percent of the plan requires modifications due to your changes, perform the cross-check from scratch one more time after the changes are made. It's always possible to "fix" errors by introducing new ones. For that reason, review your notes from the previous procedure and do it again.

One way to encourage review is to have a dedicated wall or cubicle where the latest project data is displayed. Team members can check it and flag changes or problems. Team meetings take up a lot of time and should be limited. In today's networked world, you might consider additional "groupware" tools to share project information, but don't let tools replace your involvement as project manager.

A plan that changes more than 10 percent during the cross-check demonstrates a plan that needs further work. Look at the errors to establish where they lie: schedule, budget, resources? If a definite pattern to the mistakes appears mostly in one part of the plan, consider redoing that part of the plan from the beginning.

Getting the Plan Approved

The final step before the ship sails, so to speak, is getting the project and its cross-checked plan approved by the people paying the bills. The people who approve the plan will vary by company, project, and assignment. As mentioned in Chapter 5 when we discussed the stakeholders on the project, make sure you know who will approve the work and the budget for the project. Sometimes multiple departments will be involved. Sometimes you'll get to sign the approval sheet on your own. In any case, the most important aspect of the approval is getting the money freed up (the budget) so that you can start work on the project.

> **Time Is Money**
>
> An efficient way to present a plan is with a summary presentation backed up by hard copies of the plan's WBS, worksheets, and network diagram. Presenting a management overview hopefully will avoid a line-item review of each activity, its schedule, and its budget. If it comes to that, however, the backup data you've provided will do the trick.

A Presentation of Project Priorities

Before you present your project for final approval, study the presentation of the plan from an outsider's viewpoint. Do the activities explain themselves or is additional notation required? Are the activities equal in scope (or almost)? Is the presentation clear and organized? Is the level of presentation appropriate for the scope of the project? Make sure the project sponsor reviews the project plan before you have any other decision-makers on the approval team look at it.

If you present your plan to a manager, customer, or review committee, you must be prepared to justify your choices, dates, and budgets. You'll need a compelling reason why each activity is required and the associated budget justified. (Even if the reviewers don't ask, you should be prepared.) You also need to be prepared to talk about risks and contingencies if things go wrong.

Use judgment in what you present from the plan. Always start with an overview of the plan and then move on to details. Remember, the people who approve the plan will have a copy of the complete document to review anyway; you don't need to go over every detail in the presentation. The goals of the presentation are to present the overall structure and objectives of the project, to answer questions, and to establish your credibility as the project planner (and project manager).

Too much detail in the presentation can be as devastating as too little. With too many activities in your presentation, you'll be bombarded with questions and arguments from management about the details. Managers might grandstand their opinions and try to save money on things they don't really understand. Avoid this by using milestone summaries of activities so that managers don't fail to see the big picture during your presentation. Keep the meeting short (one hour) and focused. Senior managers dislike meeting for longer than an hour. Keep it crisp, but make time for their searching questions and time to get their approval. Keep your antenna up for questions or suggestions that might cause a change in the scope of the project. If your scope gets changed in this meeting, your budget and schedule will be impacted.

The result of your presentation will be either the approval (by signature) of the project (which is unlikely on the first presentation of a large project) or a request to make revisions. Changes should be made to the general plan (scope and strategy) first and then to the details of the plan (the activities, network, resources, and so on). Remember, you must change both. You can't just adapt the schedule because the stakeholders don't like it. If you've done a good job of planning, you'll have to communicate this fact to the people who approve (and sign off on) the plans.

If real objections crop up, stop the presentation and reschedule the meeting after the plan has been modified. If more than three revision meetings are required, then either your plan has serious problems or the political agenda of the people approving it is likely to prove impossible to circumvent. Without full management commitment to your project, successful completion is unlikely at best.

If you get caught in a political situation, have one-on-one discussions with individual stakeholders to understand their concerns and then come up with a strategy for circumventing (or reducing) the politics from the process so you can go forward with the plan. Use your project sponsor to help you run the political maze that has your project ensnared.

Presenting Your Plan as an Outsider

As an outside project management consultant or vendor, you might be required to present your plan and sell it in a competitive bid. Although management will be focusing on costs, try to emphasize the quality of your proposal as well. If you're not the lowest bidder, convince the potential customer that your organization delivers consistently high-quality work, on time and within budget. (Hopefully, this will be the truth.) As for a group sold solely on schedule and/or budgetary concerns that turns down your carefully honed estimates, you probably wouldn't have liked working for them anyway.

Approval at Last

Finally, there's great news: Your plan is approved. They've signed on the dotted line. The accounting department has assigned a budget number and account codes for the project. You're ready to go.

The plan you created and got approved isn't the only plan you'll use during your project. During a project, you'll typically have three or more versions of the plan active at one time. First, there is the original approved plan. This is sometimes called the baseline plan. Second, there is the actual plan, which reflects the actual work done to date. Third, there is the future schedule based on work done to date. Finally, there could be a number of contingency plans developed for a complex project over time.

Just remember to keep the plans numbered and keep them up-to-date. A big filing cabinet is a good idea if you'll be managing big or frequent projects. A good computer program should be able to manage more than one version of the project at a time so you can compare various stages of the project as you proceed.

Bringing a Delayed Plan Back to Life

In too many organizations, your carefully constructed project plan might be shelved if organizational and market changes alter management priorities. Then, phoenix-like, the project rises later to haunt you.

Before you seek the approval of such a plan, make sure you verify all the activities, assumptions, and budgets. Don't just blow the dust off yellowing pages. Make sure the old plan still makes sense.

If a plan slips a month past its starting date, a new schedule is mandated. If it slips more than one month, the entire plan must be scrutinized. A new schedule is in order, but you must also verify resource availability and make changes to the plan to reflect management dictates. Even equipment and supply lists must be updated. Last year's order of 48 top-of-the-line computers might be superseded by newer, cheaper models. Suppliers might have closed up shop, moved, or been unable to deliver a brand they carried 365 days ago. You'll have to modify the budget to reflect the improvements in technology, market changes, and the effects of time.

> **Words from the Wise**
>
> When the company archives your plan because it's so important, it's a goner. You won't ever see it again. And it will never ever serve its purpose as a plan.
>
> —A project manager for a multinational company

> **Words from the Wise**
>
> The longer a project's duration, the less likely that changes in organizational priorities and happenstance will allow it to reach completion.
>
> —A standard project manager's axiom

From Plan to Action, Finally

After getting a plan approved, it might seem like you've done an awful lot of work and still not gotten anything done.

The central role of the plan in the project management process often leads people to the mistaken conclusion that the creation of the plan is project management. It's not. Most of the time spent in project management involves management. As you've already surmised, project management involves much more than just a plan.

Still, don't be surprised if people identify your project management skills with your ability to create a nifty network diagram and an impressive-looking planning binder. Worse things could happen, and as long as they pay you for it, well, you don't have to tell them that it wasn't really that hard.

You'll soon get to work and put your approved plan into action. Forward and onward! The executing or implementation phase is about to begin. In the next phase, you'll learn how to take the baseline and create both plans that reflect work done and schedules for remaining work. But that's to come. For now, just enjoy your completion of a demanding phase of project management.

The Least You Need to Know

◆ You need to cover all your bases in planning. A brilliantly scheduled research project in Switzerland will come in over budget if you don't remember to include the team's travel, food, and lodging expenses.

◆ Projects with a degree of significant risk might require a second look from the bottom to the top.

◆ Risky activities should be analyzed. If a less risky approach is possible, the plan should be modified to accommodate it.

◆ All planning documents from the WBS to the network diagram should be scrutinized to ensure that they match and work together.

◆ Aging or delayed project plans require revamping before going for approval.

◆ You'll probably have to present your plan to management and customers before it gets approved—and it probably won't get approved the first time around.

◆ You must sell your plan to the stakeholders and get their commitment to the plan, its schedule, and its budget before starting work on the project.

Part 4

The Execution Phase

Well, you've done it now—you've defined a project and have gotten the plan approved. You're ready to begin, and the beginning is a very crucial time in any project. If you begin the execution phase (also commonly called the implementation phase) of the project the right way, it will enhance your likelihood for success.

To start toward the finish line of a project, you must establish your leadership, organize the team for top performance, institute operating guidelines, and yes, figure out what kind of reports and other paperwork you'll need to get things going and keep them headed in the right direction.

Chapter 17

Getting Started on the Right Track

In This Chapter

- ◆ Project kickoff activities
- ◆ The first project meeting
- ◆ Getting project members in synch and enthused
- ◆ Avoiding the floating start date

At this point, you have an approved project plan in hand. You have identified most of the key team members, have sought permission to use them, and have established a budget and a source of funds to pay them. You're ready to get started. Or are you? How will anyone know what to do? What's the first step?

For most projects, these questions are answered at the project kickoff event and the first project meetings with the group and individuals. These activities are the first steps in the executing phase of any project. The big kickoff event (or at least a small one) serves to get everyone in synch with each other and to build a feeling of camaraderie. The project kickoff is like the locker-room rally before a big game. It gets the juices flowing and reinforces the goals for the project. The first project meeting is like the initial huddle in the Super Bowl. This is where you actually agree on your first play in the project and get the team lined up to win the prize.

In this chapter, you'll learn how to hold a project kickoff that motivates the troops and gets everyone moving in the same direction—toward the project finish. You'll also see how to make the first project meetings part of the key strategy in your project game plan.

Always Get Your Own Act Together First!

Before you have the kickoff event, you'll need to consider both your leadership style and your management tactics—the two are intertwined and are central to the implementation of projects. Your leadership skills and the appropriateness of the management tactics you adopt for each of the various people on your project team are of paramount importance in achieving project goals. The first time you get to try out these strategies and tactics will be at the kickoff event.

> **Time Is Money**
>
> Remember that you will never have everything completely in place and that changes will be coming no matter how carefully you have planned (we'll talk more about changes in Chapter 24).

In Chapter 18, you'll learn a lot more about becoming a leader on your project. We mention it now only because, to get a project kicked off, you must be both a manager and a leader. You can use the project kickoff to gain the trust and respect of the project team so that people feel comfortable taking your direction. You can also use the kickoff to explain the reports and administrative procedures you'll use to help people get work done on time and within budget.

Do It Now and Do It Right

Once you've decided that you're really ready, you need to decide how to kick off your project. Whether handled formally or informally, the kickoff events of the project or subproject need to accomplish the following objectives:

◆ Communicate the goals of the project to all team members to ensure that everyone is crystal clear on their own objectives and responsibilities for the project.

◆ Attain the commitment you need for the project and get people enthusiastic about making things happen.

- Establish the leadership style for the project and get the team ready to follow you.

- Identify critical deadlines and phases of the project.

- Review the overall schedule and work plan with the appropriate team members.

- Explain basic operating procedures including required reports, meetings, and other ongoing communications necessary between you and other team members.

- Explicitly give the people responsible for the initial tasks the go-ahead to begin work on the project.

If you add all these objectives together, you'll see that the overall goal of the executing phase is to establish a set of conditions so work can get done. These conditions start with clear communications about the plan and other procedures associated with your project. The project kickoff is the first step in opening up the channels.

The Formal Kickoff

Although some projects don't require more than a small meeting and a memo to get started, when a formal project kickoff event is appropriate, the event should be both celebratory and informative.

The type of event will depend on the size, importance, organization, and budget for the project. Use your judgment. Look at the kinds of events given in your company for similar projects—and ask about the events that worked and the ones that didn't. If a customer is paying the bill, keep the event simple and economical. One more reminder, if you hold the kickoff in a public place, make sure that the competition is out of earshot.

It's a Go

Regardless of the sophistication or format of the kickoff event, the event should put team members on notice that the project is a "go." The event should emphasize that each individual's contribution is vital to the success of the project. The kickoff event can also help individuals relate their goals and work responsibilities within the overall project to the efforts of other team members. This is a first step in establishing a "team" spirit.

In the more formal kickoff meetings like those described later in this chapter, always schedule the event so that your project sponsor and all other stakeholders, customers (if appropriate), managers, and key team members can participate.

Give the sponsor a spotlight (most of them love it) to endorse the project and "wave the flag." Remember that a critical success factor for projects is the support of senior management. Seeing and hearing from one of the executives from the organization gives the whole project team a sense that the company really means business regarding this project.

The kickoff event should also establish the priorities, tone, and energy for the project. The kickoff should avoid too many individual details; leave those for the first project meetings and one-on-one sessions with key project players. These meetings should take place during the first week after the project kickoff event.

Between Kickoff and Team Meeting: Use the Time Wisely

The time between the project kickoff and the first formal project meeting (we recommend three days to a week between events) gives team members time to reflect on their roles. Feedback after the kickoff event is invaluable to plugging up holes in the project plan. During the period before D-Day (the day of the first project meeting), you may have team members approaching you with questions or problems.

Based on any feedback, you can fine-tune your project plan and look into problems that team members throw at you. You can also run issues and problems by senior management to level out the small molehills before they turn into major mountains. Gathering feedback allows you to come to the project meeting prepared with answers to objections and explanations of issues that were inadequately addressed in the plan.

During that time, set up what is usually called a "war room" for the project. It is often a conference room that is reserved for the duration of the project for the exclusive use of the project team. It should be outfitted with phones, Internet or intranet connections, and plenty of wall space to post information. This is a space where project members can come at any time and work, and other members of the company can stop by and see what's going on. While it is not top secret, you should also have cabinets with locks on them to store sensitive material.

The First Project Meeting

After the kickoff event, you're finally underway! Schedule the first team meeting to take place approximately one week after the kickoff. This first meeting will be the first true test of your leadership skills as the project manager.

All working members of the project implementation team should be invited. (Customers and the executive management team should not be invited.) This is a meeting to get work started. The first team project review meeting should accomplish the following:

◆ Establish a model for future meetings:

1. Start on time.

2. Develop and distribute an agenda of objectives before the meeting and ask people to review them before they come.

3. Conduct one agenda item at a time and conclude it before moving on to the next item. (Avoid getting hung up on the order of topics.) Establish a "parking lot" for items that come up that are off the topic. The list can be written on a piece of chart paper—be sure to label it as the Parking Lot.

4. Encourage open communication; meetings give individuals a chance to express suppressed ideas.

5. Take notes. Really the only notes that are probably relevant are action items that are assigned to people with due dates and any decisions that were made by the team.

6. Establish the time and place for the next project team review meeting. We would recommend that you try to establish a regular meeting time such as every Tuesday afternoon at 3:00. It's much easier for people to manage their schedules if they know that for the duration of the project, their Tuesday afternoons are devoted to the project.

7. Agree on and reiterate any follow-up activities or action items required. Be sure to assign people to these tasks and get their commitment to complete them.

8. End the meeting on time. If you need to stretch the meeting a little longer, ask the group for permission and decide *how much longer* you will meet. Once that time is up, close the meeting down.

9. Distribute (brief) minutes to all attendees within two days of the meeting.

10. Make sure the action items and responsibilities are indicated in the minutes (so that people don't conveniently forget what they agreed to do in the meeting).

◆ Introduce the members of the team and their project roles.

◆ Review the first priorities for the project and repeat/reiterate briefly the other objectives and overall schedule.

◆ Review individual plans for getting work started.

◆ Discuss methods and tools to be used to manage, control, and operate the project.

◆ Deal with objections to the current project plan and work them out if possible.

◆ If decisions need to be made by the group, follow these steps:

1. Discuss the problems and seek opinions from all.

2. Don't allow one person to dominate the discussion.

3. Test for readiness to make a decision.

4. Make the decision.

5. Assign roles and responsibilities.

Here is a example of how minutes might look after a project team meeting for All-Star Cable Movies-on-Demand project:

All-Star Cable Project Team Meeting Minutes

Meeting: All-Star Cable Project Team

Date: 02/06/2003

Time: 2:30–3:30 PM

Chair: Bob Braveheart

Attendees: Kim Winford
Jo College
Ben Admin
Joe Goniski
Mary Scarlotti
John Andreotti (by phone)

Decisions:

Agreed to the Case for Change and the Business Case for the project.

Items	Person Responsible	Date	Status
Action Items:			
Research vendors to build the cable boxes	Kim Winford	2/06/2003	Completed
Investigate the credit policy as reported by the project team	Ben Admin	2/06/2003	Completed
Review requirements for new billing system with Accounting	Joe Goniski	2/06/2003	In Progress

Items	Person Responsible	Date	Status
Submit RFP for OTS software	John Andreotti	2/06/2003	In Progress
Analyze reporting needs for management team	Bob Braveheart	1/30/2003	In Progress
Parking Lot:			
Question of "Adult" movies being part of the offerings to work with	Project Manager Project Sponsor	1/16/2003	Parked
GUI interface for customers	Parked until more items are completed	1/16/2003 1/30/2003	Parked Parked
Data Storage and data mining	Parked until late February		

One-on-Ones: The Individual Starting Events

In addition to the kickoff and the first project meeting, you'll need to meet with key individuals at the beginning of the project to make sure they have all the information they need to get started. These initial meetings with new players may continue throughout the project as different aspects of the project get underway.

Formal meetings with project team members, known as *one-on-ones*, should be used to clarify priorities and to discuss schedules and plans. Many of the people will have worked with you on the project plan already, so you won't need to go over all the details with these folks. However, you will need to turn their focus away from planning and start delegating work to them so things start happening. This is a great place to review the network diagram and show each team member how their work fits into the broad project plan for the project.

One-on-ones with key players should also be scheduled on a regular basis throughout the project. For a short project, the one-on-ones might happen daily or weekly with key personnel. For a longer project with more players, the formal one-on-ones might be monthly or even less frequent depending on your other level of interactions.

In the first one-on-one meetings, the following should be clarified and reviewed with each individual:

Project Lingo

One-on-ones are meetings (often scheduled and formal) between two people involved in a project. These meetings are used to discuss priorities, to resolve issues, and to communicate overall responsibilities to the project.

- Why he or she was selected

- Performance expectations

- Individual priorities, tasks, and milestones

- Administrative procedures and project management methods and tools in use, such as reporting of progress on work packages and time covering both frequency and level of detail you want in those reports

- Challenges and issues

- Processes for solving problems

- A schedule for future one-on-one meetings

- Action items for future meetings

Always take notes in these meetings. Suggest that the other participant do the same.

Step Up or Flub Up?

Your ability to organize and control the first team meetings will be a major step in establishing your leadership of the project team. If you do this well, the meetings will serve as a model for subsequent project meetings and will set a tone of open communication and professionalism that will make managing your project a lot easier. If you flub up the meetings, you'll not only waste the time used on the meetings, you'll also lose credibility as the project manager. The number one criticism of most meetings is that they don't produce anything of value—don't let that happen to your meetings. Preparation, organization, and focus are critical to making the first team meetings a success.

Words from the Wise

If you go into battle, it's better to win the first time.

—Gen. George S. Patton

Information Everyone Needs to Get Started

The purpose of the kickoff and the initial team and one-on-one meetings is to inform people and get them in synch with the project plan. From the beginning, people who work on the project need access to relevant information in the plan so they can do their jobs. Tasks and schedules should never be a secret (although budget and other financial information may be held confidential when people aren't responsible for the costs). The project plan should generally be an open book to help guide people to the promised deliverable.

Provide every member of the team with a summary of the plan during the initial stages of the project. This can be done before the kickoff event, in a team meeting, or during a one-on-one at the very start of the project. For team members who will remain with the project from the beginning, we recommend presenting these documents prior to the kickoff event and then discussing them in the first project meeting and one-on-one sessions. As new team members join the project during later stages, you'll need to make sure they get the information as well.

Here are the pieces of information from the project plan that every team member needs in order to contribute appropriately to the project:

◆ A summary of the overall project goals. The project summary outlines and explains the purpose of the project, its goals, and the overall schedule.

◆ The team member's role and task assignments. The specific tasks and milestones for each team member (or subteam) should be laid out in writing. At the beginning, the milestones and task overview might be general with specific tasks being introduced by you or other supervisors and managers at a later date.

◆ A list of who's who on the project. The directory or list of key project team members should include a description of each team member, his or her role (and title) in the project, and contact information (telephone numbers, office location, and e-mail addresses).

In addition to information about the project plan, every team member needs to be informed of the administrative procedures that will affect his or her life: reports, forms, legal documents, and so on. Don't drown team members in paper. If your reports to them are crisp and timely, their reports will hopefully be on time and accurate. For a large project, you may want to provide a "Project Administration Handbook" that assembles examples of all the forms, reports, and other documents required from project personnel, along with other relevant documentation of the project plan. For small projects, a simple list and an example report will probably do the job.

Time Is Money

Always remember: What you don't know hurts you. And what your team doesn't know will also hurt you.

You should also let team members know that regular status reports are required. Explain why the reports are essential to tracking the project and keeping it on time and within budget. Set the report intervals for weekly, biweekly, or monthly intervals, depending on the nature of the project. (Note that monthly would be for an extremely long project of more than two years. If you wait for a month to find out that someone hasn't met their commitment, you are in a world of trouble with little time to catch up.) Present people with sample reports and completed forms that set the expectations for their reports. (We offer more recommendations on reporting frequencies and formats in Chapter 21.)

If confidentiality or other legal agreements are required for your project, now is the time to get them signed. If your organization contracts with the military or other government agencies, rules may be more strict. Look into the proper forms of agreement and reporting that are required and make sure the appropriate team members understand the requirements at the beginning of the project.

Avoid the Floating Start Date

Getting a project started is key to finishing a project successfully. The right information in the right hands goes a long way to make things happen. A project with a floating start date, however, never goes anywhere. If you kick off a project and then fail to follow through with clear delegation of the work to get it started, you may have a good plan, but you won't have a project.

Never rev up your team to tackle mountains unless you're really ready to reach the summit. If a project fails to happen as announced, you'll likely find that the team has lost interest by the time you decide you're ready to begin work. Team members may even find something else to do that precludes their participation. Delays also mean adjusting the dates in your carefully honed project plan and getting things approved all over again.

If you kick off the project, be sure to follow through with the next play. If you start as planned, you'll have a lot better chance of finishing as scheduled.

The Least You Need to Know

- Getting a project started right involves communication.
- All projects need starting events that clarify project goals, responsibilities, and operating procedures. These events can be simple or elaborate but should always be commensurate with the size and importance of the project.
- Prior to the first project team meeting, a review of the project by team members may point out holes in your plan that need patching.
- At the beginning, all (or at least most) major problems, whether financial or political, should be satisfied in the plan.
- Focused, productive, and informative team and individual meetings are the best way to get things started on the right track.

Chapter 18

Leadership and You: Taking the Bull by the Horns

In This Chapter

◆ Establishing your role as leader and manager

◆ Management by walking around (MBWA)

◆ The leader in times of crisis

Since it's up to your project team to complete the work specified in the plan, you, as the project manager, must employ appropriate methods to motivate, coordinate, facilitate, and administer your team. If you don't, the work may never get done. As a project manager, you must also identify and implement the appropriate leadership style for keeping the team motivated.

The Importance of Establishing Your Leadership

Whether managing the remodeling of a major hotel in downtown New York City or the installation of a new Internet wiring within an office suite, you must take command to lead your project to success. You can use every technique in this book, but without assuming leadership of the project, you'll get nowhere. You must become the leader and manager of the project if you want to succeed. And these are two distinctly different roles.

As a leader, you must command respect and take responsibility for guiding the project. One key way to command that respect will be as a trusted and reliable source of information on the project. As a leader, you will be expected by your team to be honest, competent, and in charge.

As a manager, you will monitor and control the project through to completion using specific techniques and procedures that establish the framework and structure of the project. You'll review the plan, complete reports, balance the budget, update the plan, fix the schedule, update the plan again, report on the updates to the plan, and yes, update it again. You'll also do a lot of other administrative stuff that will drive you crazy. You'll continue to "manage upward" in keeping the key project stakeholders informed and involved about project decisions.

Time Is Money

One of the single biggest mistakes that [a leader] can make at this critical time in the life [of the project] is to be either unavailable or aloof.

—W. E. "Dutch" Holland in his book *Red Zone Management*

Some people get so caught up in the management of a project that they forget about leadership. It's possible to complete the management part of the project and not attain the status and influence of a leader. That's why we've written this chapter—to make sure all those project management traits get transformed into leadership skills as well.

Wearing the *Big* Shoes

You must be a leader who provides strong guidance but at the same time offers a receptive ear to people with problems. Your team members may not always fill the big shoes you've offered them. The well-known Murphy's Law often ensures that anything can go wrong on projects from the tiniest to the most colossal.

As a leader, you should also know the plan inside and out and be able to talk to the team about priorities without sounding frustrated or rushed. If a team member has a problem that requires discussion, as a leader, you should always be seen as a resource to seek out rather than as an obstacle to avoid.

Managers go to meetings and complete paperwork. Leaders must gain the trust and respect of the project team. People must feel comfortable taking your directions; otherwise, they'll make up their own. Yes, as a manager, you must develop protocol and administrative procedures for ensuring that work is getting done on time and within budget. But establishing yourself as a leader is more important than any report or process.

Leadership style and your management tactics are intertwined and are central to the successful implementation of the project. Your skills and the appropriateness of the management tactics you adopt for each of the various people on your project team are of paramount importance in achieving project goals. There are lots of hard-nosed books on becoming a leader, but we favor a simple, soft approach involving only eight steps:

♦ Listen to the people and ask lots of questions.

♦ Be a reliable source of information when your project team needs it.

♦ Observe what is going on and take notes.

♦ Know enough to know that you don't know everything.

♦ Be available when people need you. If you need to leave for any length of time, make sure your team knows how to reach you.

♦ Make decisions when called upon to make decisions, but also know when decisions should be deferred to other stakeholders with more authority.

♦ Delegate the work that needs to be delegated.

♦ Don't micromanage. You manage the project; your team members must manage their work.

A Style That Gets the Job Done

Business writers have described a wide range of effective leadership styles that can be adapted to meet the needs of different people, organizations, and projects. You'll need to choose from three basic styles to lead your project:

♦ **Task-oriented leadership** emphasizes getting the job done and concentrating on methods for assigning and organizing work, making decisions, and evaluating performance.

♦ **Employee-oriented or people-oriented leadership** concentrates on open communication, the development of rapport with team members, and an ongoing direct concern for the needs of subordinates.

♦ **Reward-based leadership** ties positive feedback and other rewards directly to the work accomplished. The reward-based style assumes that a high level of performance will be maintained if work results in meaningful rewards that correlate directly with the quality of the person's efforts. Rewards include pay and promotion but also encompass support, encouragement, security, and respect from the project manager.

The approach of matching management style to the specific needs of a situation is often called situational management or contingency theory. Project managers must effectively apply the best style for the job—whether task-oriented, employee-oriented, or reward-oriented leadership—to meet the needs of individual team members.

As you try to implement a style, don't assume that, because you like something done a certain way, your team members will have the same preferences. Individuals differ from one another in experience and personality. Each person has a different conception of how the job should be done, who should get credit for the effort, and how each individual should be rewarded for his or her work. For these reasons, different leadership styles and management methods must be used to monitor and coordinate different projects.

How to Be a Leader

There are two components to project leadership: visibility and communication. First, you must be visible in the role as project manager. Second, you must communicate your intentions and the progress of the project to team members on a regular basis.

Taking the Reins Through Communication

Communication and leadership go hand in hand. The project managers who consistently succeed in bringing their projects in on time and within budget are those who effectively manage the interfaces and communications between people and organizations. The people working on your project, and other members of the project team, need to be comfortable with bringing issues to your attention. This goes for people who report directly to you, their managers, and your managers as well.

Three types of communications must occur for a project to be managed effectively:

1. **Vertical communications.** These are the up-and-down organizational communications based on the hierarchical relationships established on an organization chart.

2. **Horizontal communications.** Horizontal or lateral communications involve communicating and coordinating activities with peers.

3. **Diagonal communications.** The diagonal relationships are rarely shown on organization charts, but they are almost always important to the success of a project. Diagonal communications involve upward relationships with managers and officers from other departments. They also include downward diagonal communications with third parties such as contractors, suppliers, or consultants.

If you have established the requisite communications in all three dimensions before conflicts occur, when the inevitable conflicts do arise between organizations, styles, procedures, or priorities, there will be an established channel available for resolving issues. If you have established the basis for discussion before the conflicts arise, the resolution process will usually be easier.

Meeting regularly with team members, reporting to them on team accomplishments and success (or lack thereof) in meeting objectives, and becoming a resource of project knowledge, suggestions, and conflict resolution is what makes you the leader. Your team members will look to you as a central clearinghouse of knowledge and praise (and you should provide plenty of the latter).

This is not to say that some team members won't be uncooperative, but much of this eases once a project is underway and your—for lack of a better word—charm builds a cohesive team bent on meeting schedule dates and making you and them look good!

> **Words from the Wise**
>
> The greatest mistake an executive can make is to be afraid of making a mistake.
>
> —John Capozzi, *If You Want the Rainbow You Gotta Put Up with the Rain* (1997)

Good Communication from a Real Leader

If you want to be a really good communicator and a leader as well, here are some guidelines to follow:

- Hold regular meetings with team members—and don't cancel them. Effective meetings should start with the project kickoff (described in Chapter 17) and should continue throughout the life of the project.

- Meet both in groups and individually. Some things that won't be said in front of other team members in meetings may

> **Time Is Money**
>
> Projects are becoming increasingly virtually staffed by transient, dispersed teams. Achieving to potential under these conditions requires distributed project leadership using "virtual walking around" techniques via computer networks, video conferencing, and the Internet. These techniques help people communicate, collaborate, and manage shared activities in an integrated way.

come out in one-on-one sessions. In groups, simmering conflicts, which won't be mentioned in private, may rear their heads.

- Provide your team with constant feedback on the project's status. Be available, friendly, and willing to discuss anything that team members are burdened with—from project problems to personal problems. Include outside vendors in relevant project conversations as you deem appropriate.

- Keep meetings short and to the point. Team members respect leaders who don't waste their time. Have meetings over lunch (you always buy). That way, you have the benefit of a congenial conversation coupled with time required for the project. And everyone likes a free lunch.

- Save major parties and celebrations for important milestones and accomplishments. Members of your team, especially those with life commitments such as small children, may resent too much time spent on work-related dinners. Many people regard evening "get-togethers" as extensions to their workday.

- Know how you react when you are under stress. If you tend to get "snappy" with people during stressful times, the best way to keep that from causing problems with your project team is to recognize it and try to moderate those tendencies.

- Use written messages like golden bullets. Written communications are important, but fire off very few and make them count.

Good leaders know how to prepare effective messages. Here are some guidelines to help your messages achieve your best intentions:

- Always think through the politics before you communicate. Before you send any message (oral or written), consider the potential effects the message may have after it is received.

- Be aware of all the people who will receive your message, even if they're not on the address line or at the meeting. Consider the people who will be copied, given the cover sheet, or told about the message over coffee in the cafeteria.

- Decide on both the format for the message (letter, e-mail, fax, telephone, face-to-face) and the timing. Writing is permanent and not soon forgotten, so always make written messages something you won't mind being brought up again. Oral messages can be misconstrued, so if absolute clarity over time is required, put it in writing as well.

- Make sure the content, tone, vocabulary, style, length, and grammar are exactly what you want to say. Unfortunately, this is often forgotten when writing e-mails.

◆ Always follow up on the message to see if it was received and understood. Note reactions and ramifications so you can do better next time—or change the approach if the message didn't accomplish what you expected.

◆ When in doubt, don't send the message.

◆ Keep written communication brief and to the point unless complex technical instructions are involved. No written communication should exceed one or two pages; otherwise, almost no one will plod through it.

Listening Effectively

When you meet with people, make sure that you listen twice as much as you talk. Ask a lot of questions, particularly for clarification. For example, when someone on the All-Star Cable project team says they are "having some trouble" with the vendors, the project manager needs to ask a lot of questions before giving any advice. Ask questions like the following:

◆ What kind of trouble are you having?

◆ How often is this happening?

◆ How do you respond to them when this happens?

◆ What have you done about this so far?

Get them to paint a picture for you so that you can see the "trouble" they are having. Then you are in a position to help them. Don't jump in too fast and try to fix the problem.

Taking the Reins Through Visibility

The project manager's classic mistake is to climb into an ivory tower and effectively disappear. The disappearing act may be accidental as you get buried in a project problem, management dispute, paperwork, or just a lot of busy days. But the results are the same. When you're invisible, the project team assumes one or all of the following:

◆ You don't care about the project or them.

◆ The project is unimportant to the organization.

◆ You are an ineffective project manager/team leader who should be replaced.

Also note that, if team members perceive you to be invisible, they may feel free to make decisions and act on their own, sometimes to the detriment of the project. Worse, if you are perceived to be invisible and team members perceive they are working on a doomed project, they may work actively to save their own reputations (and point fingers at you) instead of pulling together to make the project succeed.

For these reasons, you must become a Visible (with a capital V) member of the project team as well as a leader. Avoid the ivory tower routine and rendezvous regularly with the troops. Pitch in. When a body is needed for anything from moving furniture around to stapling 500 copies of the agenda for a frantic project member who is putting them together for a user conference, be there if possible. Role up your sleeves and become an in-the-trenches hard worker who inspires the team as well as leads it. You'll make friends, will make your workers appreciate you as a comrade, and will get a little project-related work done at the same time. One of the best project managers we ever worked for said, "I never ask my project team members to do something I wouldn't be willing to do myself." That kind of attitude inspires trust and respect.

Use Management by Walking Around (MBWA)

Remember that the channels of communication are best opened by you being physically visible. When supervising a project, just walking around and chatting with the participants will improve both the quality and the timeliness of the work underway; it also will give you essential information on project progress. Building a 20-story condo complex? On the phone, the foreman may claim progress on the tenth story. On-site, however, you may see that only nine stories are in place. By using MBWA, you get a real-life assessment of project progress, some exercise, and the chance to work out problems team members are experiencing. At the same time, you are building visibility as project leader, are establishing and strengthening communications channels, and are making sure that everyone knows you care about the project. It helps if you appear that you love working on it, too!

Leading a Technical Project When You Don't Have Expertise

You don't have to have technical knowledge to provide leadership to a technical project or to supervise engineers working in a discipline you know little or nothing about. Instead, you need to be an efficient project manager capable of listening intelligently and understanding and handling the human and business issues at hand. Yes, it's possible that technical people may try to "snow" you with jargon, but you can work around these efforts to stall the project.

Always talk regularly to each member of the technical team, insist on periodic updates, and ask (with genuine enthusiasm) to see results, no matter how small. At the same time, never allow a single team member to be the only repository of key project data. Instead, insist that more than one member of the technical team understand (or at least be involved in) key technical areas. Keep copies of work descriptions on paper or on backup tapes/disks and archive them regularly (off-site!) as additional backup and protection from acts of God (and disgruntled workers).

Being All Things to All People

As project manager, you change roles from day to day. One day, you may feel like a hands-on manager in charge of a group of productive, motivated employees. The next day, you may be relegated to a position that's really little more than that of petty bureaucrat, shuffling papers and dull appointments all day.

The role of project manager also changes as the project proceeds. At the beginning, during the initiation and planning phases, your role focuses on creating a vision for the project and working with stakeholders (managers, customers, and other project beneficiaries) to reach consensus on the goals and objectives of the project. During this planning phase, the project team may occasionally complain that all they seem to do is crank out paper. However, gently remind them that all that "paper" will pay off when you move to the execute phase. Then, as the project proceeds into the executing phase, your role involves supporting, coaching, and otherwise guiding people to the promised land of project completion. You'll also have to spend time communicating the project status to the stakeholders to make sure they remain happy with the results you are achieving as the project proceeds.

In all these roles, you will be expected to excel. Obviously, you can't be all things to all people. But as a project manager who is also a leader, you better be—at the very least—a lot of the right things to most of the project team.

The Leader in Times of Crisis

To be the authority when things don't go right is the toughest challenge of all. You may have done 699 things right but blown it accidentally on number 700. Sadly, no one will look at the 699. Instead, they'll focus on—well, you can guess!

Avoiding problems is the obvious approach, but what can you do when your vendor doesn't deliver your cable boxes on time for the pilot? Before considering a long trip to a place where no one can find you, consider these alternatives:

- Study the mishap, whether it's a failure to deliver or a public relations nightmare. Get a firm grasp on all aspects of the problem and focus on how it impacts project objectives, budget, and schedule.

- Call the team or team managers to an emergency meeting. Hopefully, you already have a risk plan for a delay in the delivery of the cable boxes, but also ask for suggestions and recommendations from the team. Weigh each recommendation carefully and consider the cost and time for implementation.

- Adjourn to your office, home, or another quiet haven and pour over the suggestions to see which will cost the least and can be implemented the fastest with the least damage to project outcomes.

- Act to salvage the project. Be up-front and honest with management, customers, and team members. Quick response, decisive decisions, and team spirit must be used to pull the project out of the hole. If you need 24 hours to revise the project schedule, then have a couple of cups of coffee and do it. Most important, communicate the schedule fix and any new elements to bridge the gap causing the problem.

- Never let a project get the best of you. Eat well, get enough sleep, and work hard while taking care of your team members and yourself.

If you can do all the things we've talked about in this chapter and still keep your spirits up and your focus on the project goals, you'll become the leader the project needs to make it to the finish line.

The Least You Need to Know

- To lead any project, visibility and appropriate communications are essential.

- Your team members look to you for problem resolution, team management, and both positive and negative feedback. Make sure you give them what they need in appropriate doses.

- No project is an island. Your dedication is central to maintaining the schedule and controlling the budget to bring the project to successful fruition.

- Anyone with a good plan, dedication, and basic people skills can lead a project. The trick is really the people skills.

- A true leader can fix almost any project problem by adjusting objectives and realigning the project team and stakeholders.

Chapter 19

What an Organization!

In This Chapter

◆ Creating an organization that works

◆ Pointing team members in the same direction

◆ Considering various project structures

◆ Communicating, coordinating, and cooperating are the keys to teamwork

◆ Keeping focused on the end results

How can you know what the right organization is for your project team? How do you get people to move where you want them to go? Who should lead the work and who should follow orders? In this chapter, we look at some of the pros, cons, and alternatives so you can organize your players for maximum impact.

No Easy Task, but Someone Has to Organize These Guys

Creating a productive project organization is no easy task, even for a small project. Politics get in the way, people get sick, and your boxcar load of cable boxes from Mexico fails to materialize—and someone always gets blamed. As on *Jeopardy*, the answer is: "Build an adaptive structure coupled with personnel contingency plans." The question is: "How do I organize my project team correctly?" There are the three C's in successful project organizations: Communication, Cooperation, and Coordination.

Making Sure Everyone Is Pulling in the Same Direction

Structuring a project organization means more than just choosing team members and committing outside vendors to specific tasks. To function effectively, your project team members require clear reporting responsibilities and a roadmap to their location in the project. On top of this, your core team may require ancillary support such as administrative assistants, computer installers, technical help, and others who are trained, ready, available, and prepared for secondary but vital duties.

Turning all these people into a viable project team involves cementing relationships, making the right resources available in a timely manner to the right people, implementing reporting relationships, and establishing a schedule that works. Because people are involved, it sounds easier than it is.

The Human Drama—Personality, Politics, and Corporate Culture

To help you understand ways to organize the people in your project, you can compare your project team to the cast members in a play or a movie. This was a very effective metaphor used by Dutch Holland in his book, *Change Is the Rule*. You have the producers and backers of the project (managers and other stakeholders), the director (the project manager), the main actors (the workers who play a role throughout all or most of the project), the bit players (people who do one important task and then disappear from the scene), and the cameo players (the important people, such as consultants or advisors, who may add value to the project but don't necessarily stick around through the entire play). You also have the special-effects folks and the production crew, who have special skills but aren't as visible as other members of the cast. You may have prima donnas and stars in your project team, and these people need special care and attention.

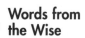

Words from the Wise

There are two ways of being creative. One can sing and dance. Or one can create an environment in which singers and dancers flourish.

—Warren Bennis

First You Need to Give Them a Script

One of the first considerations in developing your team is the same for the actors in a play. They need a script to work from. What is your script, you may ask? It is your project plan. They need to see how the role they play helps the production (the project) be successful. Without that, they will make up lines, work on things that are not important, and possibly make some poor decisions. Just like actors, if you simply ask them to ad lib, unless they are very experienced, they won't do very well.

Avoiding Casting Catastrophes

As you consider the organization of your cast, you'll need to develop some procedures to get things done. Lead players, bit players, and cameo players might possibly be directed (supervised) by assistant directors (other managers), and the production crew might work for lead crew or assistant producers.

Sometimes, after you design your ideal project organization, you'll find that the first choice for a team member in a particular role isn't even a possibility. For example, a person you would like to use in the project may not be available because of commitments to other, higher-priority projects. Or you may ask to use one person from an organization and the manager from the group assigns a different person to your project. Thus, you may not get the experience you wanted in the cast and you might have to adjust the schedule to accommodate for the less experienced actor to learn their lines.

If you say you need a person with a particular skill for your project and the line manager (middle manager) assigns a person to you, you usually must accept this person's judgment unless you can make a good case for someone you have more direct experience with. If you find out later that the assigned person lacks the required skills, you can negotiate or look at other alternatives.

Project managers often need to make these kinds of concessions to other managers to get people for a project. It's like signing up Sean Connery to star in your movie and then finding out that Eddie Murphy was assigned the role instead. Obviously, the script and direction will require some adaptations.

The Proud, the Few, the Project Team

When talented actors work on a play together, they all share and support the same goal (to produce a successful play). To this end, the actors, great and small, generally follow the lead of the director, and each player does his or her best to fulfill the specific role assigned in each play. Even the stars, like Jennifer Aniston and Brad Pitt, must follow the rules of the game. People on your project team need to play their roles in the same way.

For the people working on your project to become a real team, some specific things need to happen with your coaching and leadership as project manager. Project members need to …

◆ Realize that they'll be working on activities that involve more than one person. Therefore, they'll need to communicate and cooperate with each other to get things done.

◆ Share common methods and tools for assessing and communicating the status of the project.

◆ Identify and solve problems together—and then live with the results (together) and agree to support the common decision in public.

◆ Accept the fact that, if one person makes a mistake, the entire team suffers. Therefore, they need to help each other avoid as many mistakes as possible.

◆ Realize that new people will be joining and other people will be leaving the project as time goes on, but the overall team structure and project goals will remain the same until the project reaches fruition.

◆ And finally, recognize that changes will occur and they must be flexible enough to adjust and use the change control methods that we will describe in much more detail in Chapter 24.

When other organizations or departments are involved, positive interaction between the project manager and these organizations is also critical to creating a good team. The relationships among line, staff, vendor, customer, and project personnel must be tempered with mutual trust.

On Becoming a Team: The Basic Ways to Organize People

Even though infinite possible combinations of people are involved, there are only a few basic ways you should structure the organization of a project. These include functional (or line) organizations, pure-project structures, matrix organizations, or mixed organizational structures. These structures may be distributed over multiple locations as well, making the organization more of a virtual team in cyberspace rather than a group of people in a defined location. And as you'd expect, each organization has its pros and cons.

The Functional Project Organization

On a project that uses people from the same organization, the existing line organization can be used to manage the project. This organizational structure is appropriate when the project is clearly the responsibility of one department. Many small projects use the functional organization as the project organization. A functional project is assigned to the functional department or division in a company that has the most interest and technical ability to complete the project. Almost all tasks in a project organized as part of a functional organization will be completed within the one functional area. Existing managers in the department often double as project managers.

The advantages of using a functional organization to complete a project include the following:

◆ **Familiarity of the team.** The team members are already familiar with each other, and the skill levels of the staff are clearly understood.

◆ **Established administrative systems.** The general administrative policies and procedures are already understood by the team and cost centers.

◆ **Staff availability.** The staff is readily available to the project because the line managers control the staff assignments. Thus, there are few, if any, interdepartmental conflicts over the use of resources.

◆ **Scheduling efficiency.** The scheduling of staff can be highly efficient. As a staff member is required, the person can immediately be assigned to a task and then return to routine work without serious logistical interruptions.

◆ **Clear authority.** The lines of authority and communication are understood. Thus, the conflicts between project authority and line authority are minimized.

The disadvantages of using a functional organization include:

◆ **Project isolation.** The project may be completed in isolation from other parts of the company and may fail to realize larger strategic goals as a result. However, if new collaboration, networking, and web-based tools are employed, this isolation can be minimized.

◆ **Limited resources.** The project is limited to the technical resources within the department, which may not be adequate to complete the tasks required. Of course, outside vendors and consultants can be hired, but expertise within other departments of the company is not readily available. This may lead to inefficiencies or redundancies in the project organization.

♦ **Bureaucratic procedures.** In a functional organization, the project manager usually has very weak decision-making authority. There may be more levels of approval than really necessary for the project because of the established bureaucracy in the line organization. This may impede progress and slow decision-making.

♦ **Lack of project focus.** The project may lack focus or priority in a functional organization because it is not the only work being done. Thus, routine departmental work may interfere with project work. In addition, motivation for project work may suffer because the project is considered "additional" or "optional" work as opposed to being a clear responsibility.

♦ **Department orientation.** The project may suffer from "department-think." This occurs when the priorities of the department become the project priorities, regardless of the actual goals for the project. Work outside the department's normal concerns is given little attention, and the "finished" project may not be complete or may suffer quality problems as a result.

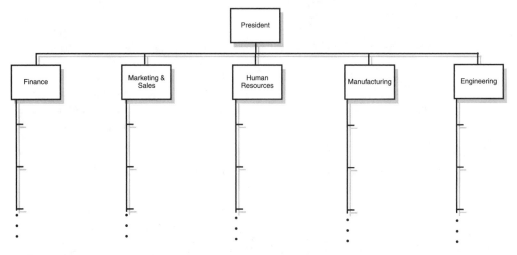

A functional organization.

The Pure-Project Organization

In a pure-project structure, a team or "task force" is put together to accomplish the project's goals. In such an organization, all the team members report to the project manager during the course of the project. The team members do not have responsibility to other managers or jobs during the course of their work on the project. When a team member's responsibility for the project is complete, the person returns to another job or is assigned to another project. Only one project and one job are assigned at a time.

In the direct version of the pure-project structure, every project team member reports directly to the project manager. This is appropriate for small projects with 15 or fewer people involved. In the indirect version of the pure-project structure (suitable for larger projects), the project manager may have assistant managers or supervisors to manage subprojects or functional areas within the project. As in an ordinary line organization, the supervisors and assistants report directly to the project manager, and the various functional teams within the project report to the second-level managers. Extremely large projects may have multiple management levels, just like a corporation.

Pure-project organizations are found in companies fulfilling large government projects or in some engineering-driven companies that produce predictable model updates for their products. Large construction projects often employ a pure-project organization as well. If work on a complex, priority project spans a year or more, a pure-project organization is often an advantage.

The advantages of the pure-project organization include the following:

- **Clear project authority.** The project manager has true line authority over the entire project. Thus, there is always a clear channel for resolving project conflicts and determining priorities. The unity of command in a pure-project organization results in each subordinate having one and only one direct boss—a clear advantage in most situations.

- **Simplified project communications.** Communication and decision-making within the project are simplified because everyone reports to the same project manager and focuses on the attainment of the same project goals.

- **Access to special expertise.** If similar projects will be completed by the company on a cyclic basis, specific expertise in the components of the project will be developed over time. It simply becomes a matter of transferring the experts to the right project at the right time.

- **Project focus and priority.** The pure-project organization supports a total view of the project and a strong, separate identity on the part of the participants. This helps keeps the project focused and integrated.

There are distinct disadvantages to the pure-project approach, however, including the following:

- **Duplication of efforts.** If a company has multiple projects with important goals in progress at the same time, some efforts may be duplicated, making the overall cost of the projects higher than necessary.

♦ **Unclear loyalties and motivations.** Project members form strong attachments to the project and each other, which is good. When the project is terminated, however, the team must be disbanded, and this leads to uncertainty and conflict. Team members fear layoffs or anticipate assignments in undesirable projects in the future. Thus, keeping technically qualified people happy over the long haul becomes a major challenge. Your staffing management plan should clearly address this problem if you use this model.

♦ **Intracompany rivalry.** Rivalry and competition may become strong between various projects in a company that uses pure-project organization for its major projects. This may result in a company that competes with itself instead of with the competition—an ugly state of affairs.

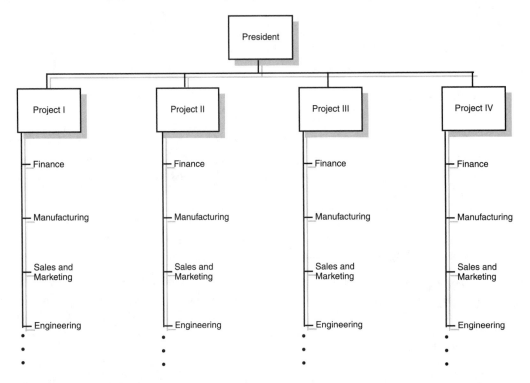

A pure-project organization.

The Matrix Organization

Implementing project management techniques sets in motion a significant change in the culture of an organization. One of the more common results of using project management in business is the introduction of "matrix management"—a situation in which people report to multiple managers. Matrix management involves coordinating a web of relationships that come about when people join the project team and are subject to the resulting multiple authority-responsibility-accountability relationships in the organization.

The *matrix organization* is an attempt to take advantage of the benefits of a pure-project organization while maintaining the advantages of the functional organization. It is rare to find pure-project or pure-functional organizations in business any more. Matrix organizations are typical today, even when other project management tools aren't involved.

Project Lingo

A **matrix organization** is one in which a project manager shares responsibility with the functional managers for assigning the priorities and for directing the work of individuals assigned to the project.

In a matrix organization, a clear project team is established that crosses organizational boundaries. Thus, team members may come from various departments. A project manager for each project is clearly defined, and projects are managed as separate and focused activities. The project manager may report to a higher-level executive or to one of the functional managers with the most interest in the project. However, the specific team members still report to their functional departments and maintain responsibilities for routine departmental work in their functional areas. In addition, people may be assigned to multiple project teams with different responsibilities. The problem of coordination that plagues other project structures is minimized because the most important personnel for a project work together as a defined team within the matrix project structure.

The management responsibilities in these projects are temporary—a supervisor on one project may be a worker on another project, depending on the skills required. If project managers in a matrix situation do not have good relationships with line managers in the organization, conflicts may arise over employees' work and priorities. Not everyone adapts well to the matrix structure for this and other related reasons.

The complexity that a matrix organization causes is clear: People have multiple managers, multiple priorities, and multiple role identities. Because of these complexities, before an organization enters into matrix organizational structures, at least two of the following criteria for the project or the enterprise should be met:

◆ A need to share scarce or unique resources that are required in more than one project or functional area

◆ A requirement for management to provide high levels of information processing and communication to complete the project

♦ Pressure from the outside by customers or agencies to have one person or group centralize control of the project even though the project may be carried out by other groups in the organization

In cases in which projects meet these criteria, the matrix organization has the following distinct advantages:

♦ **Clear project focus.** The project has clear focus and priority because it has its own separate organization and management. Most of the planning and control advantages of a pure-project structure are realized in a matrix organization.

♦ **Flexible staffing.** Staffing is relatively flexible in matrix organizations because resources from various line organizations are available without job reassignment. Scarce technical resources are available to a wide range of projects in a company that regularly employs matrix-organized projects.

♦ **Adaptability to management needs and skills.** The authority of the project manager can be expansive or limited, depending on the priority of the project. If a project manager has strong authority, he or she has command authority over most of the project, and is assigned to the project full-time, this would be called a "strong matrix" structure. If a project manager has weak authority, is assigned only part-time, and the line managers have a strong influence on project activities, this type of organization would be dubbed a "weak matrix" structure. There is also a structure called a "balanced matrix" structure that falls in between. Thus, the matrix organization can be adapted to a wide range of projects—some that need strong support from line managers and some that require independent management.

♦ **Staff development opportunities.** People can be given new challenges and responsibilities that are not as likely to be offered in a purely functional organization. People can gain exposure to new technical areas, develop management skills, and have new experiences that maintain their interest and motivation at work. Ultimately, these new experiences can lead to more effective employees with high degrees of independence and flexibility. And because people tend to be more responsible for the quality of their own work in project-oriented groups, overall corporate productivity can improve.

♦ **Adaptability to business changes.** Matrix organizations can adapt more quickly to changing technological and market conditions than traditional, purely functional organizations. This is largely because of the high people-to-people contact in these organizations. In addition, matrix-organized projects encourage entrepreneurship and creative thinking that crosses functional responsibilities.

The disadvantages and potential conflicts within a matrix organization must be understood and dealt with to take advantage of the benefits of matrix management. The more frequently reported problems in matrix managed organizations include:

- **Built-in conflicts.** Conflicts between line management priorities and project management priorities are inevitable. The question of who is in charge affects both the project and routine departmental work. The division of authority and responsibility relationships in matrix organizations is inherently complex. Matrix organizations are no place for intractable, autocratic managers with narrow views of organizational responsibilities.

- **Resistance to termination.** As in pure-project organizations, team members may prefer their project roles to their line responsibilities, creating interesting motivational challenges for managers. Because the team members have unique identities and relationships in their project roles, matrixed projects often resist termination.

- **Complex command and authority relationships.** There is no unity of command in a matrix organization—a clear violation of traditional management principles. The team member is often caught between conflicting demands of the line manager and the project manager. The discomfort and uncertainty of having more than one boss at the same time cannot be adequately described to someone who has never experienced the situation. Of course, if the two bosses are adequately trained and are open in their communications, many of these difficulties can be resolved or eliminated.

- **Complex employee recognition systems.** In a matrix organization, which manager should complete the employee's performance reviews or make recommendations for raises? If the reward responsibilities and authorities of the project manager and the line manager are not clearly identified, the employee may feel unrecognized. It is imperative that both line responsibilities and project responsibilities are accounted for in the employee's performance review process. Some form of reward system needs to be established for team members within the project—whether this is just public acknowledgment of a job well done or formal monetary rewards depends on the project and your budget.

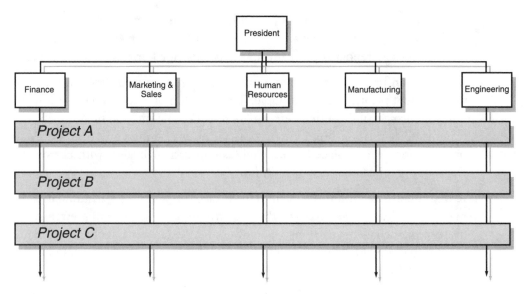

A matrix organization.

The Mixed Organization

Some companies employ a mixture of functional, matrix, and pure-project organizations to accomplish enterprise goals. In companies with a wide range of projects, a Project Management Office (PMO) may be set up to help administer projects as well. The people in this office provide expertise and assistance in planning and tracking projects. In other companies, the PMO may become a division in its own right with full-time project managers and staff responsible for project-oriented activities.

When a project has more than one purpose, mixed organizational structures are usually the norm. The space shuttle missions are a perfect example. Getting the astronauts ready for a flight is one project. Building and installing a new robot arm is another. Although someone is responsible for coordinating all the projects and making sure they get done at the same time so the launch can happen as planned, the people are organized on a subproject basis. The subprojects require a completely different set of team members and organizational structures.

Mixed organizations are not distinguishable from most matrix organizations because of the complexity of relationships, and most of the strengths and weaknesses of a matrix organization also apply to a mixed organizational structure. The unique problem in mixed organizations is one caused by the extreme flexibility in the way the organization adapts to project work. This leads to potential incompatibilities, confusion, conflicts, and duplications of effort if the managers are not adequately trained to deal with these complexities.

Which Structure Should You Use?

The organization you choose for most ordinary business projects will probably be an adaptation of a matrix or functional organization. In the All-Star Cable case study, the project manager decided to use a strong matrix organization with a mixture of functional people from the company and consultants with skills and experience that were not available within the company.

Project size, project length, the experience of the team members, the location of the project, and factors unique to the project all have influence on the selection of a project organizational form. For example, on a small, short-term project for creating a new process for bringing new customers into All-Star Cable, the organization of the project might be along functional lines that already exist with the involvement of a few outside resources and key vendors to complete specific tasks. On a larger project to design and build the next generation of cable TV, namely Movies-on-Demand, a matrix organization might be more appropriate because of the wide range of involvement and ongoing communication required across departments of manufacturing, marketing, engineering, and services.

Because large organizations may be distributed over multiple locations, management authority is increasingly being wielded via virtual management tools such as e-mail, computer networks, team collaboration software, and the web. This is a growing management challenge on large projects, but it's one that will likely continue to evolve to make project teams more virtual and easier to move among multiple project priorities. The trends toward virtual management and *just-in-time employment* almost dictate matrix-style organizations with local control of basic administrative services and reporting lines to the project managers for the working aspects of the jobs.

CAUTION

Risk Management

Be aware that the combination of team players on a task always makes a difference. The combination will work either for you or against you. Both the personalities and the skills need to be complementary, especially on long project tasks in which people are in close proximity. It's important that the sum of the people should always equal more than the total of the individuals.

Project Lingo

Just-in-time employment is a process for maximizing the value of the people you add to the project team by using them only when their needed and releasing them to their functional boss for the rest of the time.

Working with the Outsiders

We've already discussed working with outside vendors of all sorts in Chapter 15. When assembling your organization, however, it's important to remember to tightly bind outsiders into the tangled web you weave for your project organization. Most key vendors should be included in the planning phases and should be updated regularly on the project's status. This will help you avoid bills for time not worked but committed to because your project ran late. Outside vendors should also clearly understand reporting relationships, invoicing requirements, and terms of payment. If your vendors are "hooked in" to information technologies, you can employ e-mail, the web, and other e-business technologies, as well as face-to-face contact, to help you do this.

Managing Outside Resources

Don't forget that outside resources require careful tracking and management, even though the people you work with may be paid by other companies. You must ensure that the work is being completed on schedule and that your "outsiders" don't take on more than they can complete—whether it's your task, the company's workload, or client projects.

The Care and Feeding of the Off-Site Team

Many projects require resources that are available only off site. Whether essential personnel are working in the building next door or in manufacturing plants in Singapore, these groups require extra care. Without the MBWA (management by walking around, discussed in Chapter 17) technique at your disposal, its easy for project workers to assume that, if you're out of sight, the project is okay to put out of mind.

Obviously, you'll want to employ all the modern tools of intranetworking and electronic communication with these off-site people. A little human contact, however, is still a good idea for keeping team members in multiple locations on track. Make a few personal visits and phone calls to show your support and interest. If the locations are far removed, a trusted assistant project manager is often the answer. Teleconferencing and e-mail are increasingly important tools in keeping long-distance, distributed projects in synch, but you should still make yourself or a surrogate manager available on-site on a regular basis to ensure that all is well and stays that way.

Focus on the Launch

As with the larger projects, such as All-Star Cable's Movies-on-Demand project, the complexities in project organization multiply as the project goals become more complicated. Whether your project is large or small, however, the actors in your play need to know who the director is, what their role is, and the script that they have to work with. As project manager, you must balance the workload, skills, and reporting structure of the organization to achieve its goals of on-time, within-budget delivery. If you do this, it really doesn't matter how you structure the team—as long as the people make it to the opening curtain at the same time.

The Least You Need to Know

◆ In addition to the right team members, the correct organizational structure (functional, project, matrix, or mixed) is key to managing a successful project.

◆ Smaller teams are usually more efficient, but sometimes this isn't an option. Therefore, organizing the team into smaller groups is often an option to make things manageable.

◆ As project manager, you're the director for the team. If you don't make the roles clear and assign people to specific parts, the cast won't know how to work together to stage a successful play.

◆ The assignment of internal staff from other departments must be handled carefully to avoid political problems.

Chapter 20

Operating Guidelines: Setting Up to Get Things Done

In This Chapter

- ◆ The process groups within every phase of the project
- ◆ Establishing administrative procedures
- ◆ The importance of a project diary
- ◆ Ordinary and fun things to keep people motivated

When you initiated the project with the stakeholders, you already established some basic rules for the project in the statement of work (refer to Chapter 7) including authorities and reporting requirements. Now it's time to extend those rules and expand the operating procedures for the entire project team.

Before we talk about procedures, though, let's talk about processes.

The Project Processes in Each Phase

In each phase of the project there are basic project management processes that will aid you in organizing the project—these are called project processes, and they can be further divided into the following categories:

- **Initiating Process.** This *process* begins a phase of the project and authorizes the work in that phase.

- **Planning Process.** This process defines and refines the goals for a phase of the project and includes selecting the best course of action from all the alternatives.

- **Controlling Process.** This process ensures that the goals of the phase are met by monitoring and measuring progress regularly to check for any deviation from the project plan so that corrective action can be taken when necessary.

- **Executing Process.** This process consists of coordinating the people and other resources needed to carry out the activities in a phase.

- **Closing Process.** This process brings an acceptable and orderly end to a phase.

The general project processes may vary in intensity depending on the project phase. For example, the initiating processes are much more in evidence during the beginning of any of the four project life cycle phases. By focusing on the initiating processes during the beginning of each phase, it helps to ensure that the project stays focused on the business need that it was supposed to deal with. Controlling processes are important processes during the execution phase of the project, but they should be recognized and used from the beginning to control costs and schedule from the beginning of the project. Finally, the processes overlap, so that the closing of one phase provides input for the next. For example, in the All-Star Cable project, the closing of the project definition phase requires the acceptance of the project charter document by the steering committee. In addition to closing out the definition phase, the project charter defines the activities that will be undertaken during the project planning phase as the project team plans for Movies-on-Demand.

Project Lingo

The Project Management Institute defines a **process** as a series of actions bringing about a result.

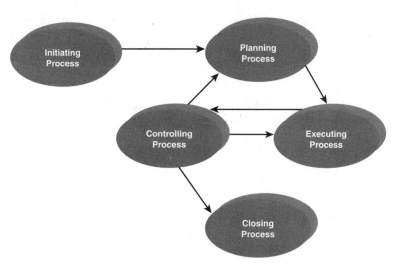

In each phase of a project, you will need to use each of these processes. Arrows represent the flow of information and represent the links among the process groups within a phase.

Project Processes vs. Project Procedures

Unlike the project processes, the operating procedures for your project should help you guide people to work on the right tasks at the right time. Operating procedures also help you stay abreast of the status of every activity and cost associated with your project. You need to delegate the work and gather information without de-motivating the team with too much administration, paperwork, and redundant communications. In other words, your operating procedures should help you manage the project but not keep you from getting the project done.

Operating procedures should also allow you to gather the information necessary to make changes in a timely fashion, thereby maintaining control of the schedule, resources, and the costs—and ultimately guiding your project to completion on time and within budget.

The Things That Need to Get Done

Getting work done on the project should always be the first priority. To get the actual work started, you'll need to delegate all the work that isn't your own responsibility. You should do this in meetings, in written communications, and through reviewing the project plan with team members. As you start the project, however, you'll also need to develop a process or work schedule for the many activities that won't be found on the work plan or task list for the project. These required tasks include the following:

♦ Coordinating activities among groups and vendors involved in your project. On large projects, project managers spend a lot of time coordinating the interfaces between people, vendors, managers, and clients as well as controlling schedules.

♦ Monitoring progress on the project. Managers must compare the time, cost, and performance of the project to the budget, schedule, and tasks defined in the approved project plan. This must be done in an integrated manner at regular intervals, not in a haphazard, arbitrary way. Any significant departures from the budget and the schedule must be reported immediately because these anomalies affect the viability and success of the entire project.

> **Time Is Money**
>
> The supervisory role may not appear to be a task, but project management is about managing projects, so you should treat the operations side of any project as a set of tasks and list them as such. Having said that, make sure you have included all these items in your project plan.

♦ Adapting the project schedule, budget, and work plan as necessary to keep the project on track. As the project progresses, changes in the original plan may be required for a number of reasons. It is the project manager's responsibility to make sure that these changes are appropriate, valid, and approved.

♦ Documenting project progress and changes and communicating these to team members. The quality and level of detail of your reports and communications need to be consistent, reliable, and appropriate for each level of the project team.

To do all these things, you'll need operating procedures and policies. Necessary guidelines start with the general approach of working together as a team and go on to include formal and informal communications and procedures for doing the coordinating, tracking, adapting, and documenting necessary to keep the project pointed in the right direction.

> **Time Is Money**
>
> When distributing project status reports, make sure they are received, read, and understood by all team members. You may want to create two versions: one for people who need details and a summary or simple format for the less technical or less involved members of the team (such as customers or managers).

Formal and Informal Ways to Tell What's Going On

Every project should have both formal and informal monitoring and reporting activities. The larger and more complex the project, the more monitoring and administration is required. Regardless of the type of administration, the goal is to keep your team working toward the final deadline, within the budget, and in line with the goals specified for the project.

Formal monitoring includes reports, audits, and project review meetings. Informal monitoring includes general conversations with the team, ongoing interactions with stakeholders, and observations during MBWA (management by walking around) sessions (discussed in Chapter 17). The size and complexity of the project, along with the culture of the organization, determine the extent and type of monitoring to use.

Keep in Touch

If any of your vendors or project participants are at a different location, a phone call now and then just to see how things are going is vital. This is also a good time to provide positive feedback about accomplishments to date.

Never be a pest in your MBWA program—whether you're a physical presence or a virtual one in cyberspace. You want to be encouraging and motivating. If you are perceived as a spy, the results of your monitoring efforts will backfire. People don't want you standing over their shoulders, especially if they have creative or thought-intensive work to complete. Think how you would feel if your boss came over two or three times an hour and asked how you were doing. For best results, make the visits unpredictable, spontaneous, and sincere.

Start with the Open-Door Policy

Your operating and monitoring activities should start with informal guidelines, and the most important of these is the open door policy (ODP). The ODP should be the premise of everyday life on the project. Every organization claims to offer such a policy in which employees can discuss a difficult problem with their boss or boss's boss, but few people actually take advantage of this "opportunity" for fear of retribution. You must make sure that your team actually believes in the open door policy (even if your open door is really an e-mail address); otherwise, all the communications, tracking, and other procedures are of limited value. ODP is not just a "gripe line"; it's also a way to keep good ideas flowing and is a key aspect of identifying issues before they turn into problems. To repair project pitfalls quickly or to minimize their impact, you must be available to all team members regardless of rank, location, or job. The open door policy must be real.

The advantage of the ODP approach is simple. When people have little experience working together, communication can become a bottleneck, especially if someone tries to conceal a problem to save face. Team members who are aware of the problem must feel comfortable presenting the project manager with their concerns. That's where the open door policy comes in. If you are a trusted leader, you'll be told about predicaments before they become disasters.

If people know your door is usually open, they'll learn to respect the times when you need to close it for private meetings or intensive work sessions. Sometimes you may want to use a closed door as a filter for trivia. The occasional closed door informs people to make minor decisions on their own that day and invites them to depend on themselves to answer ordinary questions. When the closed door is used with sensitivity and in contrast to the ODP, it can be a powerful tool for getting things done.

Establish an Environment of Motivation

Beyond the ODP, you need to cultivate an environment of motivation around your project. People often refer to the work environment as the "culture" of the organization, and you want your policies and actions to establish a positive culture for getting things done. Here are some things you can do as project manager to ensure that the culture you nurture is one of motivation (as opposed to frustration):

- Lead by example. Arrive at work on time and work hard. Get things done as promised, be respectful of others' time, be knowledgeable about the project, and ask good questions when you don't have answers.

- Adopt a positive attitude and others will do the same.

- Respect your leaders and the staff will respect you. Never criticize management in public. Be considerate of others, even if you disagree with them.

- Never make promises that you know can't be kept.

- Don't be secretive about the project. Let people see the things they need to see such as reports, customer requests, and letters of appreciation.

- Don't try to conceal problems when you encounter them. Instead, seek advice from more senior or experienced people.

- Give people the attention they require. Initiate MBWA from day one and schedule (and keep) one-on-one meetings on a regular basis.

- Offer assignments that provide challenges, but don't challenge people to the point of exhaustion.

- Clearly define performance expectations before people start their tasks.

- Make all team members aware that their efforts are important and have a direct impact on the outcome of the project.

As the project progresses, remember to always acknowledge work well done but never reward mediocrity; otherwise, you'll end up with a mediocre project. We discourage monetary bonuses and exclusively individual awards. The results of such "incentives" are often counterproductive. Instead, offer public acknowledgment of good work at meetings or in status reports and provide group rewards for meeting milestones in the form of group events or tokens of appreciation that everyone on the team gets at the same time.

It is also important to have some fun on projects. This is an important part of creating a motivated team and a positive project culture. Here are some ideas to get you started:

- ◆ Use humor (sparingly) to loosen up tense situations. Sometimes a good laugh can break the ice so people can get on with solving the problem.

- ◆ Circulate cartoons that relate to projects. The Dilbert strip is a rich source, but there are others. Encourage team members to do the same.

- ◆ Copy articles about project disasters and circulate them. These usually are educational and can help team members see that their own problems pale by comparison.

- ◆ Have pizza parties for team successes (or for solving problems). A little bribery never hurts, especially if you need to ask people to stay overtime or work weekends.

Informal Meetings and One-on-Ones

Not all operations, reports, and meetings need to be formal and planned to be effective. Just inviting a team member or a few people who are working on the project to your office to sit and chat over coffee may be appropriate. Another useful technique is to schedule regular one-on-one meetings with staff members so they can go over their own concerns, not just yours. Giving team members an opportunity to tell you about the project from their point of view can be very enlightening. People will often let you know about particular problems and concerns in a one-on-one situation that they would never reveal in a meeting or report.

Administrative Procedures That Won't Hurt

Eventually, in spite of your good attitude and informal chats with people, you'll have to ask people to do administrative tasks like writing reports and reconciling expenses. Most people won't like it, but if you have a positive culture, they'll comply with your guidelines (most of the time and as long as you make the requirements clear in advance).

As you develop administrative procedures, be sure to collect only the information you'll use. At the beginning, you may collect more information in the form of reports and updates than you really need. As you realize you're gathering too much data, make sure you give the troops a break and tell them to simplify or shorten their reports. For the data you really need, make sure the information is stored for ready access and is easy to retrieve when you need to analyze it.

If your project is one of many similar projects in your organization, there probably are established operating and administrative procedures already in place to help you complete your ongoing responsibilities to the project. These include report formats, time frames for project review, and other tracking procedures.

If review procedures and administrative reports are not already well-established in your organization, you need to develop basic administrative procedures before you begin work on your project. To establish what you'll need, you must answer all of the following questions:

Words from the Wise

When people fill out time reports weekly, without writing down what they did daily, they are making up fiction. Such made-up data are almost worse than no data at all.

—James P. Lewis, *Fundamentals of Project Management*

♦ How will you assign the work? If team members are already clear on "who is going to do what" because of their involvement in the planning process, how will you coordinate these efforts?

♦ How will you measure the project's progress? Will you ask for formal updates, just walk around, or both?

♦ What kind of information do you need to assess progress? Make sure you let people know exactly what you need, or they won't give it to you.

♦ What standards will be used for evaluating the quality of project deliverables? People like to know these things in advance, as do customers paying for the project. People will try to achieve standards they know about—they will do what they think is best, but sometimes that isn't as good as you'd like.

♦ How many project meetings will you have? Which people need to attend? Be specific, put it in writing, and don't have too many meetings; otherwise, you'll never get any work done.

♦ How often will you update the project plan? We recommend that you do it as often as necessary, and that means every time a major change is made to objectives, the schedule, the budget, or sequences. And don't forget to date the plans so you know which plan is current and which should be sent to the archives.

♦ How will you determine what has been spent on the project? How will you verify the accuracy of these amounts? Maintaining control over expenditures is key to project success. Know how to get financial information before any money has been spent, and don't forget to have the accounting folks send copies of the invoices to you to review before outside vendors are paid.

♦ How often will reports on the project be made and to whom? The number, frequency, and detail of the reports and procedures you use will depend on the management requirements for your project, your manager's preferences, and your own need for ongoing information about the project. At a minimum, a formal status report should be distributed once a month for a long project and weekly for a shorter project.

Action items for different size projects.

Reports & Administrative Guidelines for Small and Large Projects

ACTION	DAILY	WEEKLY	MONTHLY	QUARTERLY
Informal Discussions with Team	S	L		
Staff Meetings with Managers		B		
Project Review Meeting with Team		S	L	
Status Report		S	L	
Project Audit (optional)				L
Team Building Activity			B	
Report to Management			B	

S = **Small Project**
L = **Large Project**
B = **Both Small and Large Projects**

There's always an excuse to produce too many paper and e-mail messages. Like advertising, too many "communications" of the same types and duration degrades their impact. (Ever notice how, on the most boring freeway journey, you tune out the billboards after the first 20?) The basic rule of thumb is to use multiple channels and target the message specifically to particular audiences. A message that is meant to address everyone will end up addressing no one and will be ignored. That's why the communication plan must be carefully controlled.

The Reports You May Need

Your stakeholders, managers, and customers deserve informed communication about the project on a timely basis. In addition to a regular *status report*—which contains information on current progress, schedule changes, and budgets—On large projects, there may be cost-variance reports, load-leveling reports, supply inventories, and other formal documentation to track specific aspects of the project.

Project Lingo

Different reports will target different audiences. **Status reports** are targeted for project stakeholders. **Weekly update reports** are targeted to the project team, including vendors who are part of the team.

In addition to general status reports, other reports may be required to both inform and motivate team members. A daily or *weekly update report* on large projects may be a good idea. The update report is a document distributed to all team members to emphasize important priorities, issues, or deadlines. The purpose of the update report is to convey information that might otherwise fall through the cracks. (If a major snag crops up, the update provides information to keep troops focused on their own work while you deal with the problem.)

Simple Forms to Create Useful Reports

Reports allow your team to follow the project "roadmap" and stay on track, but the reports need to be easy to produce. We suggest using a good project management program (see Chapter 30) or simple forms for gathering regular report information. Here are some forms we often use on our projects that may be useful for yours.

Schedule update forms. You will need to update the schedule as the project progresses and evolves. Team members should be notified each time the "map" changes, for whatever reason, so they can review the master chart and adjust their duties to match.

Supply and equipment request forms. Team members will require supplies and possibly equipment you haven't considered. Give them a simple worksheet to complete so they can tell you what they need before they need it.

Status reporting forms. If you don't use a groupware reporting system on a computer network that reminds people about status reports and other administrative requirements, paper systems can accomplish the same goals. Simply give each team member a stack of forms for reporting their weekly and monthly progress. Add a section specifically for them to report problems and roadblocks getting in their way. You're more likely to get completed status updates when you provide the blank forms in advance and have an assigned person go around to pick them up at a specified date or time. The status forms should include blanks for providing the following kinds of information that should be included on every formal status report:

- Tasks completed since the last status report with dates completed

- Tasks in progress with forecasted completion dates

- Tasks planned with expected completion dates

- Budget expenditures

- Issues that need attention

- Recommendations for project improvements or changes

- Questions or items that require other people's approval or input

When everyone uses the same forms, it becomes easier to summarize, synthesize, and analyze the status information for the formal status report you'll write as the project manager.

Every Report Needs a Purpose

For each report (or form) you choose to use on your project, the following should be documented:

- How often is the report produced? Some reports are produced weekly. Others are submitted monthly or quarterly.

- What is contained in the report?

- Who is responsible for producing the report?

- What is the objective of the report?

- Who will follow up on action items identified in the report?

- Who is the intended audience for the report? For example, there are three potential audiences for status reports: team members on the project, company management, and customers or stakeholders (if there are any involved). The report to management and customers is typically more formal, but less detailed, than the report made to the team members. The reports that team members send to you (as project manager) probably have the most information; some of this information is for your eyes only, however, so you need to filter what you summarize for other staff and managers.

Writing status reports for various audiences allows you to synthesize the formal and informal monitoring you've been doing. It allows you to relate your progress to the original project plan and to understand any risks to meeting your planned goals.

Ask Two Final Questions Before You Start

Before any report or procedure becomes part of the bureaucratic process associated with your project, ask yourself the following questions:

Is this report or procedure the best way to communicate this information?

Is there some other form of communication or action that would be more expedient and just as useful?

Chapter 21, which is about making the most of your communications, will help you answer these questions.

Overdoing It

It's common to be too structured in organizing a project. While this sounds improbable at first, when you look at all the tasks and people that need coordinating, watch for the following problems as you proceed with the project to see if you're going overboard with paperwork and control:

- Do you feel isolated from the rest of the team because you always have reports due? If so, you probably have too many reports or other administrative procedures to do. Try simplifying and combining reports to keep the volume under control.

- Are the team members complaining of being micromanaged? You must achieve a balance between task assignments and task management. Some team members will need more structure than others. You must decide which approach best suits individual personalities and the project. Err on the side of trust and loose control as you begin the project. You can usually tighten things up later (unless the schedule is a cruncher).

◆ Are status reports always late from your team members? Either they don't regard them as important (which you can resolve by talking to them) or perhaps your report is too complex or detailed. Remember that every hour spent on forms and reports is an hour taken away from getting project tasks completed. Again, simplify and consolidate to keep administration in balance.

Dear Diary—Do You Need One?

In addition to taking notes at meetings, gathering information from project participants, and making general reports, a prudent project manager makes a personal project diary part of standard operating procedure. The daily diary should include notes on progress, problems, and any issues that impact the project in a positive or negative light. Unlike a young girl's "Dear Diary" entries, this notebook resembles a captain's log from a ship. Entries are to the point, are dated (by page), and contain as much or as little information as required to document project progress and issues. Use a computer if it's convenient, but back up your entries so this vital document doesn't suffer from disk or power failure.

The diary should contain information about the outcome of key meetings, accomplishments, conflicts, and extraordinary events affecting the project's health and well-being (not to mention your own).

The purpose of the project diary is fourfold:

◆ It tracks your progress and can be inspected by all parties concerned with project status. The diary may pinpoint project sinkholes that are hard to identify by reading a pile of status reports. Long-term problems, such as a failing team member, become easily visible as you flip through the book. Unloading the team member is easier when you can document his or her nonperformance through the written record.

Time Is Money

Document each project-day's events as they come and go. Putting it off "for a few days" may find you at the end of a project without enough data or notes to write a report or to defend yourself should something beyond your control go astray. Your project diary will have little value if it's incomplete.

- Future project managers can use your experiences to better understand their role as project managers and the ins and outs of the organization.

- If management complains about a problem such as budget overages or tardy delivery, your meticulously kept diary serves as the perfect memory of what really happened so you can explain the situation.

- Your diary is an excellent tool for doing a better job next time. Review it occasionally to see what worked and what failed last time. Employ the positive and reject the negative. A good project is fuel for laughs years down the road.

Before heading home for the night, always update your project diary. This process gives swirling thoughts and worries a place to rest and acts as the formal termination of your workday. The diary also keeps the "fossil" record intact for later review and for writing the final report. With your work done, reports completed, and diary done, you can go home and watch *Fraser* or *Friends* without a pinch of guilt.

Keeping People Up-to-Date

One of the most important operating procedures you need to develop is a way to make progress visible to team members as work progresses on the project. Seeing movement toward the finish line of the project is vital to maintain morale and to keep people focused on their contributions to the project. Here are some things you can do to make project progress visible from the onset:

- Display a large map of the project-network diagram and post it where everyone can see it. Fill in the shapes or highlight the activities on the list as they are completed. If remote sites participate, each site should have a chart so they can see what the other sites are doing.

- Use a whiteboard or other display to show current tasks and to schedule assignments. (This puts pressure on lagging team members to get with the program.)

- Display samples (where appropriate) of the team's progress. This might include brochures printed for a product launch, a sample of a new product or its prototype, or anything tangible that represents team progress. Change this display frequently to keep people interested and motivated.

- Regularly publish a project newsletter. This is a good communication tool if the contents are relevant. Articles can be used to describe team accomplishments. Include a list and photos of team members who contributed. Be careful not to leave anyone out. Focus the articles on group accomplishments. (If you don't intend to keep the newsletter going, however, don't start one.)

◆ If your project has a website or an intranet (most large projects should in this day and age), you can gather information via web-based reporting tools. You can also put all the shared reports, news items, and updates on the web—even pictures and voices of the people working on the project around the world. This really helps develop a "reality" for the team aspect of a distributed venture.

Recognition rewards don't have to be large to be effective, but they do have to be part of the operating procedures if you want to create motivation. A laser-printed (but signed) certificate congratulating team members on special-project success or work above and beyond the call of duty can make a big difference in making people feel appreciated. A coupon for a pleasant dinner out for two makes these awards more fun. Be careful not to overlook unsung team members located at a remote site or those who work quietly with little day-to-day visibility to the rest of the team.

The Bottom Line

In implementing all the operating aspects and creating the administrative guidelines for your project, you should remember that it's the management and leadership of the project that make the difference in your success, not the forms or the paperwork. You must act as a manager and a leader, not just as an administrator. With this in mind, we're ready to attack some of the best ways to keep all the "adminis-trivia" under control and to make communications more effective.

The Least You Need to Know

◆ Every project needs the project processes to track progress, report status, and move successfully from one phase to another, but no project needs long-winded reports with irrelevant details or meetings without objectives.

◆ Recognition for work done well and open communications are the two most important operating procedures any project manager can initiate.

◆ Leading a project by example and keeping a project diary are things that every project manager should do as a matter of policy.

◆ Leadership is always more important than paperwork in getting any project done, but paperwork gets noticed, so you'll need to do it anyway.

◆ The web (or company intranet) is a powerful tool for communicating with team members on large, distributed projects. Web-based technologies also can be used for many of the tracking and reporting requirements on a project.

Chapter 21

Making Your Communications Count

In This Chapter

- ◆ The various ways to distribute information on a project
- ◆ How to choose the medium for your message
- ◆ How to get your message across
- ◆ Why limiting formal communications is a good idea

Consider the U.S. government paperwork-reduction act, in which an additional piece of paper is printed to explain the paper reduction plan. Projects typically generate too much paper and too little information. Even using computer technology, the plans, status reports, and action item lists (to name just a few) use significant paper-related resources. Fortunately, most of this paper is recyclable, and large project management firms regularly recover significant sums of money from the piles of paper they recycle. They even lock down their dumpsters so no one steals the bulk of recyclables. It's a good thing, too, since reusing the paper saves both trees and money!

We noted in Chapter 20 that good administration is central to a project, but that doesn't mean you have to have lots of paperwork. Yes, in theory, you can use a computer and a whiteboard (for communication purposes), but all too often, people opt for the paper-only approach to cover their posteriors. We think this is a bad idea for most project managers.

In the modern world, there are many alternatives to the traditional memo and written report. You can communicate in person, both formally and informally. You can use the telephone for long conversations or leave short messages via voice mail. When you choose to use the written form for your messages, you can write casual notes by hand, send e-mail, transmit a fax, or when necessary, publish a formal document or dazzle people with a multimedia presentation.

In this chapter, we look at some techniques to make your project communications more effective (whether written, e-mailed, faxed, or phoned). These tips should help you improve your overall control of the project as well as the impact of your communications.

The Basics of Communications: It's All About Perceptions

Much of our understanding comes from our perceptions. Every time you communicate with people, whether it is your project team, stakeholders, or anyone else, you must keep their perspective in mind. The following communications model illustrates how perspectives influence people's understanding.

Before you communicate anything to anyone, analyze your audience. Ask yourself the following questions:

Time Is Money

According to the Project Management Institute, about 80 percent of a project manager's job is communications.

- What information they need?

- What attitudes and feelings are there to the message we're sending? You may need to alter the tone depending on how you answer the question.

- What is the best media for delivering the information?

- Who is the best person to deliver the information?

- What level of richness is required? In other words, how should the message be delivered?

- When should they receive the information?

- How will you receive feedback on how they reacted to the information?

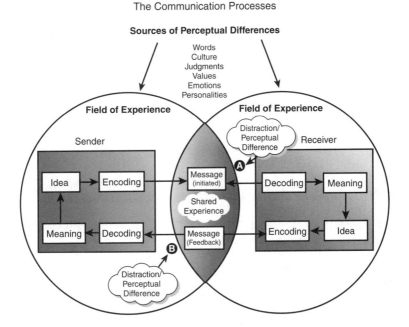

The Communication Processes

A basic communications model demonstrating that perception comes from our experiences, culture, word choice, values, and judgments. We use all these elements to encode and decode messages, and communication only occurs when the circles overlap. Otherwise, misunderstandings are inevitable.

Finally, make sure you think through the purpose of your communication. Do you want the recipient to do something? Do you want them to think or feel a certain way? To determine what kind of response you want from the recipient, complete this sentence: The purpose of my message is .... If you can't complete the sentence, how will those with whom you are communicating understand your purpose?

The Advantages and Disadvantages of Various Communications

By considering the format of your message, the time of day, and the job of the recipients, you can predict with a fair degree of accuracy whether a message will reach the intended receiver. Before you deliver any message, however, always consider the impact if it gets into the wrong hands—because it might.

To paraphrase Marshall McLuhan's wisdom: On projects, the medium is often as important as the message. In other words, the means of communication can have a greater influence on people than the information you're sending. With that in mind, the following sections present some general advantages and disadvantages of using various kinds of communication formats.

Telephone Calls

Advantages:

- The telephone is good for short, focused communications that need a personal touch or should not be put into the permanent, written record.

- It's possible to combine a personal approach while reaching people in remote locations at a relatively low cost.

Disadvantages:

- It's possible to play phone tag for days. The chance of actually reaching someone on first call is about 25 percent.

- It can be disruptive to the receiver if the call is not expected in advance.

Voice Mail

Advantages:

- Voice mail is great for getting short messages that aren't sensitive or personal in nature.

- It's a quick way to contact people in remote locations.

Disadvantages:

- Messages can be lost, scrambled, or deleted without the receiver knowing there is a problem.

- People may not pick up their messages on a regular basis.

E-mail

Advantages:

- It provides a written record without sending paper, and it allows you to attach other documents to your message.

- It's a quick way to send messages to people in distributed locations.

- Most of the time, you can find out if the mail has been read.

- It provides high credibility because people perceive it as being written by the sender (not an administrative assistant).

- It's good for precise details that can be conveyed in one screen.

- Messages can be forwarded to other people who need to know.

Disadvantages:

- People may forget to save important messages or may fail to realize that other materials are attached to the e-mail.

- It can seem impersonal if not worded properly. It's also not good for sensitive issues because it's easy to forward messages to others without thinking about the long-term ramifications.

- People may not read their e-mail messages on a regular basis.

- It requires a good, precise title so that people take the messages seriously and read them.

- Long messages are considered bad form and may alienate the reader.

- They can be risky because of the permanence of the message and the lack of privacy. (It can be forwarded to almost anyone.)

Types of Communication and Their Characteristics

Type of Communication	Group	Individual	Written	Spoken	Formal	Informal
Memo/e-mail		❏	❏			❏
Letters		❏	❏		❏	
Reports		❏	❏		❏	
Meetings	❏			❏		❏

continues

Types of Communication and Their Characteristics (continued)

Type of Communication	Group	Individual	Written	Spoken	Formal	Informal
Presentations	❏		❏	❏		
Teleconference	❏			❏	❏	
Telephone		❏		❏		❏

Handwritten, Short Notes

Advantages:

◆ Short notes are great for kudos and thanks. They're a personal approach that contrasts positively with computerized communications.

◆ They're quick, simple, friendly, and cheap.

Disadvantages:

◆ They might be overlooked if the note is small.

◆ They're limited to short, concise messages, and they work best when people are in the same general location.

Informal Visits and Management by Walking Around

Advantages:

◆ This is a great way to see things in action.

◆ It gives you a real impression of the tone and productivity of the team.

◆ You can discuss a wide range of topics and issues in detail.

Disadvantages:

◆ You might be perceived as nosy or disruptive if you aren't genuine in your interest or if you visit too often.

◆ Discussions can be forgotten or misinterpreted at a later date.

◆ You must keep the discussions focused to avoid wasting the team's time.

Formal Meetings

Advantages:

- ◆ Formal meetings enable multiple people to express opinions and issues.

- ◆ You can discuss and resolve a wide range of topics and issues in detail.

Disadvantages:

- ◆ These meetings can degrade into confrontations or be a waste of time if not managed effectively.

- ◆ Some people may feel uncomfortable offering their opinions in public.

Formal Reports and Memos

Advantages:

- ◆ If used sparingly, these are good for communicating updates and important procedures.

- ◆ They provide a permanent record.

Disadvantages:

- ◆ They can be easily misunderstood, especially if the message is negative.

- ◆ They can't be taken back and aren't easily forgotten if the message is poorly conveyed.

Faxed Messages

Advantages:

- ◆ Faxes are good for getting reports and messages to people in diverse locations.

- ◆ They provide a quick way to get important written documents to people.

Disadvantages:

- ◆ They are too easily seen by others, so this is not a good idea for sensitive messages.

- ◆ If no one is expecting your fax or if the fax machine is not regularly checked, your fax can languish, defeating the purpose of a fax.

Formal Presentations

Advantages:

♦ These are great for presenting complex status reports to audiences of various sizes.

♦ They allow effective use of graphics and other display methods.

♦ If done professionally, they can have a lasting positive impression on the audience.

Disadvantages:

♦ They require considerable planning and skill to achieve a positive impression.

♦ They are time-consuming for production and attendance and are an expensive alternative.

♦ Poorly presented material can negatively affect attitudes toward an otherwise successful project.

Teleconferences

Advantages:

♦ They allow project team members to meet over great distances and save travel expenses.

♦ This type of conference can facilitate shorter meetings when distance would require day-long or multiple day meetings to justify the time and expense.

♦ They are much better than a telephone conference call because people can see each other during the meeting.

Disadvantages:

♦ You must plan these meetings carefully because the technology isn't cheap.

♦ The technology is still growing, so there is often a delay in the video signal that makes the image on the other end look "jumpy" and fragmented.

♦ You will need to establish ground rules for allowing speakers to talk and contribute if they are in one of the remote sites.

Other Media

Many people have pagers and beepers, although contacting people through these devices is generally annoying unless you really have an emergency to convey. You can use groupware (software that lets people talk together through a computer network) for keeping status reports and general project information up-to-date. You can create a project website for a really large project to keep people informed of objectives, accomplishments, and project plans.

Regardless of the medium you choose, you need to employ common sense. You can never ignore the unexpected impact of your messages. You need to select the medium wisely. Even a casual disparaging remark to a team member can come back to haunt you later in the project.

> **Words from the Wise**
>
> You know, sometimes, when they say you're ahead of your time, it's just a polite way of saying you have a real bad sense of timing.
>
> —George McGovern, former senator and presidential candidate

Selecting the Best Medium for Your Message

To help you select the best medium for delivering your project information, consider these guidelines that we've come to appreciate through trial and error. You can avoid many of our mistakes if you take these truisms to heart.

- When you have real issues to resolve, have the discussions in person. People are reluctant to commit their opinions about controversial issues in writing.

- Never use meetings to berate people or make personal attacks. If you must discuss performance problems, limit the meetings to the people involved and keep the discussions confidential.

- Use e-mail for routine messages and day-to-day work on the project, but limit the number of messages. Don't send everything to everybody. Too much e-mail can actually waste time and can distract people from more important project issues.

- Let people know through fax, voice mail, or e-mail that a long report or other formal document is coming. This will improve the likelihood that the document will actually be read and taken seriously if you announce it in advance.

- Limit your formal meetings to those that are absolutely necessary. Have clear agendas for meetings or don't bother to have them. Limit the attendees to the people who really need to be there. Set a time limit for the meeting and stick to it. Distribute minutes of the meeting when other people need to know what was discussed.

♦ Consider the culture of your team. Some teams require more communication than others. For instance, less cohesive groups need more ongoing communication and support from the project manager. More cohesive groups will generally be more self-directed and will require less direct communications from you. Consider the individual and group issues as you choose and construct each communication.

Developing Effective Messages

Communicating on a project is an art. The better you get at it, the smoother your project will flow from beginning to end. You must provide enough information to keep team members informed without boring them. Every word counts. What you send, whom you send it to, and when you send it are always issues. If in doubt about a message, always wait. When you decide you need to say something, however, here are some guidelines to help you decide exactly what you want to say (regardless of the medium you choose):

♦ Always draft the message and then carefully edit it before you send it. This will help you to be more concise in the message and ensure that you covered all the points required.

♦ Think about the audience's expectations, any actions required as a result of the message, and your expectations after the message is delivered.

♦ Justify your choice of delivery medium for the message and the timing of the message.

♦ Start the message with an introduction that identifies the issue, context, or opportunity of interest.

♦ Make any required actions clear and specific in the message.

♦ Be as concise as possible without seeming insensitive or rude.

♦ Finally, never surprise someone with information. For example, if you will be discussing something important in a meeting, make sure all the right people know what you will say before you get there.

Listening Is Part of Communicating

In addition to the ability to construct powerful, appropriate messages, the ability to listen is one of the most important communication skills a project manager can possess. Only through listening can you determine whether your messages are understood. Focused listening also helps keep you abreast of project progress better than any status report. Observant listening can also help you foresee political issues before they start bogging down the project.

Here are some tips to make you a better listener:

- Stop talking and let others tell you what they want to say.

- Let people finish what they are saying. Try not to interrupt because you'll never hear the complete intent of the person if you do. If there is a brief pause in the discussion, don't jump in prematurely. Make sure the other person has finished before you take your turn.

- Eliminate distractions such as telephone calls or people coming in and out of the office. Give the person your full attention.

- Listen with purpose and intent. Try to hear between the words for the underlying meaning of the message. Notice body language and facial expressions as people talk. These are often the clues to dissatisfaction or issues that are not being addressed. If you see something wrong in the person's face, ask some probing questions to get at the real concerns.

- Restate what you heard people say to make sure you got the message right. You must receive and understand the message for good communication to occur.

Along the Critical Path

Remember that all members of the implementation team have four basic communications needs for which you're responsible: information about their respective responsibilities, information to help them work together efficiently, status information to help them identify problems and plan their own priorities, and information about decisions made by management, the customer, and other stakeholders that may affect the business environment of the project (and possibly their own work assignments).

You Are Responsible for What Other People Hear

If you really listen and find out that a message doesn't accomplish its goals or causes problems you didn't have before the message was sent, you've failed as a communicator. The reasons for most message failures are simple:

- The message was misinterpreted. This means your tone, vocabulary, medium, or timing (or any combination of these) was deficient.

- The message was considered unimportant or was ignored.

- The message arrived too late to be effective.

- The message ended up in the hands (or ears) of the wrong person.

> **Words from the Wise**
>
> Speak less ... No one ever put their foot in their mouth when they were not speaking. Worse, if you are speaking, you can't be listening, and we always learn much more from listening.
>
> —Mark H. McCormack, CEO of International Management Group, the sports management group that represents such stars as Tiger Woods and Andre Agassi

Regardless of the reason for your message's failure, you need to take responsibility for the problem and work harder to improve your communications. We always recommend being hard on yourself and being forgiving to others. You must constantly strive to become a better communicator and to make better interpretations of the ways in which receivers will interpret and act on your messages. Once you learn to deliver messages that get noticed in the right way, you'll have achieved one of the most important skills in leading your project to a successful conclusion—the skill of effective communication.

The Least You Need to Know

- Because you're in charge, everything you say or write counts toward helping or hindering your project.

- Never underestimate the importance of personal communications or the risk of putting things in writing.

- Carefully plan, assess, and construct every formal communication you make.

- Only through careful, focused, sensitive listening will you find out what's really going on.

- Never send a message that has more negative than positive potential to motivate people.

Part 5

The Controlling Processes

Like any good project manager, to maintain your lead in the project, you need to exercise control. Like the driver of a race car, you need to adjust your speed on the curves and compensate for the condition of the road. Control of a project starts with a detailed plan, good communication, and clear operating procedures that you've developed for the project.

To actually maintain that control over time, however, you need to deal with changes, problems, and unexpected circumstances. You need to compare the time, cost, and quality of your project at every stage—and then make adjustments to the activities, resources, and plan to keep things moving toward the ultimate goal. Sometimes you may need to slow things down to avoid an accident. Other times, you'll need to step on the accelerator to keep pace with the changes.

Learning how to use information to keep the project under control is the theme of this section. Just focus on the plan and keep your eyes on the prize, and you'll reach the project finish in first place.

Chapter 22

Monitoring and Controlling Schedules and Expenses

In This Chapter

- Why control is a good thing
- The criteria for establishing positive control over the project
- How to use status information to help control the objectives, schedule, and budget
- Keeping the plan up-to-date to help keep the project on track

Once a project is underway and you establish the operating procedures and start working on perfecting your leadership style, your key responsibility is to keep things going on time and within budget. After meticulously planning your project, you might assume that team members will simply stick to your plan and get things done as specified. Unfortunately, this almost never happens. On occasion, you'll need to intervene.

In this chapter, you're going to learn about the basic control techniques that can help you.

Taking Charge and Getting Control

Once a project is underway, it takes on a life of its own. If you were the project manager for the All-Star Cable Movies-on-Demand project (our case study), you'd know the company's future depends on getting the project done on time and within budget. Your job and your reputation are on the line. How will you know if people are doing what they promised to do? How can you meet your objectives and still get everything else done? It can seem all too overwhelming.

> **Risk Management**
>
> Never make the mistake of confusing activity with progress.

> **Words from the Wise**
>
> Trouble has no necessary connection with discouragement—discouragement has a germ of its own, as different from trouble as arthritis is different from a stiff joint.
>
> —F. Scott Fitzgerald

Getting a handle on your project isn't really that hard. You have a plan, and now is the time to use it. Your plan is your main tool for maintaining control of the project through its lifetime. This requires careful management of both the plan and its resources—especially the people—to move forward and keep everything in gear and well-lubricated. Although change is an inevitable consequence of moving through time (see Chapter 24 for more on change), you must measure and manage its effects. Otherwise, you won't meet the goals established at the project's outset. The schedule, budget, and procedures you've put together to this point provide you with the structure you need to evaluate where you are at any time.

Control Is a Good Thing

Control can imply domination, headstrong authority, or excessive power. Because of these negative connotations, people new to project management may be reluctant to implement project control. The controlling phase is not about domination, however—it's about gathering information so you can measure, monitor, and adjust progress toward your project goals. That's a good thing because, otherwise, you'll never know if your project is on the right course.

Success Criteria for Project Control

How you use your reports and communications (which we talked about in the preceding chapter) to control your project will directly affect the end results your project will achieve. Here are some guidelines for using reports and communications that can help you achieve positive control of your project:

◆ Use the project plan as the primary guide for coordinating your project. A major portion of this book is devoted to preparation of the plan because of its centrality in the project management discipline. If you diligently follow the steps laid out in previous chapters, your plan is likely a good one—and thus is something worth following.

◆ Consistently monitor and update the plan and the other control documents including the statement of work, the requirement specification, the blueprints, and the functional specifications (if these documents are used for your project). A plan or supporting specification that stays in the top drawer of your desk will not help you guide your project to a successful conclusion. Instead, it must be updated regularly to be useful. It must also reflect the current status of the project and any changes that become necessary because of new information, budget constraints, or schedule or product modifications.

◆ Remember that quality communication is a key to control. Never provide too much information. Never offer too little. Every person on your project org chart requires ongoing communication at various levels of detail. Higher-level management requires summary reports on the project. Operational members of the team require more detailed information. Some communication will be formal, and some will be informal. The objective of communication is to keep people informed, on track, and involved in the project.

> **CAUTION**
>
> **Risk Management**
>
> Be sure to gather status information from all members of the project team, even from people low on the totem pole who don't report directly to you. More senior team members may whitewash or deliberately misrepresent problems in a misguided effort to present themselves in the best possible light.

◆ As we've repeated throughout this book, you monitor the progress of the project against the plan on a regular basis. Managers must compare the time, cost, and performance of the project to the budget, schedule, and tasks defined in the approved project plan. This should be done in an integrated manner at regular intervals, not in a haphazard, arbitrary way. Any significant departures from the budget and the schedule must be reported immediately because these anomalies affect the viability and success of the entire project.

◆ Get involved. You won't have time to sit in your ivory tower waiting for results and accolades from the big boss. Instead, you'll need to roll up your sleeves and get down in the trenches with the team. That way, you not only have a finger on the project's pulse, you actually contribute to a workload that may otherwise weigh heavily on team members' shoulders.

♦ Adapt the project schedule, budget, and work plan as necessary to keep the project on track. As the project progresses, changes in the original plan may be required for several reasons. We'll cover the more common causes for changes in Chapter 24. It is the project manager's responsibility to make sure these changes are appropriate, valid, and approved.

♦ Document project progress and changes and communicate them to team members. The quality and level of detail of your reports and communications need to be consistent, reliable, and appropriate for each level of the project team.

What Should You Monitor?

To keep things running smoothly, the following must be monitored for every project, regardless of size or complexity:

♦ The completion of work packages as compared to the plan to check if you are on schedule

♦ The scope of work being performed to make sure you don't have scope creep

♦ The quality of work being performed against the requirements for the project

♦ The costs and expenditures as compared to the plan to check your budget

♦ The attitudes of people working on the project or involved with the project including key stakeholders and management

♦ The cohesiveness and cooperation of team members

Note that there is more to be monitored than just the tasks, the schedule, and the budget. The level of communication and cooperation between team members and the quality of the work being performed are also obviously important aspects of the project. In addition, you must monitor the use and availability of equipment. For example, you may be responsible for the usage of computer equipment on a large project like All-Star Cable. You also want to make sure the equipment doesn't "walk out the door," so to speak.

Time Is Money

Remember in managing a project, you need to control time, cost, quality, and scope.

On a large, complex project like All-Star Cable, the effort required for monitoring and control may take more time than you actually spend working on the project. This is okay. It is your job as project manager to be the chief integrator to bring the project to a successful conclusion. If you find yourself doing a lot of the work, that should be a red flag for you. Of course, on smaller projects, the degree of monitoring and control should be much less time-consuming.

Using a simple scorecard with the colors of a stoplight can be a very useful, and yet simple, way to show the status of the project. However, be aware that some people are color blind and may not be able to see the status if you only use colors without additional symbols.

Project Scorecard
Status Legend: Red = High Risk, Yellow = Marginal Risk, Green = Minimal Risk

Cost	Yellow	Danger of a cost overrun in the development of the customer GUI
Schedule	Green	No significant problems in the schedule for the project
	Yellow	The vendor that is building the remote control is running a little behind but believes they can catch up
Quality	Green	Peer Review set for May to test the technical interfaces
Best Practices	Green	Reviewed "Critical Success Factors for Projects" to remind ourselves of what to do
Functional Issues	Green	To discuss for billing structure with Accounting
	Green	New customer input decision for credit to be concluded next week
	Green	Ron to chair Database Working Group
	Green	Bob to chair group reviewing video streaming requirements document
	Green	Kevin working rollout issues with Marketing
Communication	Green	Project team to review and respond to the Marketing queries
	Green	Project Team to send out documentation that will be refined within the steering committee before the GUI is approved
	Green	Project group to provide complete list of known issues for the steering committee to resolve
	Green	Charles to obtain more information from vendors on their quality assurance plans
Risk	Green	None

One thing that helps minimize the time spent monitoring activities on both small and large projects is the use of simple reporting formats. Keeping reports clear and succinct is more important than getting hundreds of pages of narrative on each aspect of the project. In addition, the use of appropriate project management software that is adapted to your project needs can help reduce the time required to understand the impact of current activities and changes in the project plan. (See Chapter 30, for more information on choosing an appropriate software program to help you track progress.)

What Monitoring Should Accomplish

The tasks, milestones, and budget you documented in the plan for your project are the starting point for project coordination and control. These tasks and milestones form the checkpoints to be used to monitor progress. Whether formal or informal, project monitoring should serve one or more of the following basic functions:

 ♦ Communicating project status and changes to other project team members

 ♦ Informing management (and clients or customers) about the status of the project

 ♦ Providing the justification for making project adjustments

 ♦ Documenting current project plans compared to the original project plan

Consistency is very important in the monitoring and control process. The project must be monitored from start to finish because problems can occur anywhere along the way.

Inexperienced project managers may start out full of energy and monitor everything during the first few weeks. Then, when things seem to be going okay, the monitoring falls off. These managers often end up with a big mess at the end of the project because they've failed to keep track of progress and problems. Don't let this happen to you! Maintain your zeal throughout the project.

Getting a Handle on Project Status

Controlling a project takes time and effort, but it's not that difficult if you keep up with things. In the following sections, we'll give you some tips to help you keep on top of the workflow.

Make Status Reports Useful

Status reports are more than nice documents that fill your filing cabinets—they are a fundamental monitoring tool to identify progress and problems.

You should encourage your team members to take status reports seriously and should help them learn to write and interpret them. Whether you require formal or informal status reports, status updates should be completed by each team member (or supervisor) and then should be compiled and summarized by you, the project manager. The basis for all the status reports that come from the project team should be the work they have completed on their work packages. Remember that work packages have discreet deliverables and should fall within the 8- to 80-hour rule of thumb.

> **CAUTION**
>
> **Risk Management**
>
> Project managers fall into three basic categories: those who watch what happens, those who make things happen, and those who wonder what happened.

You should add your own comments to the summary report, draw conclusions based on the data you've received from others, and make recommendations for actions and changes before you send your report on to other managers, executives, or customers who need to be kept apprised of project status.

By reviewing status reports and personal communications, you'll discover the discrepancies between where you are and where the plan says you should be. These discrepancies are always there because no plan can predict the exact sequence you'll follow in getting from idea to finished project. But isn't it better to know about the discrepancies sooner rather than later? That's what project control is all about—being able to take action sooner so the project will still come in on time and within budget.

Gantt charts display information in two ways: the left side displays it as a table and the right side as a chart. The table portion displays information about the project's tasks, such as when they start and end, how long they are, and the resources assigned to them. The chart portion displays each task graphically, most often as a task bar. The bar's position on the timeline, and its length, indicates when that task begins and ends. In addition, the position of one task bar in relation to another indicates whether the tasks follow one after the other or are overlapping.

The best way to use a Gantt chart is to see how activities are progressing over time. You can track progress by comparing planned and actual start and finish dates and by checking the completion percentage of each task. Although you can't see them on this document, the bars are represented in different colors, to indicate various aspects of the project status. Black represents the original plan, blue indicates the float available for the activity, and red indicates where the activity has slipped in time and took more time than anticipated.

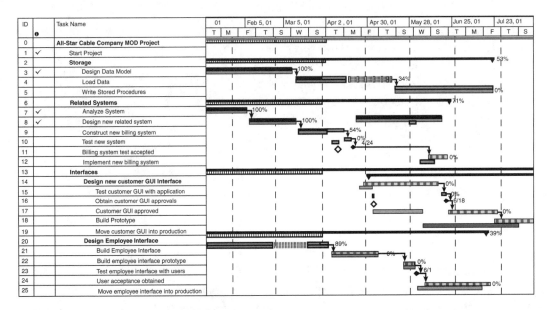

Using program software such as Microsoft Project can help you track your project. This is a Tracking Gantt chart that compares the project plan for the All-Star Cable MOD project with the current status of the project.

Time Is Money

When working with outside vendors, suppliers, and agencies, strike up friendships with their support personnel. That way, if things start running off the rails for any reason, your friends can tip you off before your project skips the tracks.

Compare, Compare, Compare

An easy way to monitor status is to use two columns to compare the current schedule and expenditures with the original project plan. The comparison allows you to understand the most immediate issues regarding your plan, and it can help prioritize your needs to adapt the plan or to make further inquiries regarding the problem areas. Always keep in mind that monitoring is used to establish the project's current position compared to the planned position. You need to make this goal clear to your team; otherwise, they'll perceive your scrutiny of budget and schedule as actions of a meddling manager on an insidious, covert mission.

The Project Review Meeting as a Control Process

Analyzing reports from your office chair will never be enough to help you guide your project to fruition. Resolving conflicts, problems, and staffing issues is almost impossible using just reports, so meetings with people are always a necessary component of project control.

The project review meeting is an opportunity for key team members, not just managers and supervisors, to get together to resolve issues. It's also a time to discuss current project status and to review performance toward meeting objectives. Project review meetings are often held at the completion of a major milestone or before or after a key phase of the project. Some project review meetings are held on a periodic basis in place of formal reports. For example, a short subproject such as the training design for new cable subscribers is best handled with brief reports and regular meetings because the project is of a short duration. A project like All-Star Cable's Movies-on-Demand may have less frequent meetings at certain stages, and then more frequent meetings when more coordination is required.

If a project meeting is necessary to resolve issues, have one now, not later. It's best to take action as soon as you are aware of a problem instead of waiting for a regularly scheduled meeting. Make the meeting short and focused on the single issue that you just became aware of and then adjourn. Long, drawn-out meetings with that wander into other issues can dampen enthusiasm and obfuscate the problem. At the end of three hours, no one cares anymore.

The Project Audit

The most formal type of project monitoring (and the process most feared by project managers) is the audit. Sometimes audits are required as a point of contract; sometimes they are necessary because the project is really off track and the source of the problem remains a mystery. The goal of a project audit is to get an accurate picture of the quality of work, current expenditures, and the schedule of the project. (These are the goals of all monitoring activities, so the audit is really no different from putting together a big status report.)

Audits are commonly performed on large government projects, projects involving multiple companies and big budgets, and projects involving customers who need outside assurance that work on the project is proceeding as planned. Audits may be initiated both during and at the end of a project. Internal audits also can be performed by project managers and team members at key milestones in a large project.

In most cases, an audit is performed by (supposedly) objective outsiders who review progress, costs, and current plans. After discussions with team members, reviews of reports, and direct observations, the objective auditors (who usually work for the customer or the government) then report their conclusions on the current status of the project based to the project manager or to executive management. They often make strong recommendations about better ways things should be done to keep a large project under control.

If your projects ever get audited, you'll be okay if you've followed all the tips for monitoring and tracking progress that we've given you in this chapter. If you've done a good job of communicating and monitoring, the audit shouldn't reveal any surprises—but if it does, take them to heart and take action. Just because you didn't discover the problem is no reason to ignore the solution.

The Project Peer Review

Another monitoring strategy is to gather some of the sharper minds both inside and outside the company for a peer review. Such reviews will usually last from one day to a maximum of one week. The objective of the peer review is to ask knowledgeable people to review your project from a technical and business standpoint and to alert you to any risks or problems that you and the project team may have overlooked. You know it's funny, but if you work on something day after day for quite a while, the whole team can begin to make assumptions that turn into oversights.

In a project like All-Star Cable, where you are trying to beat the competition, you might consider asking people from vendor companies (with whom you already have nondisclosure agreements) to participate in the peer review. Consulting firms might also offer valuable insights—just make sure that you have nondisclosure agreements with them. Just make it clear that if you are using an outside consulting firm that the review is not an opportunity for them to sell work for their firm.

Monitoring and Controlling the Budget

Reports and meetings are great for tracking schedules and performance, but budgets and cash outlays require special monitoring techniques. The way the budget tracking is set up depends on the accounting systems already in place in your company. As you make expenditures or sign contracts with vendors, you need to establish a formal tracking method to measure your actual commitments.

To help control expenditures, you should initiate review procedures for any expenditures not in the original plan. Even if expenditures are in the plan, you may want to have approval or review of any purchases that exceed a certain amount (say, any expenditures that exceed $1,000).

In most companies, if you rely on expenditure reports from the accounting department to provide the financial status of your project, you will likely go over budget or think you have more money than you actually have. Money is often "spent" in the form of contracts or agreements long before it is accounted for in the billing and invoice cycles of the corporation. Accounting reports typically report on invoices that have been "paid to date." Unfortunately, they don't usually report on invoices that have not been paid or have yet to be billed. Think of it the same way you would your checking account. You need to account for outstanding checks before you can get a true picture of the balance you really have in the bank.

For this reason, you must track actual expenditures to date in addition to reviewing the accounting reports. Ultimately, your expenditures and the accounting department documentation should match, but it might take as long as 90 days for the two systems to be reconciled.

You (and each person on your project team who will be making financial commitments to vendors or suppliers) must account for all monetary commitments as they occur. At a minimum, all expenditures should appear on the formal status reports.

A simple way to keep track of the money is to have each person provide a photocopy of each contract, agreement, or order for your project as it is approved. These go into your "project expenditures file." The total of these expenditures then becomes part of the actual expenses committed to your project. As vendors specify new prices or change their bids, these must be put into the file as well, and budget figures must be adjusted accordingly for the next status report and plan review. For larger projects like All-Star Cable, you may want to have someone with accounting skills on the project staff who can assist you in tracking and auditing the project expenditures.

When you get reports from accounting that don't match your budget file, you will have the documentation necessary to reconcile the differences. If you don't have such a file, you'll be at the mercy of your accountant or finance officer (not a desirable condition).

> **Words from the Wise**
>
> So much of what we call management consists in making it difficult for people to work.
>
> —Peter Drucker, professor, University of Southern California

Why Status Reports Don't Tell the Whole Story

Never rely on written reports alone to assess progress on your project. People often leave problems out of reports because they don't want to put them in writing. They also may fail to report schedule slips in meetings because they think time can be made up later. People often don't want to expose a problem in front of others for fear of reprisal or embarrassment.

For example, let's say that John, the customer support manager, was late on writing the new processes for the Movies-on-Demand project. Still, in the weekly report, he stated that the development of new processes were "on schedule" even though they hadn't been started. John reported this way in good faith, fully believing he would be able to make up the time next week. Unfortunately, this kind of reporting causes many problems, especially if the person never does find the time to get back on schedule. If the project manager had John turning in the work package deliverable—the new processes for customer service—he or she would have known the schedule was slipping very quickly.

The quality of performance on a project is also subjective. Performance reported as outstanding by one group may be substandard to another. In the Movies-on-Demand project, the contractors assembling the new cable boxes reported that everything was completed "to specifications." It wasn't until someone from the project team actually inspected the cable boxes being produced that it was discovered that the boxes didn't meet the requirements demanded by All-Star Cable.

For reasons like this, you need to review progress on the project on your own through direct observation and direct communication with the team members. Informal monitoring can be completed by simply listening, observing, and communicating on an ongoing basis. The goal is to spot problems before they become unmanageable.

Using Information from the Project Team

The project team is your best source of ideas for keeping the project on track. The more you allow people to adjust their own work and schedules to meet project goals, the easier it will be to keep the project on track. Thus, everyone on your project should be part of project control. People can do more than just tell you what they're up to; they can also provide ideas for speeding project progress or saving money. (Evaluate these ideas as you would any change to the plan.) In general, the best ideas come from informal sessions with the team member, not from written status reports or scheduled meetings.

While visiting team members, not only will you be able to observe people at work, they will likely have materials on hand to explain their progress and ideas. A similar meeting held in your space may find a team member without the requisite documentation, demonstration, or explanation on hand. By all means, take these opportunities to show your appreciation for a job well done, assuming it was.

Information from Other Sources

As part of your overall approach to collecting information, other sources can provide useful information as well. Vendors involved in your project provide important feedback on the performance of the team member(s) they work with. Other managers may have thoughts or opinions on project progress, especially if yours is a high-visibility project (remember the peer review). Take outsiders' comments, at least initially, with a grain of salt until you have a chance to weigh them. At the very least, document them in your project diary for future reference.

Words from the Wise

From listening comes wisdom, from speaking repentance.

—Italian proverb

Employing a Guru for Guidance

We've already touched on the sensibility of using a project guru to help in the planning stages. You can also use such a person—either an experienced project manager or a someone with technical knowledge you lack—to help control the project. This person doesn't replace your authority as project manager; instead, he or she steps in on occasion to verify project progress and to provide advice for making project adjustments. Your guru can be another manager who works for free or an outside consultant "rented" for the occasion.

Choose your project guru wisely. He or she must be someone you can work with and who won't step on your toes. The person must be affordable if you have to pay for his or her services and be truly experienced. Before hiring someone, check references and ask for specific evidence of past results. Otherwise, your guru may lead you down the primrose path instead of the path to enlightenment!

What's Really Going On?

Beyond gathering data about schedules, budgets, and outcomes, you must consider the emotional status of your team to control a project effectively. All projects involve a mix of people with different emotional requirements. Some are highly dedicated and committed; others aren't. Even though your team was carefully selected—whether by you, a previous manager, or senior management—once underway, a number of "strangers" may emerge where team members used to be. This is especially true when the pressure of missed dates puts a strain on personalities. Here are some of the folks you may encounter:

◆ The overly ambitious team member who aims to please but still doesn't get much done. (The person's skill levels may vary.)

◆ The person who always seems to be working on something, but never seems to complete anything.

◆ The procrastinator who promises results but delays progress by piddling. This person may do excellent work but deliver it late. He or she may also claim progress in expectation of completing the task later without you knowing about the inflated claims.

◆ The person who puts more effort and time into an activity than it requires or deserves because he or she thinks you're wrong in specifying a lower quality for the outcome. In project terminology, this is called "gold plating."

> **Time Is Money**
>
> When you collect data from your team, collect information on all aspects of the project at one time (tasks, budget, quality, and issues). If you keep going back to people for additional information, you'll irritate them and diminish productivity.

As you can see, each of these "new" employees requires a different management style to handle. While the ambitious team member may be hurt if you aren't overwhelmed by his or her progress, the procrastinator may require micromanagement to keep moving. Eventually, all four employees may produce equal results, assuming their experience is also equal, but you'll get them to that point with different types of control. Some require kid gloves, others a kick in the pants.

Quality and Goal Assessment

When you're up to your rear in alligators, it's hard to remember that the objective was to drain the swamp. As project manager, you will be constantly barraged with input, problem resolution, nonperforming vendors, and other issues. It's easy to get buried in day-to-day operations and forget about your real goals—to meet the project's goals with appropriate quality.

For that reason, you must make an ongoing review of project goals part of your project assessment and control activities. If the project is to repaint the Golden Gate

Bridge, the project is a failure if the painters can only meet their dates if they use gold paint instead of red. (For those of you who have never seen this monument, it's always been red, never gold.)

It may take a trained eye to see problems early in the project. On a technical project, you may need to bring in outside experts to make sure quality, as well as timeliness and careful budget management, is in place. Otherwise, at the end of the project cycle, you may end up with egg on your face when you were expecting to pop corks from champagne bottles.

Putting It All Together

Once you have complete input from your team, you can analyze project status and decide on new actions to take (if any) to keep the project moving toward a successful conclusion. This includes two steps. The first step involves—you guessed it—updating the project plan to reflect the current status. The second step is a review with the stakeholders and team to gain consensus on the revisions to the plan. We'll discuss this second step in detail in Chapter 24. For now, let's tackle updating the project plan and the related documents.

> **Words from the Wise**
>
> There are many limits to authority; so project managers should learn how to wield influence.
>
> —Milton D. Rosenau Jr., author and project manager

Updating the Project Plan and Other Control Documents

Your plan documents, including the SOW, product specifications, blueprints, budget, and schedule, are the most important control tools you can use. They allow you to present the work that's been agreed to and to communicate necessary changes.

If you're comfortable with your cross-checking of project tasks, schedules, and budgets after gathering data on the current status of the project, it's time to compare reality with the approved plan and other project documents as appropriate (such as comparing the SOW and product specifications to better predict what's going to happen from here on out). For large projects, this is most easily done with computerized tools (see Chapter 30). Plugging in the status data may predict required changes to the schedule, budget, and critical path. (Computerized project management tools allow you to see comparisons of the old versus the new by highlighting changed paths, dates, tasks, and budget variances.)

Once the new data has been used to forecast a new schedule and budget, you can look for the problems causing the variances. If your critical path suddenly goes late, you can follow the lines back to see what tasks are late and who or what is responsible. If the critical path changes, it may or may not be a major flag. Again, study the flow to see what went wrong.

Tracking the budget is a matter of having good accounting practices in place that can give you timely figures on the committed costs and expenditures of the project. The process of comparing current to planned expenditures is similar to matching work completed to the planned task network. Graphs and spreadsheets are useful for demonstrating cost variances and projections. Good project management programs will offer a number of graphing techniques to allow you to visualize the budget through time. If the bottom line suddenly jumps $100,000 in your new projections, follow the money trail back to the point of discrepancy. Look for an overall change such as the carpenters' union getting a 35 percent pay raise. Such an event may mean cutting back on the project, asking for more money, or hopping a rusty steamer to Mandalay to look for another job. (Leave no forwarding address!)

CAUTION

Risk Management

If your managers feel that your project is doomed or is seriously in jeopardy, they may take resources, including staff, from your project to work on other projects. The best way to avoid this problem is to keep everyone informed of positive results and to keep the project on track through careful monitoring and control.

The People Side of Things

Once you are comfortable with the plan and the necessary changes, it's time to look at the people side of things. Who is performing well? Who is almost burned out because a task has taken longer than expected and there's no extra time? This is an opportunity to review your notes from the on-site meetings to see how you can help your staff. A trip to the resource-leveling chart may be required to study how to change task assignments.

If a task handled by a project team seems to be constantly late, study your notes to look for personality conflicts, procrastinators, work overload, lack of experience, or lousy equipment. You may find a mix of all five as team members struggle first with too much work, second with inadequate equipment, and third taking it out on each other. No wonder they're slow! Most people try to work hard—so never blame the people until you understand the issues.

Clue 'Em In ...

The central tenet in controlling your temporary fiefdom is through monitoring and adjusting the plan. As schedules, tasks, or other assignments change, let the team members know as soon as possible—better yet, let them be part of the decision to change the plan in the first place.

The Least You Need to Know

◆ Control requires knowledge of the project status. Since the status is constantly changing, you'll need to monitor the project and compare it to the plan in some way every day.

◆ If you keep the plan and other key project documentation up-to-date to reflect changes and adjustments, your status can be more accurately determined.

◆ Reports are good tools for synthesizing information, but informal discussions often reveal a more accurate picture of the project.

◆ Always ask the team to offer suggestions when things are off track.

◆ If your project is in serious trouble, ask for expert advice before it's too late.

Conflicts: Resolving and Benefiting from Them

In This Chapter

◆ Conflicts are inevitable

◆ People are the source of most conflicts

◆ When conflicts are most likely to occur

◆ Making the most of conflicts

◆ Five basic ways to resolve conflicts

Conflicts are a way of life in projects. Just like families, all projects have them. Sometimes project managers are even described as conflict managers. But conflicts don't have to bring your project to a halt. If you know something is going to happen, you can plan for dealing with it—and that's the way you should handle conflicts.

Recognizing the difference between negative and positive, or meaningful, conflicts is vital. (Yes, some conflicts are a good thing because they bring ideas and energy to a project.) Getting control of the negative variety, however, is necessary to reach your project goals.

It's possible for just two people to bog down a project through a clash of personality, ideas, or opinions. (Don't believe it? Consider the venerable institution of marriage!) In this chapter, you will learn what causes conflicts, what kinds of problems manifest themselves at what point in a project, and how to resolve them.

Most conflicts can be resolved, but not all conflicts are worth the effort to eliminate them. Some interpersonal problems are unlikely to be fixed. Some conflicts require more effort (and time) than a repair merits. Instead, a little creative thinking to invent a way to work around the problem to neutralize the conflict may be just what the doctor ordered. In this chapter, you'll learn where and when to draw this line.

Questions to Ask to Scope Out the Issue

As you read this chapter, especially if you're looking for advice on resolving an immediate *project conflict*, ask yourself the following questions:

> **Project Lingo**
>
> Sounding like something worked out via fisticuffs, a **project conflict** is one in which something—people, priorities, or problems ("the three Ps")—begins to interfere with completing a project on time and within budget.

♦ Do I have enough information to understand the true source of the conflict?

♦ Do I have the diplomatic skills to resolve it?

♦ Will the conflict work itself out with a meeting between members?

♦ Is it self-terminating? (Amazingly, some conflicts work themselves out or burn themselves up without your intervention.)

If the answer to the first two questions is "no," whom can you tap for the task? It must be someone with enough authority for the job without overshadowing you in your role.

Create an Issues Log

Whenever conflicts or issues arise, a great tool for the project manager is an issues log. The issues log contains detailed information about the conflict or issue and includes the following elements:

♦ A description of the issue or conflict

♦ Who was assigned to work it through

♦ The impact the issue has on the project

- ◆ Who authorized the accepted solution
- ◆ When the issue was resolved successfully

It is important to keep track of any issues that arise during the course of the project. The issues log can then be used to make sure that all the conflicts have been addressed (note that doesn't mean they are solved to everyone's satisfaction) and can be used at project close-out as part of the lessons learned. Here's a sample issues log:

Issues Log

Issue	Impact	Assigned	Due Date	Resolution
Coding language	High	Bob Braveheart	4/15	ABOP chosen
Union request	Medium	Julia Robins	5/02	In progress
Software acceptance	High	Ben Samuels	5/10	Accepted as tested

Personal Conflicts Are Inevitable

As a project progresses, people conflicts enter into the picture. Properly identified in a timely manner, these project conflicts can be mitigated without affecting the project's schedule. What causes personal conflicts? Essentially, any project, no matter how mundane it looks (suggestions for how to connect new customers by cable at All-Star Cable, for example), is a creative project of sorts. Ideas may come from multiple players for planning the project. Once underway, better ways to accomplish the same objectives may appear. Team members may become out of synchronization with one another.

There are two schools of thought as to why personnel or group conflicts occur. One is considered increasingly old-fashioned but plays a role in many conflicts: failure or lack of leadership on the part of the management team. The other, considered more important today, recognizes conflicts as part of the project process. Surprisingly, they can be beneficial, as you'll see later in the chapter in the section "Conflicts Aren't Always Negative."

In a commonplace project such as laying a television cable, team members may disagree on the start date due to weather, how to route the cable, or how long the project will take. Once underway, the route may become perilous due to an old concrete sewer main blocking the original plan. Part of the team may want to route the cable differently, while the other part may want to add time to the schedule and remove

Time Is Money

According to conventional wisdom, no one is irreplaceable. But just try losing a couple of key team members in the middle of a project and see just how untrue this idea really is!

the offending concrete. This second option also requires approval from the sewer department. Further, the dig crew may be late because they must work by hand near a gas main rather than rely on a backhoe, and the wiring specialists may appear two days before they can actually start work. You may still have to pay them. Or worse, they may not be available to handle the wiring by the day you need it done. This illustrates one of the common causes of project conflict—different approaches to solving problems and the associated decisions to be made during a project.

The Four Kinds of People Conflicts

Conflicts involving project team members manifest themselves in a number of ways:

♦ **Intrapersonnel.** A team member feels he or she isn't living up to expectations or is frustrated with something on the project.

♦ **Interpersonal.** Two team members don't get along, or one member may not get along with the rest of the team.

♦ **Intragroup.** Internal feuding and bickering occurs among people working on the same part of the project.

♦ **Intergroup.** Hostilities, rivalries, or competitions appear between two different groups working on the project.

Any of these conflicts can have negative or positive consequences. Positive conflicts foster harder work, new ideas, or positive competition to excel at getting things done. Negative conflicts result in poor morale, decreased productivity, or even work stoppage.

Determine the Source of the Conflicts

Negative conflicts are resolvable but in different fashions. Before you can resolve a conflict, you must know what led to the conflict in the first place. Keep in mind that more than one source of conflict may be at hand, and it takes careful evaluation to decide which one(s) you are dealing with. The general sources of conflict are covered in the following sections.

Goal Incompatibility

It's possible that not everyone in the organization is functioning on the same wavelength regarding the project's goals. From a simple misunderstanding of the project's intended outcome to differences between the project manager's goals and team members' goals, conflict can arise. There might be a difference in perception or erroneous assumptions, or others might disagree on the precedence of tasks, dates, and performance criteria. If you sense that this is the problem, get the team together and work through the project goals that the team needs to focus on. Get clarity! It may mean using someone else as a facilitator since you will want to be able to join in the discussion and voice your opinions.

Lack of Task Focus

Tasks must be specific. You must provide detailed instructions instead of relying on brevity. For example, as part of an office-remodeling project to handle the changes in billing at All-Star Cable, you may plan to reconfigure the office cubicles in a department to handle new equipment. An ambitious facilities manager and his laborers may assume, lacking specific instructions, that the entire 10,000 square foot building is involved and may knock down everyone's cubicles over the weekend.

Administrative Procedures

As mentioned in Chapter 19, conflict can arise in a project with regard to the number of reports, their kinds, and who should receive what. Make sure your administrative procedures are helping people do their jobs and not provide "busy work" or other roadblocks to real productivity.

Role Uncertainty

A common kind of conflict is one in which people are not sure what they should be working on or they seem to be working on the same thing and are getting in each other's way. Every team member, manager, and even the project management staff (if there are others in addition to yourself) must have a clear understanding of their roles. Not having this understanding is especially problematic if

Time Is Money

Make sure each person understands the knowledge and skills they are bringing to the project and how they will use those skills.

your project is structured using a matrix management approach. (See Chapter 19 for information on project organizations.)

Technical Uncertainty

If new technology is being developed, uncertainty and conflict are sure to arise. What's the best way to do it? What steps must we take to complete the project faster? Will it work at all? At All-Star Cable, the project team is attempting to develop an entirely new technology. There will undoubtedly be real conflicts over "how" and "why" to do certain things. Don't mistake these honest differences as signs of personality conflicts.

Staffing and Resource Allocation

Staffing is a major source of conflict—from who will have to give up staff for use on a project to people perceived as having the fun tasks versus those doing dull tasks or menial labor. Even within a multi-team project, managers can act like kids assembling a baseball team. Insist on getting the choice members for your team, but realize you get them at the expense of the other team and that will undoubtedly cause conflict. Plenty of controversy is common, and even when a project is well underway, staff members may attempt to move up the ranks or undermine other team members for a variety of reasons. Please keep in mind that the best and brightest are usually highly competitive as well. Sometimes that competitive nature will cause conflict.

Budgets and Costs

Another point of conflict in every project is its budget. Conflict begins when the people footing the bill for the project fail to allocate adequate funds. Then the project manager must allocate funds with team members or groups squawking for a bigger piece of an already too-small pie. Even more conflict is generated if a group is seen as spending too freely at the expense of other less-well-endowed groups. The process repeats itself if and when the project runs out of money and the project manager must go back to the stakeholders for more.

Schedules

The schedule is usually the main focus of conflicts. People never think they have enough time to do the work right. One team may want more time than the next in line perceives as necessary. Squabbles over scheduling lead to conflict. The project may start late, and those downstream are often squeezed to make up for lost time. Anxiety and conflict result.

In resolving schedule or task difficulties, we've had good results by dragging the entire master plan into a conference room (or auditorium, if that's what it takes). We then work through the network diagram and break down the structure with the staff to see where the plan has misstated the actual work requirements. As we adjust the tasks, we work through the schedule.

By comparing the work being done to the work that was projected in the plan, you'll eventually get the team to understand why the schedule or the objectives are derailed—and hopefully, you'll get some insights about what can be done to get back on track.

Personality Clashes

We've already touched on these. Personality clashes are almost inevitable when many people work together. People with superior roles, training, and experience may look down their noses at team members perceived as less important. Sometimes people seem caustic or have different values about work and quality. Sometimes it's just a chemistry thing that can't be explained. You can minimize the negative affects of personality conflicts by building open communication and trust among the team members, but sometimes you'll just have to mediate to keep things on track.

Conflicts Are Strongest at Project Initiation

Problems such as personality conflicts can pop up any time in the project cycle, but some conflicts are more common at specific times in the project life cycle. During the project initiation phase, conflicts tend to swirl around goals, priorities, authority, and responsibility. At the beginning of the execution phase, conflicts over administrative procedures emerge but soon fade as people get used to project operations. As the project gets into full swing, conflicts move from goals to schedules and technical issues. As the project nears close-out, conflicts continue to involve the schedule but may also have growing personality-related issues. Of course, this sequence of conflicts isn't true of all projects, but it's predictable enough to help you plan for your resolutions before the problems emerge.

> **Words from the Wise**
>
> When you add power, self-esteem, motivations, and status to the equation, you'll likely see fireworks where the project team used to be.
>
> —Sunny Baker, *On Time and Within Budget* (1992)

Ignore It or Solve It? What Should You Do?

Conflict resolution requires careful consideration. The conflicting parties may both have legitimate grievances. As project manager, your task is to sort out the real problems that may be buried in the hubris of personalities. On the other hand, the clash may be the problem itself. We recommend the time-honored technique of interviewing each person or team separately and taking careful notes. It helps to have a witness with you in case legal issues come up later. (This is unlikely but not unheard of.) Then, after a period of time to reflect on the issues and a solution, present your resolution to both sides, either individually or together. Usually there is no perfect solution, but adjustments and compromise may mend the breach, at least until the project is complete.

Resolving Conflicts: The Five Options

Many people have studied conflicts and how managers resolve them. In general, these studies have identified five general ways that conflicts are resolved—and all of them are appropriate at one time or another:

- **Withdrawing** means that the manager retreats (withdraws) from the disagreement. This is often an option if the conflict is petty, of inconsequential impact to the project, and not worth spending time to figure out.

- **Smoothing** is used to emphasize areas of agreement to help minimize or avoid areas of disagreement. This is the preferred method when people can identify areas of agreement and the conflict is relatively unimportant. However, this is a weak approach; chances are, the conflict will flare up again even though sparring parties shake hands and make up. Use it to get the project moving until a better solution can be found.

- **Compromising** involves creating a negotiated solution that brings some source of satisfaction to each party in the conflict. Compromises are best made after each side has had time to cool down (if the conflict has escalated to the anger and hostility stage). The best compromise makes each party feel as though he or she "won." A well-constructed compromise will hold the project together. A poor or weak one will come apart in the future, and you should be ready for it. The solution to a collapsed compromise is usually another compromise. This works best when people have a give-and-take attitude and a shared focus on the priorities of the project. (The delicate art of negotiation is described in Chapter 25.)

♦ **Forcing** is used when someone exerts his or her position of power to resolve a conflict. This is usually done at the expense of someone else, and it is not recommended unless all other methods failed to resolve the conflict.

♦ **Confronting** is not quite as strong as forcing, but it is the most used form of conflict resolution. The goal of a confrontation (if handled professionally) is to get people to face their conflicts directly, thereby resolving the problem by working through the issues in the spirit of problem solving.

Time Is Money _____

When you have difficulties to communicate, the best way to do it is with a presentation of facts. The sooner the problem is truthfully acknowledged, the easier it will be to solve. Bad news that is covered up only grows larger over time—and damages your credibility in direct proportion to the length of time you waited to let people know about it.

Decide on the Best Approach

Almost any conflict can be ironed out, although resolution may impact the budget and schedule if the problem is complex or has been allowed to fester too long. Analyze the situation and choose the method of conflict resolution that makes the most sense and has the most chance of success.

Provide What's Needed

Attempt to provide what each party wants if possible. We once saw a conflict over computer floppy disks (still expensive then) that brought a major software development project to a halt. One team thought another was taking more than its share of disks. Buying separate supplies of disks resolved this incredibly stupid source of hostilities in minutes!

Work It Out

Best saved for personality conflicts, getting the unhappy parties together in a room with you as a mediator can work. From a mix of yelling and tears, a new friendship can often grow like a phoenix rising from the ashes. Beforehand, have each side prepare a list of grievances so that nothing is forgotten that can smolder later. Two meetings might be required to work out a complex problem. If the problem is a highly technical one on a topic in which you are not well versed, bring a third-party expert whose impeccable credentials are unassailable by either party.

Know When to Ignore It

Some problems fix themselves. A problem team member might realize that he or she doesn't fit in and find another job. This approach is only applicable to projects in which the schedule is loose and the problem isn't vital to the project's success. On the other hand, mature teams or team members may work things out themselves without your intervention. Finally, if a conflict is tangential and doesn't affect the project, it can also be ignored, at least until it does affect the project.

Employ Brute Force

As a last resort, use the chain of command to order warring parties back to work, with or without compromise. This approach is best saved for situations in which the schedule is so tight that there's no time for forging a compromise. It can also be used when one side is adamant in its position and refuses to accept a compromise solution.

The toughest problem is one you can't fix—a fundamental weakness in the project that you can't easily remedy such as an impossible schedule or a lack of resources, whether it's cash, personnel, equipment, or facilities. The only solution is either an ingenious workaround (more common in movies than in real life) or going to management, fingers crossed, and explaining the quandary and what is required to solve it.

Conflicts Aren't Always Negative

What does the conflict mean in the scheme of the universe? As project manager, you probably look at any conflict as troublesome. It slows the project, costs budget dollars, and reflects poorly on your abilities as team leader. But not all conflicts are negative in their impact. A conflict can point to real problems, can lead to better ideas for the project, or can serve as an attack on the entrenched thinking of the citadel.

When studying a conflict situation, look underneath the obvious motives to see whether there may be a better way to accomplish a task, a method for producing a better end product, or an imaginative team member constrained and confined to a lowly role. Stop, look, and listen. You may find something useful or important to the future of the project underlying any kind of conflict.

The Least You Need to Know

◆ Most conflicts can be resolved, but you may need to bring in an outside project expert to resolve a sticky conflict.

◆ To successfully resolve a conflict, you need to choose the right action for the job: withdrawing, smoothing, compromising, forcing, confronting, or, as a last resort, using brute force.

◆ Conflicts are particularly common during the project initiation phase, and the schedule is almost always a candidate for conflict at any stage of the project.

◆ Not all conflicts are negative if you know how to manage them for positive impact on the project.

24

Changes, Changes, and More Changes

In This Chapter

- ◆ Making changes to keep on track
- ◆ Accommodating the unexpected
- ◆ Understanding the trade-offs and the options for change
- ◆ Handling resistance to necessary changes

You can't predict everything, and unless you want to phone one of those telephone psychics, you're out of luck if you want to see into the future as a way to eliminate changes to your project plan. Because you can't always predict changes, we recommend that you rely on ongoing monitoring, open communications, and careful analysis as ways to deal with unforeseen changes. Of course, there are always tarot cards and tea leaves if you want to guess your way through the project.

Managing Change Is Part of Control

Some projects get completed exactly as planned—but not many. Projects often change direction, shape, or size. Goals. Budget. Schedule. Work plan. Priorities. Personnel. Any or all of these can change during the life of a project.

Some changes are under your control. For example, you might be able to shorten a schedule because you learn faster ways to do things as you proceed through the steps of the work plan. On the other hand, if the vendor who was manufacturing your cable boxes closes because of a strike, you'll have to change the schedule, like it or not. In both cases, you'll have to anticipate the impact of the change and adjust your project plan accordingly. Because change is inevitable, managing the impact of change is a key aspect in controlling your project.

> **Along the Critical Path**
>
> It is not the project manager's job to prevent change. It is the project manager's job to assess the impact of the change and to make a decision (or ask the steering committee to make one) based on his or her analysis.

A very common change is a change in requirements when you are already in the execution phase of a project. Recognizing that changes impact schedule, cost, and quality, you must balance those factors as you manage the change.

The Battle Cry of Change: Flexibility

Yes, there are project managers, often former military officers, who will tell you that the quickest way from Point A to Point B is a straight line. But after managing a multitude of projects of all sizes, we've learned that only a flexible project manager can actually complete a project on time and within budget—and that often means taking a longer or more circuitous route to get things done. If you insist on the rigid attitude of getting things done exactly as planned, you'll only frustrate yourself and your project team. Remember, plans are guidelines, not bibles. Your project plan is a living document that should be designed to be changed.

Let's turn to our All-Star Cable Movies-on-Demand case study to illustrate this point. During the project planning phase, the project manager was told that so-called "adult films" would not be part of the MOD package. However, during the execution phase, the marketing department convinced the management team and steering committee that adult films would be needed if they were going to get the revenues predicted in the future. The company president summoned the project manager to his office and told him to include adult movies in the film library. The project manager must then do an assessment of the impact of adding movies and tell the steering committee what the change in requirements will have on the schedule and the costs to the project.

The Marriage of Review and Change

Managing change and reviewing the project go hand in hand. As you monitor your project over time, you'll get feedback on the general issues, problems, and other factors that may be affecting your progress (positively or negatively) in completing the project. Lots of things enter the picture as the project proceeds; some are desirable, others are unpredictable, and once in a while, a disastrous event occurs. (We were working on a project at a major airport and were almost finished when 9/11 occurred. No one could have predicted that event, and needless to say, it had a dramatic effect on our project.) The good ideas and the unpredictable problems will all result in the same thing: the need to change the project plan in some way.

Through project review, new ideas and new ways of doing things become apparent. The realities of what can and cannot be accomplished shift tasks and goals. Then there are the changes handed down from senior management or the customers.

All these things require that you update your plan (including the SOW) for the project. As we've repeatedly stressed, updating the plan means making changes to the goals, tasks, workflow, schedule, budget, or people and getting them approved by the appropriate stakeholders. Be prepared for change. It's not a question of what to do *if* there is an issue; it's what to do *when* there is an issue.

> **CAUTION** **Risk Management**
>
> Today's purring project can become tomorrow's glitch-filled problem if you don't stay on top of things. Ongoing monitoring is always your first defense against the undesirable impacts of a changing world.

The Rules of Change

Now that you've accepted the inevitability of change, here are six rules that will help you anticipate changes on your projects:

1. During the planning phase, you should have established a decision-making process regarding changes that are requested. Be sure to follow that policy now.

2. Establish a change control board that is a subset of your steering committee or governance board. Use them to evaluate changes that have an impact on the stakeholders and the project. They should be able to handle the politics of changes within the organization.

3. The project manager must negotiate, be assigned, or have the authority to make appropriate operational project adjustments. The PM also needs authority to

control outside interference that's ill-advised. If the project manager lacks these basic authorities, uninformed changes made by people outside the project are more likely, and eventually, the inability of the project manager to control change will doom the project.

4. Establish emergency decision-making authority in case things need to be done too quickly for even the change control board to meet and discuss a change. In our All-Star Cable case study, a major decision needed to be made quickly on the movie library that All-Star Cable would use to pull movies. A vendor was in financial trouble and needed to make a deal to improve their second quarter financial reports. Unfortunately, it was the end of June, and most of the members of the steering committee and the change control board were on vacation. Fortunately, the project plan included an emergency authorization for the project sponsor to act on behalf of the steering committee, and All-Star Cable was able to secure a very favorable contract.

5. Maintain a change control log that tracks all change requests and documents the vital information needed to complete the lessons learned during the close-out phase.

6. You need a work authorization structure for handling changes. This is a big term that just means you, as project manager, need to authorize any changes in the work that people undertake. You don't want people working on activities without your knowledge. You can make this as formal (probably smart on large projects) or as informal as you think appropriate. Just make sure you have one!

Risk Management

Meddlers beware! There's always someone associated with your project who "knows" how to do things better than you're doing them. Sometimes you need to put your foot down and pinion these meddlers to keep them from getting in your way. Establish a clear process for suggesting and reviewing changes so that people offer constructive advice instead of bothersome chatter. And if you fail at a project because of outside meddling, guess who will get the blame? We bet it won't be the meddler with all those "good" ideas.

This is an example of a change control log. It tracks the information, including the tracking number that corresponds to the numbers on the work breakdown structure (WBS).

Change Control Log

Date	Change	Tracking Number	Authorized By	Impact
___	___	___ ___ ___	___ ___	___
___	___	___ ___ ___	___ ___	___
___	___	___ ___ ___	___ ___	___
___	___	___ ___ ___	___ ___	___
___	___	___ ___ ___	___ ___	___
___	___	___ ___ ___	___ ___	___
___	___	___ ___ ___	___ ___	___

Communicate with Everyone!

Yes, you've heard it before. When dealing with change, it's vital to get input from everyone on the team. Comments should also be solicited from other managers, senior management, and customers (when appropriate). Multiple inputs provide perspectives you may not have considered in your plan of change.

For example, if you make a task, resource, or schedule change, make sure the whole team is involved in understanding the need for new roles or task assignments. Have alternative activities identified if primary activities are stopped. You'll also need to ensure that all resources are aware of new job responsibilities and schedule implications.

Change and Risk

Any time you make a change in your project, you and your team will need to go back to your risk management plan and see if there is any impact. Work through any adjustments, or develop entirely new plans if the change requires it.

Change and Conflict Go Hand in Hand

In Chapter 23, we looked at ways to deal with conflicts. Many of the forces that cause conflict have to do with project changes. New ideas enter the project. Change is required. Schedules slip. Change is required. Jane and Joe are acting like children. Change is required. When a task proves impossible as originally defined, you guessed it. Change is required again.

The list of potential change sources is a long one. Some changes you can see coming, and you can make a preemptive strike to minimize their impact. Others occur without warning. Project changes also vary in their impact on your project. Some are little more than a blip easily accommodated within the project flow. Others force you to radically alter the budget, schedule, and scope of the project. Hope for the former but prepare for the latter.

Here are some of the "typical" changes we've seen in our experience as project managers:

> **Time Is Money**
>
> The best way to deal with a runaway project is to get involved as soon as you suspect a problem. The longer you wait, the less you will be able to salvage of your schedule and budget. Before you jump in, however, ask what's really wrong. Determine what precipitated the problem so you don't end up in the same place next time.

- The organizational priorities are realigned, and the priority of the project comes into question. Sometimes you can salvage the project through careful planning, justification of the project, and skillful renegotiation; sometimes you just end up on the wrong side of the corporate priorities and have to look for another project to manage. Once a project has lost the support of the stakeholders, resign yourself to the inevitable and don't try to salvage it.

- A company's restructuring or reorganization moves staff around, possibly depleting you of key team members. Again, the first step is negotiation to get whom you need. If that doesn't work, there are always outside vendors. And don't forget to consider staff development for the people you have left.

- An organization announces sweeping cuts in operational budgets. This can have a profound impact on a project with a budget that's already on the slim side. Go back to your plan and look for ways to cut back on expenses. Make sure everyone knows that the results will likely be cut back along with the budget (which is almost never a good idea or a good choice).

◆ A competitor announces a product that is similar to yours. You must get to market first, budget be damned. Now is the time to pull out all the stops and redraft the plan to get to market faster. You'll need more money as well as other resources, so expect to make a presentation to management that justifies your scheme.

◆ An external event occurs which has a dramatic impact on your project, such as a new or revised government regulation.

Understanding and Estimating the Impact of Changes

If you want to stay in control and help your project evolve in the right direction, a well-documented project plan is your first line of defense in managing change. If you want the results you expect as opposed to the consequences that just happen, you need to keep your plan up-to-date. Period. With a plan in hand, you can quickly assess the impact a change will have on the project's budget, schedule, and resources. You can also use the plan and your current status analysis to show why a new or different user requirement may have a negative impact on the final results of your project.

As you review your plan, you'll see that there are really only six major components in any project that can be changed. They are the same components that were used to create your project plan in the first place. Here they are again:

◆ The basic reason the project was undertaken in the first place, which you translated in project goals and objectives.

◆ The people who work on the project.

◆ The money (budget) you have to spend on the project.

◆ The material and technical resources you have available to support your project.

◆ The time you have available to complete the project.

◆ The quality requirements that were acceptable for the finished deliverable.

Any change in your project plan will affect one or more of these project components. Most changes will affect all six in some way. If you want to keep changes under control, you'll need to address the impact of changes by updating your project plan and communicating the changes to everyone involved.

Sometimes you'll need to replan, reapprove, and replan again. As you execute your project, things change. You control these things by adjusting the plan. As you execute the new plan, things change again. You repeat the cycle until the project is declared finished—and that means (finally) moving on to the close-out phase.

This type of change is called "balancing the project." As you find that the project is running out of time, costing too much, or short of resources, you must balance the cost, schedule, and results (goals) of the project to keep things on track. This will require involvement of all the stakeholders on the project.

The Balancing Act

Balancing a project can take place at three levels of authority, depending on the severity or immediacy of the change needed:

- **Project-level balancing** involves making adjustments to keep the project within its approved cost, schedule, and quality outcomes. The project manager and core team members should have enough authority to make these decisions.

- **Business-case balancing** is necessary when a project cannot achieve its approved cost, schedule, and quality goals. When this becomes obvious through project monitoring, the business case for the project must be reevaluated. Maybe the project will be useless if it doesn't come in on time. Maybe there isn't enough money (or profit) left in the project to make it worthwhile. Business case changes are beyond the scope of the project manager's authority alone and must involve the review and approval team of stakeholders. Most of all, the customer must agree to any changes that affect the cost, schedule, final features, or end results of the project.

- **Enterprise-level balancing** is required when a firm has to choose from various projects to spread limited resources out. This could result in a project being cancelled (terminated) or postponed. This is primarily a business management decision that is well beyond the scope of the project team, although the key team members will likely be involved in the process. The enterprise responsibility for this type of decision could lie with the customer, a government agency, or the corporation as a whole.

Maintaining control of changes is critical to keep from suffering from scope creep. We had one customer who would go to the project team members to request changes instead of the project manager. Of course, the project team was trying to please the customer and always said "yes" without the project manager's knowledge. It's easy to see how this project could get out of control quickly. To prevent these kinds of problems here's what to do:

- Establish how changes will take place before you need to make any. This should be done as a formal part of the project administrative procedures. On a large project, the change management process will likely include detailed, written steps for submitting and reviewing project changes. It may also include the formation of a change control board comprising a subset of stakeholders from all relevant areas of the project. This team will review and recommend changes for approval at various levels.

- Clearly define the expectations for the change. You are not making changes for fun but to improve something or to fix a problem. Be sure you determine how you'll measure whether the desired effect on the project is achieved. How will you know if the change is successful?

- Document requests for changes from team members as part of the change management process. If these changes meet criteria of importance or urgency, the recommendations should then be reviewed for further action.

- Plug the proposed changes into the project plan to see what happens to schedule, budget, and resource requirements. Never commit to a set of changes before assessing their impact on the project. Violators of this rule might find themselves with a failed project on their hands. Team review of the impact is vital. Others may spot an impossible task dependency that you missed, and the technical folks may have knowledge of dependencies for tasks you don't understand. When assessing the impact of the change to your project, you will need to assess how each of the elements are affected and balance time, cost, and quality. You will also need to consider if any of the elements are more important than the others. For example, if the project is time-critical, then it may require more resources and affect your cost. If you are also budget constrained, then you may need to adjust the requirements and sacrifice the quality of the project.

- Always look for alternatives before you, the change control board, or other stakeholders make a decision to change a major component of the plan. One more time, consider the budget, the staff skills, and the ability to meet the scheduled dates. Keep in mind that there is more than one way to accomplish almost anything.

- Have the changes reviewed and eventually accepted by the appropriate group of stakeholders.

- Once the changes are decided upon, document changes on the original plan, date them, and communicate them as you would a new project plan. On large projects, the documentation of the changes is often called configuration management, and it can require a full-time staff in the "project office" responsible for controlling the different versions of the project plan.

Risk Management

It's important to always get formal approval for revisions from the powers that be. Even if the disruption is minimal, managers and stakeholders should be fully cognizant of changes. For changes that impact delivery dates or the budget, written correspondence should accompany your request. Remember, if they're not in writing, agreements are easily forgotten.

◆ After the new plan is approved, inform all team members of the changes to their tasks and delivery dates. Make sure all team members are aware of exactly what will be expected of them and how the changes will impact the project. You'll also need to let team members know how the effect of the changes will be measured so that things don't end up going on just like before. This should be done through ongoing monitoring, reports, and communication. (And yes, you might need to change some of your project reports or procedures to make sure you get the new information you need.)

The Basic Changes You Can Make

In balancing a project that's missing its time, cost, or quality objectives, here are the basic things you can do:

◆ **Reestimate the project.** This means double-checking things to make sure the estimates are really valid. Don't just give in to management to reduce the cost or schedule estimates; instead, look for opportunities to do things better or differently to achieve the same goals. For example, you may be able to take advantage of the float in the schedule to resequence noncritical tasks. If you do the review of the project correctly, your new estimates should provide an even firmer foundation for meeting project expectations.

Time Is Money

Keep in mind that people get frustrated with endless rounds of picky changes. To avoid this frustration, limit the self-induced changes to those that are truly necessary and important.

◆ **Add more people to the project.** Beware of this simple-sounding solution, however; as you add more personalities, people can lock horns in what is called a "creative conflict." This can bring work to a standstill until the mess sorts itself out or a creative team member stomps off for good in self-righteous disgust. This is sad but common. Only add people if people will actually help get things done faster. Look for other means to improve productivity. If you scoped out the work and selected a good team in the first place, you may need to change objectives instead of the team.

◆ **Reduce the scope of the tasks.**
Sometimes the best way to get a project done is to scratch some of the work from the list. This can turn an impossible list of tasks into a doable (and scoped down) project. Before promising to do less as a way of dealing with change, however, make sure the downsized project is really worth doing. Also make sure the stakeholders agree to the downsizing. If not, you'll need to negotiate what you really need—more time or resources or a bigger budget—to get the project done right.

> **CAUTION**
>
> **Risk Management**
>
> There's a dimension in many projects that you might call the twilight zone—the unreality between the actual time and resources available and the demands by the customer or senior managers in your company. Try to avoid entering the twilight zone by being firm and honest with people who attempt to pressure you into unrealistic goals, schedules, or budgets.

◆ **Increase productivity by using in-house experts.** Some people are simply more productive than others. By reassigning people, you may still be able to meet your original cost and schedule performance. Sometimes this is a good solution for the project but a bad one for the company, however. For example, it's not always a good idea to put all the best engineers on one project; the other projects may suffer as a result. Some of these engineers might end up doing work for productivity's sake that's well below their capabilities. Be sure there isn't a better way to make the staff more productive such as training people or prudently using new technologies.

◆ **Use outside resources.** Assign part of the project to an external firm that can manage and complete it within your original guidelines. (This is called outsourcing.) This moves the work to outside experts who will hopefully be more productive. However, this may create more risks in terms of lost in-house control and the gamble that the outside experts will actually be able to do what they say they can.

◆ **Use overtime.** Use it prudently, however. It can backfire in lost productivity and morale problems if this option becomes the default action. If you're using hourly employees as opposed to salaried ones, it can end up pushing the budget out of control.

◆ **Shift some of the work to the customer.** If a project is high on cost or short on people resources, this can be a good choice—if the customer agrees to it. You and the customer should identify tasks that the customer's staff can perform.

This only works if the customer agrees with the plan and has adequate resources to take on the tasks. It can also create political problems between your project organization and that of the customer. Be careful when you consider this option; it needs to be done in a way that preserves the integrity of the project and your authority as project manager.

♦ **Crash the schedule.** This involves compressing the tasks on the critical path to reduce the time required to meet the desired finish date. You'll need to produce a cost/schedule/trade-off analysis, which can help analyze the cost of reducing the schedule. Sometimes the increases in cost to get things done faster will outweigh the need for speed.

♦ **Adjust the profit requirements for the project.** A reduced profit margin can free up cash for needed resources. If the project won't bring in enough money for the company to survive, however, this is a bad idea. A decision to reduce profit is clearly the territory of the company executives—not the project manager.

♦ **Adjust the project goals.** This is like playing on thin ice. Although it may be appropriate to reduce some of the functionality or scope of the project end results, it's not usually a good idea to reduce the performance characteristics (quality) of the project. Remove some of the functionality only when it doesn't affect the performance of the product overall. Performance cuts may initially save time, but these cuts result in cost increases in the long run due to reworking broken or deficient parts or damaging the reputation of your firm. Remember that quality is never free.

Comparing Changes with Trade-Off Analysis

Trade-off analysis is one method of dealing with change that lets you evaluate the impact of various alternatives. "We can do this if we skip that. Which is more important?" Analyzing trade-offs is also a way to understand the pressure change is placing on the project. Understanding trade-offs clarifies the changes that affect later tasks and milestones. Here are some considerations for understanding the impact of various options (or trade-offs) when implementing a change to a project:

♦ Determine the underlying rationale for the change. Are the changes motivated by rational thinking or a political agenda? Does the change really make sense?

♦ Are the project goals still appropriate? Will the change also affect the eventual outcome of the project? Imagine if God set out to make the eagle but, due to project changes, created the dodo bird instead. Make sure your dodo will still be a desirable species—or figure out how to make the eagle you really wanted.

♦ Do the options affect the likelihood of completing the project successfully? You should have already reviewed how the various options impact schedules, budgets, and team member availability. When changes increase the risk of failure, this needs to be carefully analyzed and then clearly communicated to all involved. Sometimes the risk is for good reasons, but sometimes it's just a plain mistake. Make sure you know which it is before you choose one change over another.

♦ Analyze the options at all levels. Try to hold the budget and objectives constant and then evaluate how you can accommodate the changes. Look for alternatives, tasks that can be deleted or shortened, or dollars that can be moved around in the project. This is usually a team exercise. Be patient when trying to come up with alternatives. Don't always jump on the first ideas. It's often at 11 P.M. over a seventh cup of coffee that a team member suggests the perfect compromise that hadn't occurred to you during the first review of the problem. Only after looking at all options should you ask for more money or more time.

Use the Zero-Based Budget Approach

Sometimes you need to prioritize what really needs to be done in order to understand the things that should be changed on a project. If you're building a hot new computer system with many new multimedia features, for example, maybe some of the features could be released in next year's model. To make this kind of decision, we often use the zero-based budget (ZBB) approach to establish the priorities and the bottom line for a changing project. ZBB is an approach that separates the must-do from the would-like-to-do work. (This is different than a trade-off analysis, which looks at one option for change compared to another.)

Assembling a ZBB is simple. Make a list of all the elements you would like to see done at completion (see the following chart). Then rewrite the list according to priority. List the most important must-do tasks or goals at the top and work your way down to the less important tasks toward the bottom.

Next, review your list. Rewrite it if you've made lots of notes, erasures, or arrows to move things around. When you have a prioritized list, starting from the top, write down the costs and schedule significance of each goal or task and weigh the time and budget required. As you work down the list, when you run out of resources, draw a line under the last goal or task you can accomplish within your budget (or schedule).

Items above the line can be done. Items below the line should be scrubbed since the resources required to complete them successfully are not currently available.

A zero-based budget is a simple tool for understanding and simplifying priorities based on the cost of getting things done.

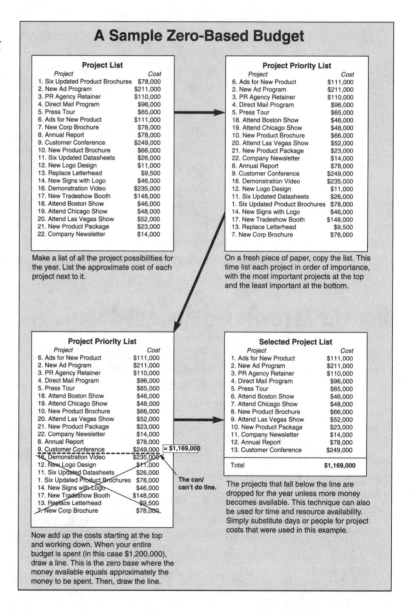

A Sample Zero-Based Budget

Project List

Project	Cost
1. Six Updated Product Brochures	$78,000
2. New Ad Program	$211,000
3. PR Agency Retainer	$110,000
4. Direct Mail Program	$96,000
5. Press Tour	$65,000
6. Ads for New Product	$111,000
7. New Corp Brochure	$78,000
8. Annual Report	$78,000
9. Customer Conference	$249,000
10. New Product Brochure	$66,000
11. Six Updated Datasheets	$26,000
12. New Logo Design	$11,000
13. Replace Letterhead	$9,500
14. New Signs with Logo	$46,000
16. Demonstration Video	$235,000
17. New Tradeshow Booth	$148,000
18. Attend Boston Show	$46,000
19. Attend Chicago Show	$48,000
20. Attend Las Vegas Show	$52,000
21. New Product Package	$23,000
22. Company Newsletter	$14,000

Make a list of all the project possibilities for the year. List the approximate cost of each project next to it.

Project Priority List

Project	Cost
6. Ads for New Product	$111,000
2. New Ad Program	$211,000
3. PR Agency Retainer	$110,000
4. Direct Mail Program	$96,000
5. Press Tour	$65,000
18. Attend Boston Show	$46,000
19. Attend Chicago Show	$48,000
10. New Product Brochure	$66,000
20. Attend Las Vegas Show	$52,000
21. New Product Package	$23,000
22. Company Newsletter	$14,000
8. Annual Report	$78,000
9. Customer Conference	$249,000
16. Demonstration Video	$235,000
12. New Logo Design	$11,000
11. Six Updated Datasheets	$26,000
1. Six Updated Product Brochures	$78,000
14. New Signs with Logo	$46,000
17. New Tradeshow Booth	$148,000
13. Replace Letterhead	$9,500
7. New Corp Brochure	$78,000

On a fresh piece of paper, copy the list. This time list each project in order of importance, with the most important projects at the top and the least important at the bottom.

Project Priority List

Project	Cost
6. Ads for New Product	$111,000
2. New Ad Program	$211,000
3. PR Agency Retainer	$110,000
4. Direct Mail Program	$96,000
5. Press Tour	$65,000
18. Attend Boston Show	$46,000
19. Attend Chicago Show	$48,000
10. New Product Brochure	$66,000
20. Attend Las Vegas Show	$52,000
21. New Product Package	$23,000
22. Company Newsletter	$14,000
8. Annual Report	$78,000
9. Customer Conference	$249,000	= $1,169,000
16. Demonstration Video	$235,000
12. New Logo Design	$11,000
11. Six Updated Datasheets	$26,000
1. Six Updated Product Brochures	$78,000
14. New Signs with Logo	$46,000
17. New Tradeshow Booth	$148,000
13. Replace Letterhead	$9,500
7. New Corp Brochure	$78,000

The can/
can't do line.

Now add up the costs starting at the top and working down. When your entire budget is spent (in this case $1,200,000), draw a line. This is the zero base where the money available equals approximately the money to be spent. Then, draw the line.

Selected Project List

Project	Cost
1. Ads for New Product	$111,000
2. New Ad Program	$211,000
3. PR Agency Retainer	$110,000
4. Direct Mail Program	$96,000
5. Press Tour	$65,000
6. Attend Boston Show	$46,000
7. Attend Chicago Show	$48,000
8. New Product Brochure	$66,000
9. Attend Las Vegas Show	$52,000
10. New Product Package	$23,000
11. Company Newsletter	$14,000
12. Annual Report	$78,000
13. Customer Conference	$249,000
Total	$1,169,000

The projects that fall below the line are dropped for the year unless more money becomes available. This technique can also be used for time and resource availability. Simply substitute days or people for project costs that were used in this example.

Haul your entire network diagram and schedule into a boardroom and lay it across the table. Your convincing arguments to senior management may persuade them that the change is not a good idea when you review the impact on the plan in detail.

Often, simply telling them how much extra cash the change requires is a very persuasive tactic in managing expectations and change.

Sometimes Quitting Is the Only Choice

In spite of looking for reasonable options to keep your project on track, there are some changes that force only undesirable options. We're sorry we don't have better news. As frustrating as such unforeseen problems are, sometimes no amount of planning or management will fix the problem. You'll just have to start over or quit the project. That's why it's always a good idea to have a contingency plan when opening a new business or bringing out a new product—along with some extra income sources in the background—just in case Murphy's Law prevails.

The Steps for Engineering Organizational Change

The final product or products of any project must ultimately be used by people in the operations part of the business—whether the customer is an internal or external customer. Whenever that product is introduced, it creates change. You can either manage that change, just like you manage the changes to your project, or you can throw fate to the wind and hope everything turns out okay. For example, at All-Star Cable, the billing department will be impacted tremendously by the Movies-on-Demand project. Getting the billing department ready will be very important to the ongoing success of the operations of the entire company.

Here are the five requirements for *operations integration*:

- ◆ Create a vision for how the project deliverable will benefit users. They must be able to see how it will be used in their day-to-day life for them to accept and embrace it. If you ignore this picture of the future, then everyone will make up their own picture and you will have confusion about the product. For All-Star Cable, their customers must understand how the new service of Movies-on-Demand will be better than the "old" pay-per-view system and see themselves watching movies and stopping and starting the film just like when using a VCR, with the added convenience of not needing to go to the store to rent it!

Project Lingo

Operations integration means the full implementation of the product or service to achieve the intended value outlined in the business case for the project.

◆ Make sure that people have the skills to use the product. They may need to be trained or be given instruction guides to help them use the product effectively. If they don't know how to use the product, they won't use it! At All-Star Cable, if the project team doesn't develop and execute training and instruction guides for the customers, customers won't sign up for the service.

◆ Give users incentives to try something new. At All-Star Cable, the project team decided that a couple of free movies in the first week might be the right incentive to get people started. Without incentives, it is very difficult to get people to change their behavior—there has to be some reward.

◆ Provide resources to assist people as they make the change. For instance, All-Star Cable will need to have a 1-800 number that people can call if they have questions or problems figuring out the new Movies-on-Demand system. Without the resources in place, people will get frustrated and they won't accept the change— in this case they won't order movies!

◆ Finally, people need to know the schedule for rolling out the new product. The project team has let them know, at the appropriate times, what is happening and when. Just like the local newspaper prepares the TV guide for the next week, the All-Star Cable project manager must prepare the company's customers for the results of their project.

When you do all these things, you will have very little resistance to organizational change.

The Least You Need to Know

◆ Changes are a natural and expected aspect of any project, but changes made through a defined process will be easier to control.

◆ Change is not a negative word; many changes on projects are made for positive reasons.

◆ The end result of changes affects the budget, schedule, and goal outcomes. This means the plan must be updated on a regular basis to reflect the impact of changes.

◆ Change should be resisted when unnecessary, frivolous, or obviously detrimental to the successful completion of the project.

◆ Engineering organizational change will ensure that customers adopt a project's deliverable.

Chapter 25

Quality Management: Making It the Best It Can Be

In This Chapter

◆ Planning for quality

◆ Ensuring the quality of the product

◆ Controlling quality during the project

The issue of quality will always surface as you attempt to balance the four main elements of your project: time, cost, quality, and scope. We've spent a lot of time on monitoring and controlling your schedule and costs (Chapter 22), and now it's time to work on assessing and ensuring the quality of the project's deliverable. In reading this chapter, keep in mind that even though we will refer to the "product" of the project as a deliverable, in reality, it can mean a service as well as a physical good.

What Exactly Does Quality Mean in a Project?

In its simplest form, the definition of *quality* is conformance to requirements. Remember when we talked about developing the requirements in

Chapter 4? That's the starting place for developing your quality plan. During your quest for quality, you will need to identify which quality standards are relevant to your project and determine how to satisfy them.

Project Lingo

The Project Management Institute defines **quality** as conformance to requirements. **Grade** is the ranking we give products that have the same functional use, but different characteristics.

Often, a project team may confuse quality with *grade* and end up hurting the project overall. For example, a software product may have high quality because it does what it is supposed to do with few problems. However, it may have a low grade because it has very few appealing features. On the other hand, we have all had software that had a ton of features, but so many "bugs" that we wanted to throw it away. That product would be defined as having high grade (a lot of features), but low quality (too many problems).

Determining the right balance between the quality and the grade is the work of the project manager along with the project team. In our case study of All-Star Cable, the project manager and the project team will need to see how many features they can successfully add to the Movies-on-Demand product while still meeting the requirements for cost and schedule they have developed.

Planning for Quality Is the Starting Point

When you begin to plan for the quality of the product your project will produce, you need to first go to the statement of work and review the scope of the project. Review with the team what is clearly in-scope and out-of-scope on this project. For example, the project team at All-Star Cable decided that they would initially target their existing customers as the primary audience for this service (in scope) and not target new customers with MOD (out of scope). Also, they decided to use a film library from an outside source (in scope) since they did not want to maintain a library of movie titles (out of scope) and outsourcing the library would allow them to change titles more frequently. Continue with a review of the requirements and specifications that you were given when you were handed the project and the process you used to refine them during the definition phase.

You will also need to review other aspects of the project to gauge the impact on quality. For example, you may need to review the procurement process for selecting vendors who will supply you with products or services to be sure that the quality requirements for the vendors you choose will meet your project requirements. This will also help you control the quality of the vendors' work during the course of the project. The project manager and the project team for All-Star Cable developed a very specific set of requirements on the size, features, and video signal capabilities for vendors before they sent out the request for proposal (RFP) for the cable boxes and remote controls for Movies-on-Demand.

Quality Planning Tools and Techniques

There are several tools and techniques that you can use to plan the quality of your project's deliverables. In this section, we will cover the more common ones.

Cost/Benefit Analyses

One of the most useful techniques is to do a *cost/benefit analysis* as part of the planning for a project. As you work to balance time, cost, scope, and quality, you will need to weigh different factors and come up with alternatives to satisfy your stakeholders. For instance, to determine which features to include in the Movies-on-Demand screen menu, the project manager for All-Star Cable will do a cost/benefit analysis of the features. Some of them may be almost a given, such as a parental control feature that prevents children from ordering movies without their parents' knowledge or consent.

Other features may be far more optional, such as how long the customer will have access to the movie after ordering it. In this example, allowing the customer to have access to the movie for 24 hours versus 72 hours will have a very different economic impact on the company. The project manager will need to show the steering committee how these two alternatives might affect the profit margin for MOD. The project manager will need to discuss them with the stakeholders, provide them with the cost/benefit analysis, and let them make the decision.

Project Lingo

A cost/benefit analysis is an estimate of the costs and benefits of various alternatives and then using financial measures, such as Return on Investment (ROI) or payback period, to determine which of the alternatives is the most desirable.

Benchmarking

Benchmarking can also be a very useful in quality planning tool. Benchmarking involves comparing your project plan or practices to those of other projects to generate ideas for improvement or to provide a sound standard you can use to measure your project's performance. You may want to benchmark against other projects within your organization, if they are available, or you may want to use standards developed by the Project Management Institute. Either way, it should help you to plan and execute your quality process within your project.

Cause-and-Effect Diagrams

Cause-and-effect diagrams, also called Ishikawa diagrams or fishbone diagrams, can also help identify how a problem may be solved by showing the linkage between various factors. The basic idea is to find the cause of a problem and separate that from the effect it is having (similar to a doctor noting a high fever—the symptom or effect—and the cause which may be an infection or a virus). As you measure the progress of your project, any potential quality problems should begin to show up and you will need to take corrective action. The cause-and-effect diagrams can give you and your team a visual linkage between factors to see if the problem lies with manufacturing, people, a technical specification, and so on. Also, you will need to collect data that helps to …

◆ Define the problem: What has been observed or reported?

◆ Identify where is the problem occurring

◆ See any patterns for when the problem is occurring

◆ Determine how often the problem occurs

Cause-and-effect diagrams can help the project team to uncover problems by showing how various parts are linked together.

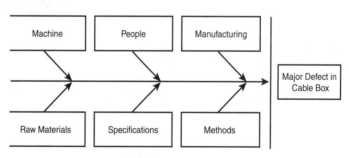

Finally, system or process flow charts can illustrate how information flows during a process or throughout an organization. They can also be used to help the project team by showing them where quality problems might occur so they can plan to prevent them. The pictorial representation can help people see what is happening and when. As a result, detecting the source of a problem, or potential problem, may be easier to identify.

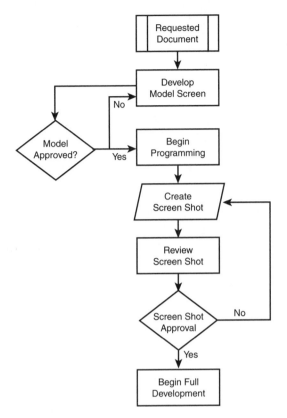

Flow charts can help the project team spot potential areas for quality problems.

As you use these tools, you and your project team should develop a quality management plan that explains …

◆ How you will implement your plan.

◆ What operating guidelines you will use to measure quality.

◆ Which checklists you will be using to verify that you have implemented your plan.

Quality Assurance: The Real Proof

There are a variety of ways to ensure that the project will meet the quality requirements set out in the quality management plan. The quality tools mentioned earlier are a great start. Doing benchmarking to see how a successful project operated is an easy way to ensure your project team will know how to succeed. All the quality tools are also helpful in keeping the quality of your project deliverables on track.

You may also want to consider conducting a peer review. The peer review is a formal review of the project, usually during the design phase, that can provide an unbiased assessment of your project plans.

The Peer Review

To set up your peer review (which we discussed at length in Chapter 22), you will want to gather a small group of people (probably no more than 10) who have the knowledge and experience to effectively evaluate your project plan. They should probably not come from your stakeholder group since you want an unbiased review. However, you should give the stakeholders a briefing on the results of your peer review when it is completed. For All-Star Cable, the project manager would probably invite people who know a lot about cable systems from the perspective of various disciplines, such as IT, accounting and billing, content management, marketing and sales, and operations and management.

These people evaluate the plan and provide insights on potential risks that may be present that the project team had not considered. Don't ask the reviewers to approve or disapprove the project. They are just there to evaluate and help the project team with a "sanity check" on the approach to the project.

We have been involved in dozens of peer reviews and they are one of the best quality tools around to handle quality assurance.

Quality Control: It's All About Results

In quality control, as project manager, you and your project team are monitoring very specific project results to make sure that they meet the requirements of the project. Some organizations have a quality control department; if yours does, be sure to get them involved early on in the project so they can help with quality planning. Or maybe you have a quality expert on your team, if so, he or she should also be involved in the planning process. If you don't have that expertise, don't fret, there are still some things you can do. One of the most common methods of quality control is simple inspections. For example, as project manager for All-Star Cable you might want to assign a team member to visually inspect and test the cable boxes that the manufacturer is producing for the company. The purpose is to make sure that the boxes conform to the requirements established in the quality management plan. Far better to learn of some mistakes *before* the customer gets those faulty boxes!

If there are too many boxes to inspect individually or you are short on time, you can conduct a statistical sampling. This means that instead of inspecting all the cable boxes, the team member will look at a certain percentage of them—say, every tenth cable box being made. Or maybe they will look at three boxes in each large container of twenty-five. There are a number of books on the market with detailed approaches to sampling and the evidence that it works. This can also reduce the cost of conducting quality inspections, usually a primary consideration in cost-conscious projects!

Once you've inspected the product, you can use a Pareto diagram to put the information you collected into a usable format for control quality. A Pareto diagram is basically a histogram that shows how many results were generated by an identifiable cause. It will show you were the problems are and help you and your team to establish priorities for tackling any defects.

A Pareto diagram is a special type of histogram that helps us to identify and prioritize problem areas. It involves collecting data and types of problems from the various sources. In the diagram, the sources of problems are the video signal, audio signal, remote control, power cable, and cable connection. This is the source of the famous 80/20 rule that says that 80 percent of your problems will come from 20 percent of the sources. You are trying to evaluate where the greatest source of problems are occurring and take corrective action. In this case, the video components seem to be the greatest source of problems, so it becomes the highest priority for corrective action.

Using checklists and the whole suite of quality tools that are available will aid you tremendously in getting the results you and stakeholders want.

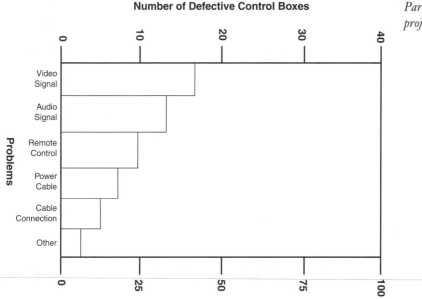

Pareto diagrams can help the project team set priorities.

The Least You Need to Know

- ◆ Focus on quality, not on grade.
- ◆ Plan for quality right from the beginning.
- ◆ Use quality tools to help you.
- ◆ Remember that quality control is all about results.

Chapter 26

Common Project Problems: Get Them Before They Get You

In This Chapter

- How to recognize the urgency of the problem before you take action

- A dozen or so common problems to expect on any project of any size

- Identify problems in the making before they undermine project objectives, schedules, or budgets

- Strategies to help you solve or avoid the most common project problems

Okay, you've read every chapter so far, and as hard as you try, some of your projects aren't getting done better. They're taking too long. They're not reaping results. Your team doesn't seem interested in meeting the deadlines. Your boss keeps asking for changes. The customers want more results. Even Dogbert's advice and Dilbert's humor don't seem to help when deadlines are slipping and expenses are skyrocketing.

If you think that project management techniques will eliminate all your problems in getting things done on time and within budget, forget it. All projects have problems. In some ways, project management success depends on problem-solving techniques more than any other processes.

Recognizing All Problems, Large and Small

The successful project manager is able to maintain a perspective that allows honest, objective evaluation of each issue as it comes up. Like personal conflicts, not all problems require immediate action, and some don't require any action at all. They just need to be monitored to make sure they don't get out of hand. At this point, you might want to review Chapter 3 and the seven reasons that many of these problems occur.

Large problems typically have multiple owners and involve several resources or significant amounts of money with jeopardy to budget, schedule, and quality. These frequently require immediate attention and take a great deal of time to resolve.

> **CAUTION**
>
> **Risk Management**
>
> Safety problems may be associated with the potential for loss of life. These must be analyzed and resolved immediately.

On the other hand, small problems may be solved quickly and with the help of only one or two resources. Nonurgent problems are those that can be deferred until later without impact to the project, the customer, or the organization. In fact, a great many of these become nonproblems as time passes.

The good news is that most project problems, whether large or small, are predictable. To help you anticipate problems in your projects and thus minimize their impact, we'll describe some of the common project problems in this chapter. Like a Boy Scout, expect to encounter them and be prepared to minimize their impact.

The Floating Start Date

Some projects just never seem to get off the ground because other priorities keep getting in the way. Unfortunately, even though a project may start late, everyone expects it to finish on the original schedule. If you find that your project never gets started, consider these strategies for solving the problem:

- ◆ Reanalyze the business case for the project. Maybe the project really isn't that important after all.

◆ If the project really needs to be completed as scheduled, work with your project sponsor to communicate the problem to management and adjust your own work habits to make time for it.

◆ If the project starts late, communicate (in writing as well as verbally) the new finish date to management and the project team. If you need to keep the original date, complete a trade-off analysis of time, cost and quality that the changes will require as described in Chapter 24.

◆ Analyze your daily activities and determine whether you are wasting time on less important tasks. If you need time-management training, get some. There are many good books that offer guidelines for identifying the time traps in day-to-day work—get one and implement its advice.

> **CAUTION**
>
> **Risk Management**
>
> Never assume that people will be available when dates slip. If you don't ask about the new schedule and people's availability, you may be the last to find out that you don't have the people you counted on to get things done.

There's Not Enough Time for Everything

Things always seem to take longer than we anticipate, and there are always more things than we have time to do. In a search for solutions to the ever-present problem of finding more time for the project, look into the following alternatives:

◆ If the team is falling behind, don't try to catch up all on your own. Delegate more of the activities and involve other people in the prioritization and assignment of work.

◆ Eliminate work that isn't really necessary. Always question the necessity of each task on a project. Skip tasks that don't count.

◆ Learn to politely say "No" (or if this isn't possible, at least say, "I'll think about it") when someone asks you to add tasks that may interfere with more important project priorities.

◆ Change the priorities for the work. Some things may get done later than originally planned, but this is better than nothing getting done. Of course, you must communicate this change to the other people working on the project.

◆ Work longer hours when this is an option, but don't overdo it for too long; otherwise, you and your team will become less productive and less motivated. All work and no play are ingredients for disgruntled project teams and poorly executed projects.

Too Many Reports and Not Enough Communication

Reports are not a substitute for one-on-one communication with your project team. Too many reports also bog projects down in unnecessary paperwork, and this affects quality, schedules, and motivation. To ensure that reports are not substituting for communication, do the following:

◆ Make a list of all the reports being produced for the project, the people responsible, and the content of each report. Then critically review each report and make sure it is really necessary. Also make sure that the reports are as simple as possible while still conveying the required information.

◆ Create a card file, or tickler file, reminding you to visit key team members on a regular basis. Note the last date you spoke with each person. Write a note to yourself in your calendar or organizer to talk to specific team members each week or day as appropriate.

◆ Take people to lunch when you have time and ask them how things are going. Informal get-togethers often result in more open communications and more honest updates on progress.

◆ Keep your door open unless you're really in a private meeting. There is nothing more intimidating than a project manager who is always locked behind a closed door.

They Always Need It Faster

Shortening the schedule is a frequent request because of predictable business demands, especially competitive pressures to get products out faster or to generate the revenue anticipated from the completion of a project. It's always good to consider faster alternatives for completing a project. However, implementing a "crash" schedule may cause your team to "crash and burn." You must consider the trade-offs in terms of other business priorities, the use of resources, and the costs of getting things done faster. The ways to do this were explained in Chapter 24. You can also see if tasks or work packages can be done in parallel rather than sequentially.

Time Is Money

Project managers use the term "crashing" a project to indict that they are adding additional resources to complete a project faster. Just be sure that more resources will help you get things done faster.

The 90-Percent-Done Syndrome

Many people are optimistic about their ability to make up for lost time. Others simply attempt to look good on paper. For these reasons, whenever we see the phrase "90 percent done" on a project status report, we know there's a big problem.

What is hiding behind that unfinished 10 percent that no one wants to admit? Why does it seem that 90 percent of the effort only takes 30 percent of the time, and the last 10 percent takes 200 percent of the original schedule?

If you see that 90 percent or some other large percentage of a complex task is completed very quickly, but then the work only inches up to 91 and 92 percent over the next couple of status reports, you need to figure out what is really going on by talking to the staff in an environment of support and understanding.

Here are some guidelines for getting to the root of the 90-Percent-Done Syndrome:

- Investigate the scope of the remaining work through meetings or one-on-one sessions with key project members. Are there technical difficulties that the team doesn't want anyone to know about? Should the task be broken down into smaller, more measurable tasks?

- Consider whether the remaining 10 percent of the work is really predictable. Creative tasks, such as inventions or coming up with ideas, are often difficult to schedule. In the development of a new technology and in other high-creativity situations, the breakthrough that is required to complete a project may not happen as scheduled. Creative tasks need to be more realistically assessed. You can't schedule spontaneity, so don't try. Just be honest about the creative blocks and document the schedule changes accordingly.

- Help the team be honest in its assessment of project status by encouraging open communication and by pointing out the problems with being too optimistic about risky endeavors. Team members may be giving you the estimates they think you want to see—not the real ones. Reward yourself and the team for honesty and effort rather than false statements of accomplishment or unrealistic commitments to impossible dreams.

Moving Target Objectives

Changes in project plans are valid for many reasons, as we discussed in Chapter 24. However, sometimes the changes in project goals and objectives seem to occur more frequently than they should. Because there isn't time to plan and adjust for these daily or hourly changes, you might not bother to update the current plan. This is a bad idea.

Not adjusting the plan is just about the easiest way we know of to end up with a project disaster. When changes are requested frequently and arbitrarily on a project, it is an indication of a lack of consensus regarding the original plan or some other political problem between your customer or client, the project, and the stakeholders. Here are some ways to save yourself in this situation:

◆ Make sure the authority for making project changes is clearly documented in the project plan.

◆ Don't start a project until the plan is approved by all appropriate levels of management and other appropriate stakeholders (customer or client).

◆ Don't promise to implement changes in a project until you have time to analyze and document the impact of the changes. Follow all the other rules for making project changes that are discussed in Chapter 24.

The Key Person Always Quits

Many projects depend on the special skills of a single person. If this person leaves, the project could be doomed. However, there are a few basic ways to keep the departure of a key person from becoming a catastrophe:

◆ Keep the key person happy in the first place. Listen. Be aware of problems in advance. Most people don't just walk out; it takes time for them to become disgruntled. If there is a reason for the dissatisfaction, try to find it and fix it.

◆ Cross-train people as work proceeds on the project. This training can minimize the impact of losing a key person on the team because others will be familiar with the project.

◆ Make sure the key person is also part of the team. Try to have someone work with this person to document his or her work. If the key person works in isolation, the impact of this person's absence could be disastrous. On the other hand, if the work is documented, you can usually hire someone else to take over where the other person left off.

Costs Spiral Out of Control

Budget and cost-control problems occur for many reasons including lack of skill or discipline in estimating costs in the original plan, inadequate detail in the plan that results in vague or inaccurate budget allotments, schedule delays that cause more resources to be used than planned, unforeseen technical problems, changes in material or service costs that weren't anticipated, and changes in the scope of a project that are not reflected in the updates to the budgets—along with a myriad of other "justifiable" events.

In spite of excuses to the contrary, there is only one way to control costs: Keep on top of expenses through regular monitoring and appropriate accounting controls. There simply isn't any other solution.

Cost overruns don't just happen. Costs increase because of poor communications, lack of control, inaccurate reporting, or inadequate documentation of project changes. Through diligent monitoring of expenditures during the project, money problems can be dealt with when budget problems first appear—before the costs get out of control.

The Staff Has More Enthusiasm Than Talent

Unfortunately, the most likable people are not always the most competent. If you choose people for their personalities alone and not their skills, you can end up in a situation in which a congenial team just doesn't get the work done.

What should you do when you have a great group of fun people working on the project, but they just don't seem to deliver what you need? Here are some guidelines to help you decide:

- Develop an objective skills appraisal system to select team members at the beginning of the project. This can help keep friendly but unskilled people off the team.

- Watch the team to see if too much time is being spent in social activities. Sometimes the problem isn't a lack of competence at all; instead, the schedule suffers because of too much socializing during work hours. Usually, a simple meeting to reemphasize the priorities of the project can solve this problem.

- If a congenial but unskilled person (or group) is willing to be trained and has potential, additional education is sometimes a solution. However, getting people up to speed is only an option if the schedule can absorb the time required for training.

Words from the Wise

I always figured that I've learned the most about projects from the ones that fell apart. It's a lot like taking the rings off a partly rotten onion. You can't tell what's worthy inside until you see the whole thing. Then you become a project leader: like it or not.

—A project manager with 30+ years experience

♦ If competence is the root of the problem, a consultant or outside vendor can sometimes make up the difference in skills, allowing the friendly person in question to remain on your team in a lesser capacity.

Ultimately, you may need to tell your "friends" that they aren't making the grade. Give people every opportunity to do the job, but if everything else fails, you'll have to find someone else for the team. When this is necessary, cut the ties earlier rather than later. Getting rid of dead wood on the team is one task that most managers dread and put off. In business, if the goals for the project are important, the project must take priority—no matter how much you like the person (or the group).

The Impossible Remains Impossible

In an attempt to look good, novice project managers often commit to more work than is possible. Even worse, they commit to projects that are impossible from the start. The budget and schedule may be so unrealistic that there is no possibility for completing the work as specified.

Here are some examples of impossible projects:

♦ Projects that stem from poor plans or lack of support. Any enterprise that begins a project must have a commitment to complete it. Sadly, some projects never reach completion, and you may become the scapegoat for a failure for which you are not wholly responsible.

♦ Projects already in the works that have no hope of completion. If you're assigned a project that's already in progress, make sure you interview the team to ensure you aren't being handed a loaf of day-old bread.

♦ Projects with no staff and no budget to hire a staff. Don't laugh. Lots of people get handed objectives with no commitment of resources and no support from the stakeholders.

♦ Projects that have been underway for more than six months with no perceptible progress. If this happens to you, you need to evaluate the reasons. It may be that people are trying to do the impossible or have no idea what they're supposed to be doing. Either way, the project won't get done.

♦ Projects that assume you will bring in the money on your own to keep the project rolling. Common among modern corporations and a long-time standard among not-for-profit organizations, you become a fundraiser as well as a project manager. No one person can do both roles, and it's unfair of the organization to demand that you bring in $2 million in capital to fund your $75,000 salary.

♦ Projects in which a senior manager is fighting with others in upper management to cancel or significantly modify the project. This type of project needs some concerted effort in the "stakeholder management" arena.

♦ Projects with impossible or unfocused goals (more common than you would think). Here's an example: "Develop a cure for the HIV virus while using the same team to build a suspension bridge like San Francisco's Golden Gate Bridge capable of linking England's south coast to that of Calais, France."

It is difficult for project mangers to admit defeat, but often the best solution is to realize that some things just won't happen as planned. Like walking on water, some projects are outside the realm of possibility for ordinary people.

The best way to avoid an impossible project is to never start it in the first place. Document the risks before the project is approved. Let everyone know in advance that the project may be impossible. If you still find yourself caught in an impossible situation in spite of your realistic communications, the best way to get out is as quickly as possible. As soon as you know the project is impossible, try to convince the powers that be to stop it and quit spending the money. Prolonging the agony makes the problem worse and has brought many a company (and project manager) down in the process.

Politics, Politics, and More Politics

Politics in human endeavors is unavoidable because people always have different opinions and motivations. If the political attitudes are annoying but don't affect the end results of your project, ignore them. It's only when *political* agendas start undermining project goals that they pose a problem. When this happens, treat the politics as any other conflict and resolve the situation by following the conflict resolution options covered in Chapter 23.

Project Lingo

A **political** situation can be described as two people in a room trying to get something done.

Management by Best-Seller

Senior management may push one of many ineffective, concocted-over-cocktails ideas on your team. Gently agree to consider the idea no matter how stupid or insufferably dopey the book or seminar from which the idea came. Then, if forced into management-by-fad, put the process into practice but complement it with the basics of good project management, inspired leadership, and common sense to make sure you actually get things done.

Basic work and organizational concepts, like the scientific method, have been honed, refined, and repaired since the dawn of time. The proof of their timeless truth is the many large projects, such as the Golden Gate Bridge (1937), that have worked thanks to astute project management and good planning. Imagine if The Watermelon Workplace or another equally shallow fad had been used instead. We'd still be taking the ferry from San Francisco to Sausalito and points north.

Taking Care of Yourself to Remain Sane

Does your family treat you like a boarder because they never see you? Does aspirin seem like candy in relief of your headaches? If this sounds familiar, it's time to get a life.

Sometimes the best way to handle problems is to take care of yourself first. Stop everything! Get a handle on the problems that are causing you to live at work and then use your leadership to fix the problems. Or choose to scale back or step down from the project. Your life is worth more than any project—even if your boss may express other sentiments.

After gaining some perspective, pick up the pieces (if possible), ramp the project back up in phases to maintain control, and eliminate the snarls that dogged it previously. And the project workers? If they're freelancers, as little fun as it is, furlough them. If they're employees, either put them back on their regular jobs or ask for their help analyzing and reconstituting the project. Listen closely to their complaints. This might be the source of the problem—and your exhaustion!

A Parable of Last Resort

As project manager, you'll be faced with pressure from both above and below in the organization. Things often seem impossible when you have too many roles and too much to do. When you feel that way, consider the following story, which according to a computer industry wag, probably originated at IBM. The story goes something like this:

A new project manager proudly walks into her new office. She arrives just as her predecessor is walking out the door in disgrace. The departing manager tells her that he has left three envelopes numbered 1 through 3 in the top desk drawer. The departing manager instructs the new manager to open an envelope and follow the instructions only when an impossible-to-rectify problem occurs.

Several weeks go by and the project problems seem overwhelming to the new project manager. Everything is behind schedule, and the new manager must explain the failures to the steering committee in a review meeting. Not knowing what to do, the project manager decides to open the first envelope before going to the meeting. The note inside instructs, "Blame it on the last manager." The new manager decides this is a way off the hook. In the meeting she points her finger to the last manager's inept handling of the project. The committee agrees and reluctantly approves more time and money to complete the project.

Time goes by and the project once again becomes mired in the murk. Stalled and without a clue as to how to handle the problems, the manager must approach the steering committee for more project moola. Opening envelope number 2, she is advised to blame the problem on the inept project team. Again, this tactic proves successful, and the grumbling committee caves in and offers the project more time and more money. Upon leaving the meeting, the committee admonishes the project manager with, "This better not happen again!"

Six months fly by with winter changing to spring. Again overwhelmed with problems, the project manager feels trapped and helpless. The project is late again, is way over budget, and is probably doomed to failure. She pauses, takes a deep breath and then opens the third and final envelope. The instructions are simple: "Prepare three envelopes ..."

You should remember this story when faced with the fatalism that infects some projects. Before you give in and write your envelopes, remember that almost anything can be fixed—but not if you blame the wrong source for the problems. You, as the leader, must use what you know about project management to pull the rabbit out of the hat that others are assuming won't appear. If you do your work to plan and scope the project at the beginning and keep track of things as they go along while always keeping communications open, you'll probably never need the three envelopes. Yes, you'll have problems, but they will probably be solvable—or at least not fatal.

The Least You Need to Know

♦ Ask questions, listen, observe, and communicate with candor and clarity. If you do these four things, you'll reduce the impact of almost every project problem.

♦ Remember that problems and change go hand in hand. Change may cause new problems, but change handled well can often be the best solution to keeping a project on track.

♦ Always be honest (but not brutal) in your assessment of project problems and make sure to support your honest appraisals with documentation.

♦ Tell your boss or customer as soon as you know something is wrong. Waiting will only delay the inevitable and make the problem worse.

Part 6

The Close-Out Phase

Whether it's a summer vacation or a visit to the dentist, there comes a time when all things good (or bad) must come to an end. Likewise, your project must move through the close-out phase so that you can wrap up the details, pay the bills, and move on to the next project with a sense of satisfaction. That's what this short section is all about—the steps to bring a project to a proper conclusion so life can go on.

Chapter **27**

Will the Last One Out Please Turn Off the Lights?

In This Chapter

- The steps for closing a project

- Moving team members from the project into other roles

- Projects that have taken on a life of their own

- Deciding whether to fix a project or end it now

If you've successfully completed your project, the close-out phase is a time of celebration and accomplishment. But not all projects end gracefully. Without a proper closing, some projects ramble on forever like a rickety truck on a bumpy road.

In this chapter, you'll learn how to close down any project including those that finish successfully, those that must die a natural death, and the more annoying ones in which team members never seem to leave. Closure is important because it is the point at which, while wiping your sweaty brow with relief, you say to yourself, "It's over." (And regardless of the outcome, break out the chilled champagne! You deserve it.)

Is There Life After Project Termination?

When the end is near, project members get nervous. What will their next assignment consist of? Will there be a next assignment at all? Unfortunately, this morale problem occurs with the worst possible timing—when a project is almost complete. The problem runs deeper than just the risk of unemployment or a new assignment in a part of the company that resembles Siberia. It means the end of budding friendships, interesting after-hours at the tavern playing poker for pennies, and the other good times that accompany a well-run project. Your people will miss it. You will, too ... really.

Why Is a Close-Out Phase Necessary?

There are several good reasons for a formal close-out to a project. Some involve people issues and others involve you personally learning from the experience and recording what you've learned. People need to be acknowledged for goals that are achieved and to feel like the work is complete. Because project managers need to evolve their skills for managing projects, the techniques, processes, and procedures used on one project should be analyzed so they can be adapted and improved in the future. These are the most fundamental and underlying reasons to formally close a project. You may want to hold similar closing, acknowledgement, and review meetings at the close of major milestones or phases in a larger project as well.

The Final Shutdown

The following tasks are part of the final termination process for most projects and are necessary to bring them to final closure:

- ◆ Meet with stakeholders to get their final approval of the project. They are the reason for the project existing in the first place. Their approval signals the project's completion. For larger projects, you may want to request a formal memorandum acknowledging the completion of the project by the project sponsor or customer.

- ◆ Finalize all contractual commitments to vendors, suppliers, and customers. This may include reports or final payments. It may also include letters thanking vendors for a job well done when appropriate.

- ◆ Transfer responsibilities to other people if required. For example, the end results of some projects are inputs for operations or new projects to be managed by other people. Consider our case study of All-Star Cable. Once the project is finished, the company's operations group will take formal control of Movies-on-Demand. The team members for development of the billing database will finish and turn over the maintenance of the database to the information systems department. The team members who were responsible for answering customers' questions during the pilot test will turn over the ongoing responsibility to customer relations to handle future questions. These activities are all part of the final termination of the product design project.

◆ Reassign people in the project and redirect efforts to other priorities or projects. People may be returned to their functional areas, assigned new projects, or both. This should follow the human resource plan you developed earlier for rolling people off the project.

◆ Release nonhuman resources, such as equipment and materials, so they can be disposed of or used for other work. Some construction and manufacturing projects also require cleanup tasks to prepare the facilities for new activities.

◆ Complete the final accounting of the project. This includes totaling the costs, paying all the bills, and closing the books on the project.

◆ Document the results of the project and make recommendations for the future. More information on the final reports and documentation required for a project can be found later in this chapter. The amount and detail of final documentation will vary based on the size, importance, and issues associated with each project.

Risk Management

Like a living entity, projects grow, mature, and finally become memories after the work is complete. On the other hand, some projects become like the Energizer Bunny and just won't quit.

Projects that aren't closed formally may continue to consume resources required elsewhere. Most projects should end as soon as either the goals have been achieved or you recognize that there's no hope for success.

Closing a Small Project

For small projects, the formal closing (also called a termination by some project managers) can be a simple matter of having a meeting with the team and the stakeholders to acknowledge attainment of the project goals and writing a brief final report on the project. The closing meeting should focus only on the accomplishments of the completed project so that people feel satisfied with the work performed.

Closing a Large Project

For large projects, the closing phase can be a time of stress and anxiety. Team members may have friendships and a sense of family. Some team members will be going their separate ways, adding to the anxiety. Termination of a long project with a close-knit team is always difficult, and it can be complicated. However, the frustration can be reduced if the team members are acknowledged for their current accomplishments and then given new assignments and challenges as soon as possible. It's also a good idea to have a formal celebration to close down the project.

Because some people fear leaving the security of an established project team or changing roles after the project is complete, it is often difficult to get the final details of a large project completed. People may continue to work on insignificant tasks related to the project. Remember your work authorization system! If they are working on work packages that you haven't given them, then you need to stop that work—gently of course.

As a project manager, it is your responsibility to see that the project ends. The project manager should help the people involved move forward into new challenges and opportunities. To reduce the stress associated with project termination, remind your team members of the overall goals that have been achieved and that the stakeholders consider the project completed. Emphasize the importance of the project to the business and their contribution in meeting the project objectives. Then remind them of the new goals and objectives they have yet to achieve on other projects and assignments.

In addition to having a formal meeting or even a party to acknowledge project completion, many projects involve other formal termination tasks, some of which were mentioned earlier: reassigning personnel, auditing the final expenses and closing the books on the project, archiving any drawings or other project materials, passing the end results of the project on to another organization (for example, setting up a product for manufacturing or installing the final product at a customer's site), informing other departments (including purchasing, finance, manufacturing, or whoever needs to know) that the project is done, and completing other miscellaneous documentation of the project. And, of course, there will be an extensive final report.

The closing tasks for a large project are not always clear-cut. When such a project is almost complete, there may be some small details that need to be resolved. The project manager must decide when a project is "finished" so it can move into the termination phase. Don't drag the close-out phase and clean-up details to keep the project alive. This is a common problem in large projects. Get on with it because there are always more projects—and the next one will offer new relationships and new challenges.

Because of loose ends, the termination of a large project may be a mini-project in its own right, demanding schedules, priorities, and budgets. Identify the major steps in the project close-out and implement them as quickly as possible. Follow all the steps and methods for managing any other project.

For many projects, large or small, a checklist is useful in determining the requirements for termination. An example of a termination checklist for a complex product development project is provided later in the chapter to demonstrate the kinds of tasks that might be required to terminate a large project. Of course, the checklist you develop may include entirely different elements that require shutdown, but our example should give you the basic idea of what to consider.

Write Out Your Lessons Learned

Closure is also the point at which management evaluates your success in meeting the goals and your skills as a project manager. In project management circles, this is part of a process called "lessons learned." Big success? Dismal failure? The termination process is essentially identical except that the smiles may be replaced with frowns.

Write out what you and your team learned during the project. What worked well and what would you do differently if you had to do it all over again. These types of reports can be very helpful for you in the future, but they can also help other project managers who may read your report as they tackle a similar project in the future. At least they won't make the same mistakes you did—they can find some of their own!

Project Shutdown

The cleanest closure of a project comes when all work is done and team members already have other work or have returned to their permanent jobs. The easiest project to close down is the small one in which tangible (visible) results demonstrate completion to one and all. For example, when the All-Star Cable Movies-on-Demand project is finished, everyone will know because customers will be able to order movies on their TV!

On the other hand, closing down the project of building a large refinery in Houston is much more complex. Not only are there multiple subplans, but for the uninitiated project manager, reaching the state of completion may seem impossible. Yes, the plant itself may be up, but all the little details may seem endless. In addition, some work may linger on. After completion, repairs may be on the project manager's shoulders as necessary. In a sense, the project continues rather than winding down in a planned and predictable process. Although 99.8 percent of the work is complete, that other .2

Project Lingo

Project murder may sound like the plot from an Agatha Christie novel, but it's really the sudden termination of a project for reasons that range from rational to absurd. An attempt on a project's life may take place during economic downturns, acquisition of the parent organization, or the unexpected death of a company's visionary founder.

Time Is Money

The formal ending of a project takes you off the hook for the budget, so everyone concerned must be fully aware that the deed is done. Otherwise, miscellaneous charges may pop up and be assigned to your now-closed project accounts. Should bills be unavailable upon termination of a project, ask whoever handles finances to build separate accounts for each one with your review before payment.

percent must be addressed by the remnants of the team, or outsiders must be hired if former team members are no longer available.

The most frustrating kind of shutdown is rightfully called *project murder.* (Yes, that's the real term used to describe the cancellation of a project.) You won't read about such murders in the newspaper (usually), but it does materially affect the lives of the project team and its leader. In this kind of termination, work may be suddenly halted even though the project is proceeding on schedule and within its allocated budget. Then we can only watch dumbstruck as the murderer pulls the trigger.

To shut down a project, steps should be taken toward an orderly closure. On a large project, shutdown may occur in phases. One major component of the project may be completed earlier than others as projected in the project plan. Shutdown of each facet should be treated similarly to the termination of the entire project. After all, each of these facets amounts to a project unto itself and deserves the celebration that accompanies completion of any project. The steps to project termination are as follows:

1. **Decision to terminate.** Careful scrutiny of the project task list discloses that the project is (or should be) complete. Visual inspection must accompany this conclusion. It's always possible that a loose end remains or that a part of the team has been feeding you overly optimistic information of its progress.

2. **Task list.** Make a list of small tasks that need to be accomplished and get them taken care of. For example, if the project requires user documentation and it's not fully "user ready," this must be done now!

3. **Consensus.** You, the team, and the other project stakeholders agree that the project has satisfactorily met its goals. Have your project sponsor or the chair of the steering committee sign a project completion memorandum that the project is completed and meets their requirements.

The Project Closing Process

The steps for an orderly close-out phase for your project.

Identify Final Tasks that Require Completion

Reassign Staff if Required

Release Equipment and Materials for Other Projects

Final Accounting and Close Books

Final Report and Final Meeting

4. **Meetings.** Hold individual meetings with team members and team managers who reported to you. Thank them for their contribution, even if they did a lousy job. (They're someone else's problem now.) Take notes on what they thought of the project's highlights and lowlights, your leadership (take a deep breath first), and what they would like to do in the future if you don't already know their intentions.

5. **Communication.** All team personnel must be instructed in writing when the project will end. This puts pressure on the stragglers who need a little more time to complete their role. If you suspect that more time is needed, set the end date several weeks into the future with weekly reminders of the drop-dead date. For real problem people, visit them daily to assess their progress and remind them of the date.

6. **More communication.** Outside suppliers and vendors must be notified that the project will cease to exist in X number of days, weeks, or months. Since the project is ending, tell them that bills not received within 30 days of the termination date will not be accepted. (Be flexible on this one. It's really a tactic to get the bills coming in the door from vendors with tardy billing practices.) It also saves you interest charges, and really prompt payment may knock a percentage off the total project bill. If possible, check purchase orders to see what's outstanding.

7. **Even more communication.** Let managers of "borrowed" employees, temporary agencies, and contractors know—in writing—that the project's termination date is near. This provides the managers time to find other opportunities for these people or to move them back into their usual job responsibilities.

8. **The books are closed.** Assuming you are working with a finance department, once a project is complete, finance must close the books so that wayward bills aren't charged against a nonexistent budget. Most companies assign code numbers to accounts for projects. Assuming your project receives one or more codes, have finance render the codes invalid. That way, you can review any invoices that pop up for legitimacy prior to payment or rejection.

9. **The celebration.** Once a project is (successfully) completed, a beer-and-pizza-type event should be held. Awards may be in order for team members who performed above and beyond the line of duty. This event is not only fun, it marks the official end of the project in everyone's mind. If the project was a flop but not because of team failure, such an event should still be held, even if the occasion is somewhat more subdued. If you or the team failed, save the pizza money.

10. **Dispersal of resources.** Take an inventory of supplies and equipment. Borrowed and rented equipment should be returned, unused supplies need to be sent back for credit where possible, and unrecyclable trash must be hauled off to the landfill. If the project was large and ends up owning a lot of surplus equipment, an auction can be the ticket to parting with 12 table saws or 48 slightly dated computers. Money from such an event can go into the organization's general fund, be distributed to team members in the form of profit sharing, or be donated to charity.

11. **The new kids.** Bring in and train the operations team, if one is needed—these are the people who will staff the project after it is disbanded. In the All-Star Cable Movies-on-Demand project, the operations team will be people at All-Star Cable who will run Movies-on-Demand once the project is complete.

12. **Handing over the keys.** Transfer responsibilities to the operations team, if there is one. Again, the Movies-on-Demand will now become part of the regular operations of All-Star Cable and they must now take responsibility for the day-to-day running of MOD.

Checklist for Closing a Large Project

DESCRIPTION	NEEDED? YES	NEEDED? NO	REQUIRED DATE	RESPONSIBLE PERSON	NOTES
Identify Remaining Work	☐	☐			
Closing/Termination Plan	☐	☐			
Personal Evaluations	☐	☐			
Close-Out Work Orders	☐	☐			
Audit Final Changes	☐	☐			
Pay All Vendors	☐	☐			
Close-Out Books/Audit	☐	☐			
Final Delivery Instructions	☐	☐			
Customer Training	☐	☐			
Notify Purchasing of Completion	☐	☐			
Equipment Redeployed	☐	☐			
Materials Returned to Inventory	☐	☐			
Staff Reassigned	☐	☐			
Close-Down Procedures	☐	☐			
Engineering Documentation	☐	☐			
Final Staff Meeting(s)	☐	☐			
Final Report and Review Meeting	☐	☐			

A checklist for terminating a project.

After Implementation Review

A common practice among experienced project managers, particularly on large projects, is to conduct an after implementation review. A meeting is scheduled, usually between three to six months after the project is closed-out, with the key team members and some of the stakeholders. The review is a discussion about what has happened since the project was turned over to operations. Often getting a little distance from the project will help everyone gain some insights on what went well and what they would do differently in the future. Also, any problems or surprises that occur will happen in those first few months, and that information can help in crafting your lessons learned.

Three Ways to Deep-Six a Workforce

Tony Soprano might have other ideas, but there are three ways to terminate a project that are standard in the project management biz: inclusion, integration, or extinction. You need to choose the right method for your project, or you'll have lots of unhappy campers with nowhere to pitch a tent.

> **Time Is Money**
>
> Leave good documentation for your successors. When you consider the project to bring water from upstate New York to the Big Apple, you'll understand why this is a good idea. Scheduled completion is around 2007. Given current job tenure across the nation, it's entirely possible that at least three different people will run the project over the next five years.

Inclusion

Inclusion is a happy ending of sorts. Your project proved successful, and upon nearing completion, it was absorbed into the organization. Again, it may become a part of the company or be run as a separate organization. In the happiest scenario, many of the original team members keep their jobs and continue to contribute. However, it may be that all staff members are replaced because they are deemed unsuitable for the post-completion phase of the project. Some team members may choose to leave anyway because, while they found the project phase exciting, the thought of running day-to-day operations makes them yawn. You may find yourself the head of a hot new company or updating your resumé and looking for another project.

Integration

Integration is the most common technique for dissolving a project workforce. Team members are reintegrated into the organization from which they were borrowed. On a long project, integration becomes complex because management may have been forced to fill slots held by the team members. A new position must be found for the returning team member that is satisfactory to the employee and the headcount. Often new skills acquired by the project member open the door to new job responsibilities.

Extinction

The dinosaur route—outright extinction of a project and everything related to it—is an all-too-common route to unload personnel. Once a project is closed down, the people are simply let go. (There's a theory that a large meteorite striking the earth off the Yucatan invented this kind of staff reduction.)

Give It Up!

At the end of a project, especially a major one that has absorbed six or more months of your life (some take decades), there's a letdown period for which you should be ready. It's like postpartum blues. You've spent nine months devoting your energies to a specific project (a baby). You've been so focused on that one goal that, once it is successfully achieved, you feel lost, directionless, and sad. You feel these emotions even though you know what your next project will be (raising the baby). Think how much more difficult it would be to cope if you didn't have the prospect of a new project and had to adjust to your former everyday routine.

Suddenly, you are no longer the head honcho of a project with team members constantly seeking your advice and decisions. Instead, you return to civilian life with your normal job duties and responsibilities. There may be a period of letdown in which the project stays on your mind. You may keep thinking of improved ways to accomplish some tasks, or ideas may come to you that might have better met the project's goals. Your "symptoms" may indeed be real. But if it's your skill and desire, freelance project managers do well and make good incomes depending on their experience and success. This could be you! Be encouraged: There's always another project to manage somewhere.

Along the Critical Path

A project that is terminated for unforeseen changes in the environment is not a failed project; it's just a project that wasn't brought to fruition. Projects that fail due to unforeseen circumstances or changes in the organization's requirements, culture, or direction are not true project failures either, although you may have trouble convincing the person paying the bills otherwise. Projects that are extremely late, come in over budget, use too many resources, or leave participants and clients unhappy are projects that were not properly managed. Depending on how much the problems impacted the budget and schedule, give yourself credit for completing the beast. At least it got done.

Right now you should have a celebration. Your project is done (except for the final report, which you'll learn how to write in the next chapter. You didn't think you'd get away without another report, did you?).

Get your team together. Revel in your accomplishments. Then move on to the next project.

The Least You Need to Know

◆ Dissolving a project takes time and deliberate effort on your part.

◆ All projects must come to an end. Period.

◆ Closing down a project is a process that follows a predetermined series of steps.

◆ After a project is finished, team members will either be included in the operations component of the project, reintegrated into the organization, or terminated.

Chapter 28

The Final Evaluation: The Short and Long of It

In This Chapter

◆ Understanding your successes and shortcomings

◆ Talking back: the final report

◆ Team member performance appraisals

Now that your project is shut down, you may think you're finally done. But there's one more important step—the final project evaluation. The purpose of this step is to appraise your actions: what you did well and what you could have done better. Only through a final project evaluation will you learn how to better manage your next project.

Evaluating Your Project

Through an effective *postmortem*, lessons learned from this project can be effectively applied to the next one. The final evaluation should happen whether the project achieved its goals or evolved into a dismal failure.

Small leftover tasks, such as installing the built-in office coffeemaker or screwing in light bulbs, shouldn't delay the final evaluation from going forward. Large leftover tasks indicate a project that's incomplete, however, making it too early to analyze results—even if the scheduled completion date has come and gone.

Project Lingo

A **postmortem** for a project means to examine all parts of the project to determine its successes and its failures.

There are three components to the final evaluation: project assessment, a final written report, and team member performance reviews. A final meeting of the core team is often in order as well because this will assist you in evaluating the project and producing input for the report. The team's technical expertise and experiences may provide data that you hadn't previously considered.

Meet with Core Team Members

Before you formally evaluate your completed or closed-down project, you need input from your core team. Ask for a brief written report or provide them with a simple questionnaire to complete. Then schedule an informal meeting with key players and ask them their opinions about the project and what they would do better next time. Take notes so you remember comments and confirm that you value their input.

The first question when evaluating a project is whether the desired results were accomplished. Then consider the project life cycle from start to finish to understand what worked and what didn't. Look closely at problems and how you and your team coped with them. Picking up the pieces and successfully gluing them back together is an art. Consider when you did this well and when you could have done better.

Compare Goals to Achievements

There are no hard-and-fast rules for project evaluation. Essentially, you match your achievements to the project's goals. If what you produce lines up clearly with well-defined goals, chances are you've succeeded. If you have met the goals only part way, your project may be considered a success by some and a failure by others. The toughest evaluation is one in which the goals were fuzzy to begin with. That's why it's so important to clearly define a project's requirements during the planning phase.

To evaluate your project's success (or lack of success), make a list of the project's accomplishments and place it next to the goals page(s). Study each list, checking off goals as you consider your list of accomplishments. This is the best way to evaluate your project.

With the exception of the smallest projects (and sometimes even for those), a final report is mandated by management at the close of the project. The final report for a megaproject is more formal and obviously longer than for a small, simple project. As previously mentioned, reports are necessary for both successfully completed projects and those that are canceled. On a successful project, the final report may precipitate bonuses for the team members and their project manager. If the project went belly-up, the report serves to document the problems and to help others avoid the quicksand you and your team slipped into. The report can also document why a project problem wasn't your fault.

Writing the Final Report

The final report is both a history of the project and a final evaluation of performance. While the final report for a small project may be no more than a two-page memo, the report for a large project may be 10 or 20 pages in length. If you kept a project diary (refer to Chapter 20), producing the final report will be relatively easy.

All of the topics covered in the project report for a simple project should be included in the final report for a large project, but they should be covered in more detail. These are the main things to include in the final report:

- ◆ An overview of the project including revisions to the original project plan

- ◆ A summary of major accomplishments

- ◆ Analysis of achievements compared to original goals for the project

- ◆ Final financial accounting and an explanation of variances from the budget

- ◆ An evaluation of administrative and management performance

- ◆ The team's performance (this section should be confidential when it applies to specific individuals and their performance)

- ◆ Issues or tasks that require further investigation

- ◆ Recommendations for future projects of this type

- ◆ Special acknowledgments to team members

In addition, the following elements are appropriate to include in the final reports for more complex projects:

- ◆ A summary of performance issues, conflicts, and resolutions

◆ The results of each phase of the project including actual versus forecast dates and the budget versus actual expenses (budget use, additions, and so on, require thorough documentation)

◆ A description of ongoing project-related activities that will require further team member participation (if any)

◆ Recommendations for changes to future projects so they will run more smoothly and be more compatible with the sponsoring organization

◆ In-depth analysis of reporting procedures and recommendations for improvements

◆ Analysis of the project management process as a whole

In each section of a final report for a project, the procedures used in the project should be analyzed. Things that worked should be acknowledged. Things that didn't work should be explained. Recommendations for improvements in future implementations of the project methodology should be made, and there should be clear examples and rationales for the changes. All key team members should either contribute to the report or review its contents for accuracy before the report is finalized. You can have others write and submit their relevant portions of the final report and then, after editing, add your own two cents' worth as an overview to cement the document.

Packaging Options for the Report

Your final report should be reviewed by everyone involved in the project from your management to the project stakeholders to the administrative assistant who makes the copies. You may want to break it into five sections, as outlined here:

The Executive Summary

This one- to two-page document summarizes the report's content for people who need a quick briefing and don't have time or are unable to digest the entire document.

The Report, Part A

This section contains information that can be disseminated to all team members, managers, and other interested parties. It includes a detailed review of the project and a goal-by-goal assessment of the project's success in meeting each one.

The Report, Part B

This section includes information for management only or that may be confidential in nature.

Confidential reports are the most difficult to manage. They contain information not appropriate for team members' eyes, such as salaries, team-member performance, and recommendations for using the results of the project. It can also include the financial reports for the project or even highly confidential government and military material that your own boss isn't authorized to read it. All such documents must be kept under lock and key, whether in a locking desk drawer or a sealed document repository much like a large bank vault. In CIA terms, a portion of a report may be "for your eyes only" while the rest is available for distribution. If you find yourself in the awkward situation of not knowing what to release, get advice from someone who is privy to the report's contents anyway.

The Project Plan

The project's overall plan should be included along with copies of the goal information. If it fits and makes you look good, include the original plan and the final plan so that readers can see how you met the scheduled dates.

Miscellaneous Components

If tangible proof of a project's success is possible, such as the opening of a new store or the discovery of life on another planet, photos can be included in this section and referenced from report parts A and B.

The Political Impact of Final Reports

In a politically sensitive organization, a negative report can cause problems. Before you state emphatically that a particular vice president was the major roadblock to successfully completing the project, you had better be in line for another job or an unemployment check.

As was strongly (if wrongly) suspected of the Warren report on the slaying of President Kennedy, for political reasons there were two versions of the report: one for the public and another for high-level government officials and operatives. You may want to consider this tactic for presenting complete information to your managers while, in a second brief report, withholding proprietary or personal information from rank-and-file team members.

In the building of the atomic bomb for World War II, a few senior government officials knew what was being developed. Thousands of project team members, however, learned only about the part, system, or explosive components they were personally responsible for designing and building. It wasn't until months after the surrender of Japan that some of these people put the pieces together, so to speak.

Who Accomplished What and How Well?

If your project involved people, you'll likely be called on to evaluate the performance of each team member. This may be limited to core team members, or it may apply to all team members and even outside vendors, consultants, and suppliers. The evaluations can be used for anything ranging from promotions to new assignments to layoffs. In a project in which a team member's contribution is made before the project terminates, a review should be held when the team member departs rather than waiting for project closure. Why? Because on any really large project, the time between an individual rolling off the project and the actual time for the review may be a considerable amount of time. It may be hard to remember exactly the points you want to emphasize if too much time has passed.

> **Words from the Wise**
>
> I'll need everyone's help on this project. I hope you can overlook the cloud of doom that hovers nearby.
>
> —Dilbert, from the strip by Scott Adams

Many companies have standard evaluation procedures that must be followed, and the human resources department will insert itself into the evaluation process. Chances are, HR will provide standard evaluation forms for both you and the employee to fill out. In a matrixed project organization (refer to Chapter 19), other managers who work with the team member may contribute to the written evaluations as well.

The basic criteria for appraising team member performance include the following:

- Quality of work
- Cost consciousness
- Timeliness
- Creativity
- Administrative performance
- Ability to work as part of a team
- Attitude

- Communication skills

- Technical ability

- Recommendations for improvement

- Consistency in meeting deadlines

When giving a performance review in person, try for a relaxed atmosphere away from other team members. For stellar performers, this is a good time to hand out any bonus checks, with the agreement that the team member will keep it quiet so as not to make other members unhappy.

The Bottom Line and You

In addition to the formal review of a project, every project manager needs to do some personal soul-searching to understand why a particular project went well or why it went poorly. After the project has been completed for a while and the emotion is gone, stand back and look at the project and your own management skills as objectively and dispassionately as possible. What did you do well? What could you have done better? What do you still need to learn? These are the observations, if acted on and taken seriously, that will help you prosper, develop, and improve as a project manager. A good time to complete this exercise is after the after implementation review we discussed in Chapter 27.

At this point, you have been exposed to the complete process of project management. You have learned how to complete project management calculations and develop diagrams, reports, and communications that will help you plan, monitor, and control your project to a successful conclusion. Congratulations—and good luck in your role as project manager!

But wait! Don't forget about the last section of this book. There you'll learn how entire organizations are realigning their operations to improve project productivity, and you'll discover the wealth of new software tools available to help you in your project management ventures.

The Least You Need to Know

- After a project ends, take stock of what went right and what went wrong.

- On most projects, a final report is required to inform all participants and stakeholders of the project's results.

- Not all report information should be available to team members and outsiders.

- Performance should be formally or informally (depending on the organization) reviewed when team members depart the project or when the project is completed.

Part 7

The Organization and Tools to Make Project Management Prosper

In this section, you'll learn the requirements for putting the discipline of project management to work throughout your organization. We'll start by looking at ways a company can use the lessons learned in the project management discipline at the organizational level. In the final chapter, you'll learn how an empowered project-oriented organization can benefit from using new project management software to help implement the planning, control, administration, and communication aspects of project management with less effort and more consistency. And you'll discover how new Internet-enabled collaboration tools can assist in facilitating the interactions and work among team members, even when the people are separated by international borders.

29

The Project-Enabled Organization

In This Chapter

♦ Focusing your business culture on project success

♦ Adapting your organization to focus on projects

♦ Establishing a portfolio management strategy

♦ Creating the "project office" for supporting projects

Project management offers many opportunities for creating consistency in meeting goals that can be applied to entire organizations. If a department or even an entire corporation can institutionalize the factors that lead to project management success, the entire organization should be able to achieve successes consistently.

Firms that have adopted zero-defect or *total quality management* strategies now view project management as one of the necessary components for achieving dependable, quality results. They have discovered that the consistent, defined processes of project management are a foundation for improving not only quality but productivity and profitability as well.

In this chapter, we'll look at some of the steps an organization can take to move from ad-hoc project control to becoming an efficient, projectized organization. Projectized is the term used by the Project Management Institute (PMI) to describe an organization in which most of the resources are focused on project work.

Understanding the Benefits of Formalizing Project Management

In Chapter 1, we specified several general factors that contribute to the success of projects and project managers alike. Here's are those factors again; consider how it applies to the work in your organization:

◆ Agreement among the stakeholders on the goals of the project and the measures of success

Project Lingo

Total quality management is a common approach to implementing a quality improvement program within an organization. To some it means meeting or exceeding the customer requirements. To others it means delivering quality products at the right time and at the right place.

◆ Support by the senior management of the organization for the project priorities and resources required

◆ Effective, consistent, quality communication between the project team and the stakeholders involved in the project

◆ A project plan that describes a clear path and unambiguous responsibilities that can be used as a baseline for measuring progress as the project proceeds through time

◆ A clearly defined scope that is both controlled and understood by project stakeholders

Is Your Organization Ready to Be Projectized?

If projects are becoming a larger and more important aspect of the work in your organization, project management offers potential for increased quality and efficiency. To determine the degree to which your organization can benefit from consistent employment of the project management discipline, you need to ask yourself some tough questions about your current organization:

◆ What's your organizational style now and should you change it to better match your priorities? The organizational models presented in Chapter 19 (functional, pure-project, matrix, and mixed) can include a wide range of organizational styles.

◆ Every company has projects and ongoing operations. In most cases, favoring one comes at the expense of the other.

◆ How much of the budget is spent on projects now? If you spend the majority of your cash (or earn most of your money) on projects, then a project-oriented structure makes sense.

◆ Do your projects include multiple functions such as IT personnel, accounting staff, engineers, and marketing experts? Do you have to borrow these resources from the functional departments? If so, the cost of communicating and coordinating with these functional areas (if you work in a functional organization) is increased. The more frequently you need to depend on the functional areas for support, the more a project-oriented style will improve efficiency.

◆ How large are the projects in your organization? The larger the projects, the more sense it makes to organize around them. Size is measured in terms of duration (projects lasting a year or more are considered large), level of resource utilization (if most of the team members are employed by the project on a full-time basis, then it's a major project), the size of the project team (any project with more than 50 team members is a large project), and the size of the budget in proportion to your organization's budget. Obviously, when a project consumes a large portion of an organization's budget, it demands more focus. (In all of these examples, an organization could be a department, a division, or an entire company. Project size is always relative to the size of the organization you're considering becoming projectized.)

◆ How similar are the projects in your organization? Projects are always unique, as you've learned already, but in some firms, there is a great deal of similarity among projects. The more similarities there are, the greater the opportunity to manage projects as ongoing operations. The more projects produce unrelated or dissimilar results, the more the project-oriented structure makes sense.

◆ How complex is the work and how important is knowledge transfer from one project to another? This is an especially important question in engineering-oriented organizations. The complexity and size of major engineering endeavors often favor projectized organizations. However, in functional organizations, people organize their careers and expand their expertise within that function; the knowledge is maintained within the company. In a project-oriented structure, knowledge transfer from one project to the next requires conscious effort. If this isn't done (and it often isn't), technical innovations or special skills may be lost when the project is over. This the short-term benefits of a projectized organization can result in losing valuable institutional knowledge unless a structure and process is designed within the larger organization to prevent this from happening.

As you consider your own project experiences and forthcoming endeavors, remember these factors and determine whether your own organization should become more or less project-oriented. The size and complexity of modern corporations defy a definitive recommendation for an organizational style. Any organizational format has strengths and weaknesses. The key is to adapt the organization of projects at the right level and in the right way for the organization in question.

Define the Organizational Boundaries First

The first decision in projectization is defining the organizational boundaries for the change. Should projectization occur at the project, department, division, or corporate level? In your analysis of organizational change, you can use the risk management techniques you learned in this book. Ask yourself how much risk there would be of losing the information gained from one program to the next if each were being managed as an independent project organization. What is the risk of losing quality and productivity if you don't organize in a project-oriented manner?

We've provided three examples of projectized organizations to demonstrate how different organizations can incorporate the project-oriented approach at different levels.

In business, when catering to fast-changing markets, each division may be largely autonomous with complete start-to-finish control of a product. This way, a separate division of the company such as manufacturing won't slow throughput as it copes with other orders.

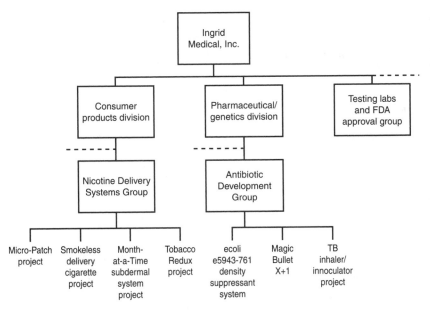

Not all organizations can use the "top-down" project development management scheme. There may be too much expense to completely duplicate all functions. Instead, one or more elements—here, the testing and FDA components— are shared. This reduces expenses but also creates a potential bottleneck for all parties if not properly implemented.

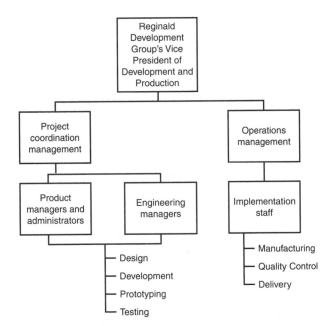

Many manufacturing and software-development houses run development on one side and operations on the other. The key to this kind of project is communication, often a thankless task handled by the most senior person (where the "org" chart trees grow together). This system has the necessary economies of scale to both market and deliver existing products while developing new ones.

Now Come the Standards

Once you've decided that the projectization of all or part of your organization is a good idea, you'll need to work on developing consistent procedures for implementing project management. This book can help you do that, but be forewarned. You can't buy *standard* practices for your organization in an off-the-shelf format; you need to adapt the standards to your own projects and organizational preferences.

Project Lingo

Standards often begin as guidelines that describe a preferred approach. As these standards enjoy widespread adoption, they become *de facto* regulations. **Regulations,** on the other hand, are rules for which compliance is mandated (usually by a government agency or corporate management). It's important in discussing requirements for projects to differentiate between standards (which enjoy some flexibility in implementation) and regulations (which are dictated and absolute).

As you develop the procedures for your own organization, here are some of the procedures and support tools you'll need to consider:

♦ Common project roles including authority levels, roles, and responsibilities for the project manager and other key players. Who will have the authority to approve a project or cancel it? Who will be able to assign people (or remove them) from a project? To whom does the project manager report? What responsibilities do the functional managers have, if any? What exactly is the sponsor's and steering committee's role and responsibility to the project? Who will have the ultimate authority to approve major changes to the project scope? Don't be vague in these definitions. Don't leave authorities and responsibilities subject to interpretations.

Risk Management

Don't weigh your projects down with excessive amounts of bureaucracy. Guidelines that are appropriate for a project to build All-star Cable's Movies-on-Demand would be inappropriate for a project to develop a training program for the sales force. Standards are important, but make them flexible enough to accommodate the differences in projects of various sizes.

♦ Support staff for projects. Will you have a formal project office to assist with administrative duties and coordination? Or will you have a full-time staff for each project? Maybe you'll borrow staff time from the functional areas. Whatever is appropriate, make sure it's clearly documented in your standards.

♦ Standard formats and criteria for project deliverables. This will often consist of templates for the statement of work, work plans, project plans, status reports, and other deliverables; there might be multiple sets of templates required for projects of different sizes. For example, the standards for complex projects in multiple locations with multiple customers and the employment of outside resources would require more standardization than small, internal projects.

◆ Approval processes for projects (sometimes different processes will be required for projects of different scopes) and criteria for making approvals.

Where Do the Standards Come From?

Ideas for project standardization can come from reading a number of books including this one. The best sources for standards, however, are the project histories from your own organization and those from expert project managers who may be called upon to help you as you projectize your organization.

People who have been project managers in your organization in the past can help you define the success factors and problem areas in past projects. That's why the documentation in the close-out phase of the project is so important: It provides key information for improving processes in the future. By addressing both success factors and problem areas in your standards, you'll be able to emphasize the processes that will lead to triumph within the culture of your company.

Establish a Life Cycle Standard

You likely remember the discussion of project life cycles in Chapter 4. All efforts at improving project management start with the definition of a consistent life cycle. This life cycle definition can help you define consistent project management practices for each phase in a project. You might need two or three different life cycle definitions for different types of projects in your organization.

In the four phases life cycle we discussed in Chapter 4 (definition, planning, execution, and close-out phases), each phase emphasizes a certain type of activity, and each phase requires approval from the key stakeholders to move to the next phase.

You can also have a life cycle with as few as three phases, which might be defined as initiate, implement, and close-out. A single approval and the initiate phase might be appropriate for a small project that must be done quickly.

Then again, you might want a life cycle with five, six, or even seven phases that require more approvals at each life cycle phase to help reduce risk in a complex project or to add time to hire project staff.

We've provided a diagram of different types of life cycles used in different industries to give you an idea of the type of life cycle that might make sense for your projects.

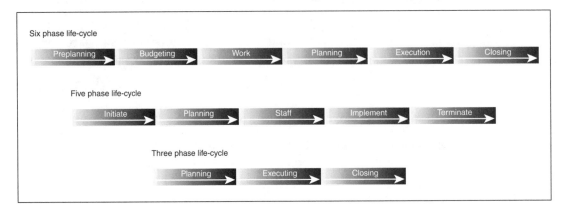

Three life cycle possibilities with common project deliverables by phase.

Be sure that your life cycle is more than just words on paper. The life cycle should include a clear definition of deliverables, stakeholder roles, and approvals required at each phase. In your life cycle definitions, create a document that answers questions like these: What must you achieve to move to the next level? Who will approve your movement into the next phase? What criteria will the stakeholders use to make this approval?

You may want to bring in outside resources with the experience and expertise to assist in building a project life cycle tailored to your organization.

Manage Projects Like an Asset for Your Future

A major institutional step in developing a consistent project management framework is to begin managing projects as a portfolio, just like you'd manage a portfolio of assets. This means that you'll need to develop a systematic approach for choosing, monitoring, and canceling projects. Projects, like assets, that are underperforming are eliminated, while projects that are performing well deserve additional investment. To do this, accurate information, consistently formatted, is required from every project.

Managing your projects as a portfolio also requires clear authority for the steering committee or governing board who have been granted authority to manage the portfolio (which includes initiating, reviewing, canceling, and continuing projects).

Furthermore, project portfolio management requires clear operational and strategic goals for evaluating projects and a disciplined process that requires regular review of projects and clear guidelines for proposing, reviewing, and approving them.

Portfolio management also depends on the use of a quality project reporting system or enterprise resource management system. (You'll learn more about project management software for this purpose in the next chapter.) In defining the right type of information systems to support the portfolio management process, you'll need to ask questions like these:

- ◆ What information is needed?

- ◆ Who needs the information and for what purpose?

- ◆ Where does the information come from?

- ◆ How often is the information needed?

- ◆ Does the information exist already or does it need to be created?

Without a portfolio management system in place, these simple questions are almost impossible to answer.

Putting a Project Office in Place to Support the System

Without visible and ongoing support for project management, it's likely that standards and policies will degrade and return to their previous, unproductive state. One common way to prevent this from happening is to employ a group for continuous development and support of the standards, practices, and information systems that define project management. This group is often known as the project office.

The project office is called by many different names including the Program Management Office (PMO), the Project Center of Excellence, the Project Support Office, and so on. In general, these offices are responsible for various levels of planning, budgeting, scheduling, and hiring assistance. The objective is to help people put good project management practices in place.

The project office can be assigned various levels of authority for a project from basic guidance to complete authority. In some cases, project offices are temporary—they exist only during the development of a long program. In other cases, project offices are at the top of the authority structure and oversee all the cross-functional projects in an organization.

The responsibilities of the project office (regardless of what it is called) will vary based on the degree to which the organizational structure favors projects and embraces project management processes. Here are some of the responsibilities that a project office can assume:

♦ Maintaining project management standards

♦ Providing training on project management

♦ Consulting on technical and procedural issues

♦ Scheduling assistance

♦ Creating and tracking budgets

♦ Providing staff, including project managers, for the organization

♦ Providing enterprise-level project information

♦ Supervising project managers

♦ Procuring resources

♦ Participating in project portfolio management

♦ Making project management decisions

The most successful project offices will provide expertise in the discipline of project management and enthusiasm for its value in getting things done on time and within budget. The simple presence of a project office, in any form, helps breathe life into the organization's commitment to project management principles.

> **Words from the Wise**
>
> There are two things to be considered with regard to any scheme. In the first place, "Is it good in itself?" In the second, "Can it be easily put into practice?"
>
> —Jean-Jacques Rousseau

In the End, It's Leadership That Makes It Work

It's critical that you understand the nature of your organization's projects to organize project management. It's even more important, however, that the changes required to reap the benefits are supported by management for the long haul.

Joining the Project Management Institute can be a great way to start. If there is a local chapter in your area, attend monthly chapter meetings to learn more about PMI and chat with other project managers. There is also a professional certification from PMI called the Project Management Professional (PMP) that signifies both knowledge and experience in project management. Some organizations are requiring senior project managers to have the PMP certification as part of the requirements for attaining that title.

No matter what you do, change won't happen overnight. There are few higher risk projects in business than consciously attempting to change the cultural and operational practices of an organization. It will take both discipline and commitment. If you make the standards optional, that's exactly what you'll get: optional project management and optional results. But if you provide authority and funding to the endeavor, you'll win cynical employees over to your side.

People will take project management standards seriously if the authority of the project managers and the project office is taken seriously. This means the organization must grant enough authority to the project managers to be taken seriously. While this might sound obvious, it's not easy. Project managers must have a career path that's well-defined and well-rewarded. Nothing speaks louder about management commitment than what's rewarded.

Time Is Money

Red Zone Management, by Dutch Holland (Dearborn Trade Publishing), has an excellent chapter on making organizational culture changes.

Even enthusiastic supporters of the organizational changes may be bogged down as things proceed. Learning a new process can be tedious, especially when ordinary work must get done in the process. To eliminate this frustration, break the projectization process into phases—just like any other project—so the work is doable. People also need to be supplied with appropriate training and support.

Changing the organization to embrace project management can entail significant risk if people aren't convinced of the need to use the processes. Thus, your critical task in this endeavor is to win those people to your side through leadership, training, and persistent communication. (Sounds a lot like project management work, doesn't it?)

The Least You Need to Know

- ◆ Reorganizing for project management requires planning, management support, assigned authorities, training, and time for implementation.

- ◆ Projectized organizations employ consistent standards to help guide their projects to success.

- ◆ The structure of a project-oriented organization will vary based on the products produced, the size and frequency of the projects, and the culture of the organization.

- ◆ The forms and names for project offices may be different, but the support functions, in terms of planning, budgeting, and staffing assistance, are similar.

- The authority level of the project office will vary depending on the degree of projectization of the organization.

- Without management support for the processes, a projectized organization is doomed to return to older, less efficient ways of getting things done.

Chapter 3

Software for All Projects Great and Small

In This Chapter

◆ The things software can do to help your project

◆ The things software can't do

◆ The types of project management software

◆ How to choose the right software for your projects

Creating a detailed project plan and keeping it up-to-date for most nontrivial projects can be a very time-consuming process if completed manually. The complexity of figuring in vacations, holidays, weekends, early-starts, and other factors can be overwhelming to someone inexperienced in project management techniques or short on pencils. The details involved in producing networks and work breakdown structures seem daunting, and assembling a budget can be tedious. Just producing the plan is a lot of work for a project. And, as you've hopefully concluded by now, project management entails more than just creating a good plan. Producing the reports, updating the charts, and incorporating changes to a project plan along the way add complexity and more paperwork. Of course, if you need to manage multiple projects at the same time, the calculations, graphs, and reports can seem impossible.

Just like any job that you do, having the right tools can make it easier. That's what project management software really is—a tool for the project manager to use. In this chapter, you'll learn about software that can help you keep it all straight. And because the programs are easy to use, you won't have any excuses for not keeping your plans up-to-date.

Software That Simplifies the Details

All the graphing, changing, and reporting in project management can drive you crazy. Some naive managers simply reject project management methods because of the reports involved. Instead, they choose to manage projects with intuition and guess-work (and much of the time they guess wrong). The benefits of project management methods are too important to ignore just because the charts and graphs take time to produce. Today, thanks to computers and the World Wide Web, solutions are available that enable everyone to benefit from using project management methods. There are easy-to-use project management programs such as Microsoft Project that anyone can master in a few hours. There are also highly sophisticated systems that can integrate projects across the organization and can help teams collaborate on their efforts from around the world.

With the right project management program or information system, you can concentrate on the management of the project, leaving you more time for thinking and planning. You can let the computer provide tactical support in the form of charts, graphs, schedules, resource allocations, and virtual communication capabilities.

This chapter covers the basics of selecting and using computerized project management programs so you won't give up on project management before you get started.

What Can Project Management Programs Do?

Project management programs range in capabilities from simple scheduling programs that produce Gantt charts to prodigious mainframe applications, for engineering and aerospace projects, that are integrated with the corporation's budgeting, marketing, manufacturing, personnel, and other management information systems.

The underlying methods supported by most project management programs are similar to those presented in this book. Depending on the capabilities of the program, you enter task sequences, resources, dates, and costs, just as described in this book, and the program calculates or modifies the schedules, budget, or resource utilization for you. Most programs even draw the networks or can convert one network format into another. Most of the time, you'll enter your project data into a form that looks like a spreadsheet with columns and rows; this allows you to define WBS levels and to describe tasks, precedence, resource requirements, and almost anything else that's relevant—including resource calendars, labor costs, and overhead allocations.

In addition to helping you calculate schedules and costs, project management programs produce a wide variety of reports from simple to comprehensive. If you have a special project management requirement, such as a custom report or chart, there is probably a program out there with the capability to produce the output you need.

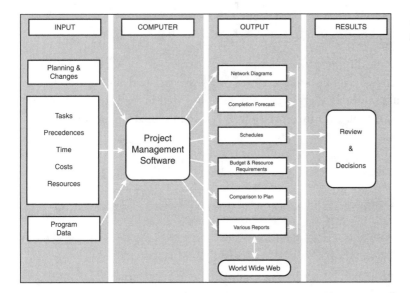

How project management software works.

Not even the most sophisticated software package is a substitute for competent leadership and skilled decision-making, and by itself, it can't correct any task-related problems or human-centered conflicts. Project management software can, however, be a terrific boon to the project manager tracking interrelated variables, schedules, resources, costs, and tasks that come into play. Software development companies such as Microsoft are continually improving project management tools that can enhance communications among team members and can facilitate collaborative problem solving. Although not all programs do everything, most of them can help you do some or all of the following:

♦ Graph costs, schedules, and resource utilization using Gantt charts, histograms, line diagrams, and a variety of other charts.

◆ Create standard and custom reports including standard accounting and tracking. Some programs will even produce special report formats required by government agencies such as the Department of Defense (DOD).

◆ Maintain resource and project calendars that record the availability of staff and equipment. These internal program calendars are used to create optimum schedules. This feature allows the project manager to establish workweeks based on actual workdays and to specify nonwork periods such as weekends, holidays, and vacations. The project calendar can be printed out in detail or in a summary format.

◆ Make schedule changes based on a variety of resource-leveling parameters (for example, no overtime!) and priority scheduling attributes.

◆ Maintain skills inventories that match resources to task requirements.

◆ Track and schedule multiple projects at the same time. Some packages feature a single, comprehensive database that enables cross-project analysis and reporting. Cost and schedule modules share common data files that allow integration among projects and that minimize problems of schedule inconsistencies and redundancies.

◆ Allow multiple people to access, input, and report on project data at the same time.

◆ Collapse the view of projects by work breakdown structure or organization structure, subproject, or milestone.

◆ Calculate and display the critical path for a network.

◆ Display alternative schedules, task assignments, and cost criteria so that the immediate impact of schedule, sequence, and resource changes can be evaluated.

◆ Assign early-warning parameters that let the program inform you of potential trouble including schedule problems, resource conflicts with other projects, and cost overruns.

◆ Integrate with material management, purchasing, and accounting systems to assist in ordering materials, supplies, equipment, and contractor services.

◆ Produce presentation-quality graphics for making reports to management and customers about the plans and status of a project.

◆ Display actual and planned data simultaneously.

◆ Summarize data in a variety of ways including expenditures, timing, and activity data.

♦ Complete cost analyses, cost accounting, and variance analyses.

♦ Create free-format reports with an integrated word processor or other report generator for incorporating personalized project annotations.

♦ Display relevant information on the web or corporate intranet so that project team members can view the status and schedule of the project and their own assigned tasks.

♦ Communicate and collaborate with the project team across project locations.

The Virtual World of the Project Needs Virtual Tools

A virtual project is a collaborative effort toward a specific goal or accomplishment that is based on "collective yet remote" performance. Some experts have called this "working together, apart." This increasingly common mode of work needs information management tools that enable communication and coordination at a distance.

You may recall from Chapter 20 that management by walking around (MBWA) is one of the most effective methods of tracking work and motivating people. The trouble is, today's "teams" often have team members scattered across the city, state, or continent. The solution is to visit project resources virtually rather than physically, a variation that might be called management by web surfing—and you need not leave your office to do it.

Virtual project management (VPM) is the Information Age equivalent of management by walking around. The rise to dominance within organizations of Internet-based collaboration tools offers many possibilities for group-based and web-based project management. Virtual project management requires several layers of information system support:

♦ *Multimedia communication* incorporates e-mail, phone calls, memoranda (hopefully as e-mail attachments but possibly as paper), and other media.

♦ *Collaboration* goes beyond basic messaging to sharing information. This is often done using the collaboration capabilities of the World Wide Web using tools like Webcast and Netmeeting.

♦ *Tracking and leveling of resources* are functions performed by traditional project management products that must be shared across spatial boundaries in virtual project management systems.

♦ *Access to project-related information systems* such as computer-aided design (CAD) and corporate information databases is advantageous. For complex projects, this project information may reside in specialized repositories such as CAD programs, CASE tools, simulation software, and data warehouses in addition to the information contained in project management software.

◆ Some organizations are required by regulation or self-imposed standards to use a specific methodology (such as ISO 9000) to maintain complete configuration control over project deliverables. A pharmaceutical firm, for instance, might need to store not only the final specification for a new drug but all alternatives and iterations leading up to it. In such cases, the dimension of process management can consume as many resources as the projects themselves. The new virtual tools should also help with maintaining this ongoing documentation.

The Power of Networking

Drug manufacturers and bridge builders weren't exactly on hold until the advent of distributed computing. All of the activities mentioned so far have been handled for years with pencil and paper and human ingenuity. How do electronic information systems change this? How do web-based applications in particular add value? The answer is in the power of networking and the Internet.

Because of networking, e-mail allows ideas to flow asynchronously (that is, without parties online at the same time), enabling work to flow across time zones. E-mail doesn't require incremental labor and provides a searchable audit trail; this is key to many formal project processes.

Networking also enables remote collaboration. With modern client/server technology, it is possible to work in collaboration with people all over the globe on a project. However, to be effective, you will need to have shared drives that all project members can access and set up a protocol for controlling the editing of various documents. There are a growing number of client/server collaboration products coming to market that allow multiple contributors to share and add content to project information. Some of these products allow project members to collaborate directly from a web-based browser.

Increasingly, companies are using web-based portals to allow project teams access to integrated environments that bridge project domains and applications. The goal of integrated process management through a suite of cooperating tools is becoming the standard in large-scale project management.

So What's in It for Me?

One of the most powerful benefits of using software to assist in the implementation of project management methodology is the "what-if" analysis capabilities facilitated by interactive software products. Even the products that aren't web-enabled allow you to do this. Changes to the time estimates of individual tasks can be made, and a new schedule is immediately displayed for review. The sequence in tasks can be changed and then put back the way it was almost instantaneously. The same thing can be done with costs and resources. Imagine trying to do that with a pencil and eraser. It would take hours. With a computer, it takes seconds!

To facilitate what-if analyses, many programs establish a separate, duplicate project database, often called a "sandbox" or test environment, before changes are entered. The software then performs a comparative analysis and displays the new against the old project plan in tabular or graphical form. This makes it fast and easy for managers to review the impact of changes and come to better, more-informed conclusions.

Simple Versus Complex Projects and the Software They Need

If you manage your projects using manual techniques, you will probably limit yourself to Gantt charts and simple precedence or PERT networks. Early project management programs were also limited to these simple displays because they used "character-based" graphics. The imprecise resolution of character-based project management graphics makes it hard to build projects and more difficult to view results.

For a project management software program to be considered for general business use today, it must facilitate interactive changes and support high-quality graphics. And, by modern standards, it must have the ability to use collaborative capabilities provided by networks and the World Wide Web.

Traditionally, project-driven organizations preferred client/server software. Organizations that were less project-driven looked for less expensive, personal-computer software that was either networked or not, depending on the size and consistency desired in project management procedures.

The Types of Project Management Programs

For purposes of easy classification, project management software products can be divided into three categories based on the functions and features they provide. These include single-project programs, corporate-level programs, and mega-project programs. Let's take a closer look at each of these.

Single-Project Programs

Full-featured software packages designed for managing single projects are a step up in sophistication from scheduling programs. These products are still relatively simple and easy to use, and their output is easy to understand. Most of them provide the ability to produce Gantt charts in a variety of formats, network diagrams (either PERT or precedence), and a number of standard reports. These programs sometimes offer simple resource management and cost control capabilities.

Single-project programs are best for projects with fewer than 200 tasks. They provide only a limited analysis of the data, and since programs at this level often fail to provide automatic rescheduling based on specific resource changes, they are not useful for projects that require extensive staffing changes and what-if analyses. Programs in this category cost as little as $200 and are almost always less than $500. You can receive big discounts for larger purchases these days since software vendors are often in financial straights right now.

Corporate-Level Programs

There are many programs in this category. These corporate-level programs extend the features already discussed for single-project software, and many run on personal computers. Others run on servers, and their manufacturers often provide a personal-computer version for smaller projects. These programs typically allow sophisticated cost accounting, resource leveling, charting, and what-if analyses. Most provide some sort of web-based reporting. The specific features vary considerably as do their ease-of-use, flexibility, and reporting capabilities.

> **Words from the Wise**
>
> The installation is successful. I have 128 kilobytes of access to the Internet. As tradition requires, I do the engineer's victory dance.
>
> —Dilbert, from the strip by Scott Adams

If you intend to regularly manage projects with 100 or more tasks or if you coordinate programs that include multiple projects, you need to start looking at software in this category. Some corporate-level programs offer a beginner's and an expert's mode that allow you to start out simple and add functions and capabilities as your project management skills develop.

Corporate-level programs begin at $1,000 for each licensed user. Network, multiuser, or minicomputer versions, when available, can be considerably more expensive. The most sophisticated programs in this category may offer add-on modules for contract control or specialized reporting functions that rival the capabilities of the mega-project programs.

Mega-Project Programs

Mega-project programs, which may or may not have more features than the most sophisticated desktop computer programs, are typically designed for use on servers. Mega-project programs can handle thousands of tasks and hundreds of resources. They almost always have sophisticated cost-accounting modules and resource-leveling functions. They are sometimes difficult to use and can certainly be difficult to install, but they offer advantages in processing speed and information exchange including advanced collaboration capabilities. Most important, their success depends on a commitment from management to standardize the program and use it consistently across projects.

Mega-project packages (with sophisticated accounting and cost-analysis modules) are priced from $50,000 to $150,000—and that doesn't count the equipment, training, and other implementation costs for a complex system. Some of these programs come as modules for different functions so you can buy just the modules you need or add more as you learn to use the first ones.

If your project management requirements include the management of thousands of tasks or complex multiple projects with shared resources, adherence to government contract specifications, and integration with corporate accounting and information systems, then one of these mega-programs may be necessary.

How Do You Choose?

After you determine the category of software you need for your project management efforts, you should consider several critical factors for evaluating software before you make a purchase decision. Complete the following worksheet and then consider the factors in the following sections.

Cost/Feature Analysis

Prices for project management software vary greatly. Depending on the kinds of projects you intend to manage, study the features of products under consideration to match your requirements. The most expensive products are not always the most capable. On the other hand, unless your budget is heavily constrained, rule out programs that skimp on features just to save a few dollars. A product that lacks basic functionality will be frustrating to use because it won't do what you need it to. After a couple of poorly managed projects, you'll once again be out shopping for software.

As you evaluate different products, add features to your requirements list that you hadn't considered before studying the software options. Don't make the mistake of selecting a package simply because it has more features at its price than any other package. Consider the other factors discussed later in this section, but make sure there are enough features for your current needs and those in the foreseeable future.

If you have the opportunity to evaluate products before purchase (either at a dealer's showroom or through a demo disk or the company's website), try using the package to assemble the plan for a small project. That way, you can test the package's reliability and see how it performs. Also check the program's speed when saving to disk, its recalculation after new tasks are added, and its printing efficiency. A program with a strong features set that takes all day to print a network diagram is probably not the one for you.

Requirements Checklist for Project Management Software

Scheduling Programs
- [ ] Schedules
- [ ] Gantt Charts
- [ ] Presentation

Single-Projects Programs
- [ ] Network Diagrams
- [ ] Simple Resource Tracking
- [ ] Actual versus Planned Reports

Corporate-Level Programs

[ ] Tracks Multiple Projects	[ ] Email/Group/Network Communications
[ ] Internet/World Wide Web Publishing	[ ] Multiple Budget Types
[ ] When-If Analysis	[ ] Reporting by Resource
[ ] Task Splitting	[ ] Reporting by Milestone
[ ] Sub-Project Tracking	[ ] Multiple Calendars
[ ] Variance Reports	[ ] PERT-Least to Most Likely Projections
[ ] More then 200 Tasks per Project	[ ] Integration with General Applications
[ ] More then 50 Resources per Project	[ ] Resource Leveling
[ ] Multiple Operating Systems	[ ] Audit Trails

Mega-Project Programs
- [ ] Integration with Corporate Mainframe Programs
- [ ] Over 2,000 Tasks to Be Coordinated
- [ ] Government Requirements for a specific Program or Report
- [ ] Advanced Cost and resource Accounting

If you check boxes at more than one level, choose a product in the highest category checked.

An example software requirements checklist.

Once you select what appears to be the right product, try to purchase it from a source that gives you a 30-day money-back guarantee. That way, if the product performs poorly or ultimately doesn't fill the bill, you can return it and try something else. If you purchase software through mail order, use a credit card. You'll have more leverage returning the product because your credit card company may take your side.

When considering the cost of the software, don't forget system configuration requirements. Will the program work on your existing system or do you need to buy new hardware?

Ease of Use and Consistency of the Interface

One of the most important aspects of choosing software for managing projects is to select a package that's easy to use and that responds consistently throughout its interface. The easier the product is to use, the more likely it is you'll keep using it.

For example, if you choose the most feature-laden package, you may get a product with a number of menus, commands, dialog boxes, and cryptic functions that not only get in your way but actively interfere with laying out and managing projects.

Although these may be important functions for a professional project manager, unless you have four months to learn the package, it may get shelved and never used. Such a package forces you into overmanaging even comparatively simple projects, thereby negating its usefulness.

Flexibility to Adapt to Various Projects

Because projects in business vary from small to large and from simple to complex, you want a package that's flexible in how it adapts to various project requirements.

Compatibility with Other Programs

In many cases, you will want to take network diagrams and other project-oriented charts and combine them with documents such as reports and presentation materials. If this is important to you, look for a package that can save or export images in a format compatible with the word processing, page layout, or presentation software you own or plan to acquire.

Use this project management software selection worksheet to compare products and to make the best choice for your needs.

Project Management Software Selection Worksheet

Product Name _____ Date _____

Price: List Price $_____ Street Price $_____

Dealer Name and Address _____

Rate each product from 1 to 10 with 10 being the highest rating:

Features ☐   Ease of Use ☐   Flexibility ☐

Compatibility ☐   Documentation ☐

Reputation of the Manufacturer ☐

Experience of Others with the Product ☐

Technical Support ☐   Training Availability ☐

Overall Rating ☐

Comments:
_____
_____
_____
_____
_____
_____

Documentation and Support for the Program

When learning how to use a product, your first point of reference when looking for a solution to a problem is the manual (whether it's online or printed in a book). Check the documentation and help menus carefully before purchase.

Study the documentation carefully. The information should be well-organized, have a detailed index, and offer plenty of screen shots showing how the product works. A lengthy troubleshooting section doesn't hurt either. Keyboard templates, quick-reference cards, and disk-based sample projects are also useful. Complex products with skimpy manuals should be avoided at all costs. Also, make sure the company offers training options for the program that are commensurate with the complexity of the software.

Reputation of the Product Manufacturer

If you are purchasing an expensive product that will get considerable day-to-day use, check up on the company that designed the product. If the company discontinues the product or closes its doors, you'll be on your own with the software. Look for a stable company with a strong track record of designing useful software and providing regular updates and bug fixes. Once a product becomes incompatible with the current version of your computer's operating system, project plans that could have been revamped for future use become unavailable if the software is not updated.

Word of Mouth Experiences

Talk to other users of a particular package to get feedback on how well the product performs with real-world projects. The users you query should use the package for projects similar in scope to the ones you plan to carry out. If calling references provided by the manufacturer, take anything less than a glowing tribute to mean that the product performs less adequately than expected.

Technical Support

When considering any software product, evaluate the technical support provided by the manufacturer. Find out if it's free or if you must pay an annual fee after 90 days or a per-use fee after a certain number of calls. Do they provide a toll-free number? Must you listen to an automatic telephone system recite a long list of options before connecting you to a technician at your expense? Dial the number and see what happens. Check out the technical support information on the company's website. If you're fortunate enough to have other users to ask for recommendations, query them on the quality of technical support.

So which computerized tool is best for you? The one that meets your feature requirements with the most flexibility, with an acceptable learning curve, from a reliable and supportive vendor, and at a price you can afford. (This is pretty much the standard formula for choosing any software or computer product, not just project management software.)

Software makes creating network diagrams and schedules a breeze. You also can easily update precedence and task relationships as the project proceeds. Here you see a project that's sending information to a corporate database.

Things Project Management Software Can't Do

As powerful and efficient as project management programs are, many aspects of the project management process are not within the computer's realm. Using computer-assisted project management streamlines administration, reporting, analysis, and even communication, but the following are things the computer can't and shouldn't be allowed to do:

◆ Project management software can't gather data. You'll have to decide how much and what type of information you need to manage the project. You or members of your team will still need to gather data regarding the project status, as described in Chapter 22. The computer only helps compute and display the information after it is gathered and entered.

◆ Project management software can't make decisions. The computer can make it easier and faster to look at alternatives, but it is ultimately you and your project team who will have to make the choice between the alternatives and take responsibility for the decisions.

◆ Project management software can't solve problems that require subjective judgments. Sometimes human intuition is the most important ingredient in project management, especially when dealing with people. People require understanding. Software is programmed and is not intuitive. It only reports back what you put into it. You still have to manage the conflicts, solve the problems, and use your own judgment.

◆ Project management software can't find the errors in your input. If you put biased, incomplete, or erroneous data into the project management program, it will output biased, incomplete, and erroneous project reports. Don't blame the computer for human error. The best way to eliminate this problem is to check the reports and entries a couple of times before they are distributed.

◆ Project management software can't communicate for you. Software is great at producing reports that look good and contain a wealth of detailed information, but there is more to reporting on a project than sending out the report. You still need to communicate with people face to face, build interfaces between people and departments, and listen to what is going on around you.

◆ Project management software won't save money by reducing the need for project personnel. Automation almost never really reduces the personnel costs on a project. The software can make you more efficient and make decision-making more effective because the information is better, but project management software will not significantly reduce the need for project management people. In fact, in a large projectized organization, you'll probably need to add a person or two just to help keep the computerized project definitions and website up-to-date and the project personnel supported when they have questions.

Go Get Yourself Some!

Now you have been introduced to the features for selecting project management software for your needs. Start talking to store personnel, reading computer magazines, and asking friends and colleagues about the programs they use. Then go out, select a program, and get started in computer-assisted project management. Follow the step-by-step guidelines for implementing the project management process you have read about. As your projects come in on time and within budget, you will have achieved membership in the league of successful project managers, and the opportunities available to you and your company will take on new perspective. With each success, you will contribute to the business, the economy, and your own career—no mean feat for just learning a few project management skills. Go for it!

Software Products for Project Management

The following companies sell or distribute project management software. This is by no means a comprehensive list. There are many other companies and products out there, and more are added every day. The companies listed here offer either products we have worked with or products that have been recently reviewed in computer literature. A listing in this book should not be considered a testimonial for the functionality or suitability of any of these products—it is only provided to get you started in your search for project management software.

Company	Project Management Products
AEC Software, Inc. Phone: 703-450-1980 Website: www.aecsoft.com	Fast Track
Artemis Management Systems Phone: 1-800-477-6648 Website: www.artemispm.com	Views, Artemis, and KnowledgePlan
Ballantine & Company, Inc. Phone: 978-369-1772 Website: www.ballantine-inc.com	QuickGantt
IMSI Turboproject Phone: 415-878-4000 Website: www.turboproject.com	Turboproject
Enact Phone: 650-325-6900 Website: www.netmosphere.com	Project Home Page and Action Plan, among others
Primavera Systems Inc. Phone: 610-667-8600 Website: www.primavera.com	Primavera Project Planner and others
Project Invision International Phone: 1-888-763-3555 Website: www.projectinvision.com	Project Invision

The Least You Need to Know

- There are project management programs for projects of all sizes and complexities that run on most common personal computers.

- Project management programs incorporate network-based and web-based communication tools to assist with collaboration, data gathering, and ongoing reporting.

- To get the most benefit from its features, choose your project management software carefully.

- No software program can replace the communication, negotiating, assessment, and other management skills required to manage a project.

Glossary of Project Terms

action plan   A plan that describes what needs to be done and when it needs to be completed. Project plans are action plans.

activity   A specific project task that requires resources and time to complete.

activity-on-node (AON)   The two ways of documenting and drawing a network: placing the activities on the arcs or on the nodes.

after implementation review   The review that is completed between three and six months after the project is completed to evaluate the success of the project's implementation into operations.

answer-back diagram   If a process is highly technical, involves creative effort, or is large or complex in scale, an answer-back diagram can help. In an answer-back diagram, the vendor takes your specs and builds a simple model that demonstrates (or doesn't) a clear understanding of your project specifications.

arc   The line connecting two nodes or representing precedence in a PERT or CPM network.

audit   A formal and detailed examination of the progress, costs, operations, results, or some other aspect of a project or system.

baseline plan   The initial approved plan to which deviations will be compared as the project proceeds.

benchmarking   Establishes a point of reference and set of standard metrics for measuring the success of a project or activities within a project.

budget decrement   A reduction in the amount of money available for a project task or activity.

buying the job   When a vendor bids at a loss to blow away the competition and get the work. An unusually low quote amidst a pile of higher but nearly identical quotes is either a "bought" job or the effort of a vendor who doesn't know what he's doing. Before you accept the low bid, make sure you know which it is.

Change Control Board   A group of stakeholders who evaluate changes that have been proposed, make a judgment on the value of any change, and then instruct the project manager on whether to implement the change or reject it.

conflict   A project conflict is one in which people, priorities, or problems (the three "P's") begin to interfere with completing a project on time and within budget.

contingency plan   An alternative for action if things don't go as planned or if an expected result fails to materialize. *See* padding.

control   A process for ensuring that reality or actual performance meets expectations or plans. Control often involves the process of keeping actions within limits by making adjustments to a plan to ensure that certain outcomes will happen.

cost-benefit analysis   An analysis, often stated as a ratio, used to evaluate a proposed course of action.

crash   Conducting a task at an abnormally accelerated pace to meet a deadline. Crashing is completed at a greater cost than a normally paced task or project.

critical activity   An activity or event that, if delayed, will delay some other important event, commonly the completion of a project or a major milestone in a project.

critical path   The sequence of tasks that determines the minimum schedule for a project. If one task on the critical path is delayed, the schedule will be late.

Critical Path Method (CPM)   One of the two most common forms of networking systems. CPM uses a one-time estimate for creating a project schedule. *See* Project Evaluation and Review Technique (PERT).

critical ratio   A ratio that measures an important characteristic. This ratio is often plotted or tracked in some way to determine priorities among items or events.

cross-check   One of the best tests of completion, whether referring to doors on an airliner or the workability of a project plan, is to cross-check it. To cross-check a plan, one person lists a procedure and another verifies it. With two independent bodies carefully verifying the plan, chances for error are much smaller.

Decision Support System (DSS)   A sophisticated computer program to assist managers in making decisions. It may include simulation programs, mathematical programming routines, and decision rules.

deliverables   The clearly defined results, goods, or services produced during the project or at its outcome. Deliverables and goals are often synonymous. Deliverables, like goals, may include organizational attributes, reports, and plans, as well as physical products or objects.

dependency diagram   Another name for a network or precedence diagram that shows the dependencies (precedence) among tasks.

duration   The period of time over which a task takes place, in contrast to effort, which is the amount of labor hours a task requires. Duration establishes the schedule for a project. Effort establishes the labor costs. Each task in a project has a duration, usually specified in workdays or portions of workdays, that may or may not be different than the amount of effort (or labor) required to complete the task.

effectiveness   A measure of the quality of attainment in meeting objectives. This should be distinguished from efficiency, which is measured by the volume of output achieved for the input used.

effort   The amount of work or labor (in hours or workdays) required to complete a task. Effort is used to establish the labor costs associated with a project. Effort is in contrast to duration, which is the span of time over which the effort takes place. *See* duration.

element   *See* subtask.

event   In CPM and PERT networks, the end state for one or more activities that occurs at a specific point in time.

extinction   The end of all activity on a project, usually before meeting its stated objectives. The end results of a project terminated by extinction are terminated by neither inclusion nor integration.

facilitator   A person who makes it easier for other people to accomplish objectives by offering advice and assistance in solving problems either with technical issues or with other people. Project managers are often referred to as facilitators.

float   The amount of time for a task to be freely scheduled without affecting other tasks in a project. Also, the difference between the duration available for a task and the duration required to complete it. Float is also known as *slack* or *slack time*.

functional management   The standard departments of a business organization that represent individual disciplines such as engineering, marketing, purchasing, and accounting.

Gantt chart   A chart that uses timelines and other symbols to illustrate multiple, time-based activities or projects on a horizontal time scale.

go/no-go indicator   A level of measurement that quickly tells a reviewer if an object's dimension is within certain limits. In the case of project management, this can be any monitoring or observation that allows a manager to decide whether to change, terminate, or continue an activity or a project.

grade   A ranking that compares items that have the same functional use, such as a glass bottle, but do not share the same quality requirements, such as the ability to withstand internal pressure without breaking.

hierarchical planning   A planning approach in which each managerial level breaks planning tasks down into the activities that must be done at that level. Typically, upper-level planning establishes the objectives for the next-lower-level manager's planning.

inclusion   A way of terminating a project by incorporating the project operations and team into the organization as an ongoing entity. The project work still exists, but the project is no longer separate from the business operations.

integration   A way of terminating a project by bringing project team members back into the organization and distributing project results and outcomes among existing functions. The project as an entity no longer exists after integration.

interface management   Managing the problems that often occur between people, departments, and disciplines, rather than within the project team itself.

interfaces   The formal and informal boundaries and relationships between people, departments, organizations, or functions.

lag   The amount of time after one task is started or finished before the next task can be started or finished.

lateral communication   When information exchange occurs across lines of equivalent authority or between managers at the same level in an organization's hierarchy.

lead   The amount of time that precedes the start of work on another task.

lessons learned   The knowledge gained from the process of planning and executing a project.

leveling   The process of shifting the use of resources to even out the workload of team members and equipment.

loading   The amount of time individual resources (people, vendors, and so on) have committed to a project. A team member or other resource who has a large block of time committed to the project can't work on other projects. If the load exceeds his or her work week, you'll have to pay overtime or add resources.

make-or-buy analysis   A decision that determines whether it makes more sense to build something from scratch or to buy a standard product on the open market.

Material Requirements Planning (MRP)   An approach for material planning and ordering based on known or forecast demand requirements, lead times for obtaining each item, and existing inventories of all items.

matrix organization   An organizational structure that uses functional supervisors as well as project supervisors to manage the same people, depending on the assignment. A strong matrix is similar to a pure project organization, while a weak matrix operates more like a functional organization.

milestone   A clearly identifiable point in a project that summarizes the completion of a related or important set of tasks. Milestones are commonly used to summarize the important events in a project for managers and stakeholders who don't want or need to see the details in a project plan.

mixed organization   This organizational structure includes functional groups, pure project groups, and perhaps a matrixed group in its hierarchy. It is similar to a matrix organization.

model   A way of looking at reality, usually for the purpose of abstracting and simplifying it to make it understandable in a particular context. A plan is a type of model used to describe how a project will be completed.

negative float   The state at which all the float in a project is used up and any imposed or approved schedule dates are impossible to meet. In essence, a project with negative float is another description for a project that will come in late.

network diagram   The logical representation of tasks that defines the sequence of work in a project. Networks are usually drawn from left to right with lines drawn between tasks to indicate the precedence among tasks. On a large project, several network diagrams may exist: one for the overall project based on the project milestones and one for each subproject that represents the completion of a milestone.

padding   A standard project management tactic used to add a little extra time or money to estimates to cover for the uncertainty and risk in trying to see into the future. Also a type of contingency planning. Too much padding can get you into trouble. Padding of 15 to 25 percent is probably the most you should ever use. If you need more than this to feel comfortable with your plan, you need help with the estimates from experts or more experienced managers.

Pareto diagram   A histogram that shows the frequency of occurrence and shows how many results were generated by a single cause.

path   A sequence of lines and nodes in a project network.

portfolio   A group of projects or other items that are being worked on at the same time or that have been completed and are used as an indicator of ability.

postmortem   *See* after implementation review.

precedence   When one task must be completed before another task can be started, the first task is said to have precedence over the second.

product development life cycle   The specific set of phases and steps to bring a product to market within an industry or company. Most product development lifecycles comprise multiple projects as well as ongoing operations.

pro forma   Projected or anticipated. This term usually is applied to financial data such as balance sheets and income statements.

project   A sequence of tasks with a beginning and an end that uses time and resources to produce specific results. A project has a specific, desired outcome, a deadline or target date when the project must be done, and a budget that limits the amount of people, supplies, and money that can be used to complete the project.

project charter   The document used by senior management that formally authorizes the expenditure of resources and money on a project.

project duration   The time it takes to complete an entire project from starting the first task to finishing the last task.

Project Evaluation and Review Technique (PERT)   One of the two most common forms of networking systems. PERT uses three time estimates to determine the most probable project completion time. *See* Critical Path Method (CPM).

project management   The combination of systems, techniques, and people required to successfully complete a project on time and within budget.

Project Management Information System (PMIS)   A system used to chart activities and data and to track progress and information flow in a project. It is most frequently computerized but not always.

Project Management Institute (PMI)   A professional organization that studies and promotes project management techniques. If you want to join PMI to learn more about project management, contact information is provided in Appendix B.

project management process   The five phases of initiating, planning, executing, controlling, and closing that can help people bring projects in on time and within budget.

project manager   Any person who takes overall responsibility for coordinating a project, regardless of size, to make sure the desired end result comes in on time and within budget.

project murder   The sudden termination of a project for reasons that range from rational to absurd. An attempt on a project's life may take place during economic downturns, acquisition of the parent organization, or something entirely unexpected. In the case of a well-known computer map-making program, the unexpected death of its visionary founder sunk a hot new project the next day. A knife in a project's back may lead to not only angry team members, but possible lawsuits.

projectized organization   A organization that provides the project manager with full authority to assign priorities and direct the activities of all the people assigned to the project.

quality   The characteristics that are defined for all the deliverables of a project to meet the stakeholders requirements.

quality management plan   The document that identifies quality standards that are relevant to the project and lays out how to satisfy them.

risk analysis   An evaluation of the feasibility or probability that the outcome of a project or policy will be the desired one. Usually conducted to compare two or more alternative scenarios, action plans, or policies.

sampling   The technique of using a representative sample to determine the characteristics of the whole.

scope   The magnitude of the effort required to complete a project. As you would rightly assume, the project scope for bringing a new toy airplane to market is much smaller than the project scope for designing a new attack jet.

scope creep   The process of adding work to a project, little by little, until the original schedule and cost estimates are completely meaningless. Always make sure that any "creep" in the statement of work (SOW) or project plan is agreed to in writing along with the schedule and budget changes.

situational management   The approach of matching management style to the specific needs of a situation. Project managers must effectively apply the best management style for the job—whether task-oriented, employee-oriented, or reward-oriented leadership—to meet the needs of individual team members.

slack   *See* float.

stakeholders   People who have a personal or enterprise interest in the end results of a project. Not all stakeholders are involved in completing the actual work on a project. Common stakeholders include customers, managers, corporate executives, and representatives of government agencies.

standard task unit   An agreed-upon description and amount of effort for a common task used in multiple projects.

statement of work (SOW)   An integrated set of task descriptions, goal descriptions, risks, and assumptions that accompany the evolving master project plan during its development. When completed, the SOW will detail the work to be completed on a project and the contingencies for dealing with known risk factors.

subcontract   Delegating tasks or subprojects to contractors or other organizations.

suboptimization   The optimization of one component of a system or project, such as task sequence or schedule, often to the detriment of the overall plan or project.

subproject   A portion of the whole project that can be viewed as a project in its own right. An example would be building the new Trip to Jupiter ride (a subproject) within the project of building a new Disneyland theme park in Africa.

subtask   A portion of the complete task. For example, the task might be to write the articles for a newsletter, while a subtask might be to write the lead article for the newsletter.

systems approach   A wide-ranging method for addressing problems that considers multiple and interacting relationships. This approach is often contrasted with the analytic approach. Project management is a systems approach to managing projects.

task   A generic term for work that is too minor to in the work breakdown structure (WBS), but could be part of the work package, which is the lowest level of the WBS.

task description   A description that defines all the work required to accomplish a project activity including inputs, outputs, and quality specifications.

termination team   A project team responsible for wrapping up the administrative details of a project.

work breakdown structure (WBS)   A basic project diagram or listing that documents and describes all the work that must be done to complete the project. The WBS forms the basis for costing, scheduling, network diagramming, and work assignments.

work packages   The lowest level of the work breakdown structure that has a discrete deliverable.

Web Resources for Project Managers

The following World Wide Web resources provide general information about project management or offer special training programs for project managers.

Project Management Institute
130 South State Rd.
Upper Darby, PA 19082
Website: www.pmi.org

Project Management Institute (PMI) is a not-for-profit organization dedicated to the advancement of project management methodology and the training of project managers. The quarterly *Project Management Journal*, published by PMI, includes timely articles about project management procedures, experiences, and techniques. The institute holds regular seminars and meetings for members. PMI also offers a certification program for people who want to verify and document their project management expertise. As of this writing, the membership fee is $119 per year. A subscription to *Project Management Journal* and *PM Network* is included as part of the membership fee.

Project Management International
Website: www.infoser.com/infocons/pmi/

This site provides information on project management activities and standards around the world.

PM—Project Manager: The Industrial Project Management Site
Website: www.project-manager.com/

This site provides links to a wide range of industrial project management resources.

The SMG PM Iqnet
Website: phl.smginc.com/smginc/marketing/pmiqnet/demo/

The demo of the PM IQnet from SMG (Strategic Management Group) illustrates the training, consulting, and other resources available from SMG to help develop project management skills within the corporation.

Online Project Management Course through UC Berkeley
Website: learn.berkeley.edu.

Sunny Baker (one of the authors of this book) offers an online project management course (Management X.470) through the University of California, Extension. You can find out more information about this open enrollment course on the site.

Index